Divorce
in Wisconsin

The Legal Process,
Your Rights, and What to Expect

Linda S. Vanden Heuvel
Attorney at Law

Addicus Books
Omaha, Nebraska

An Addicus Nonfiction Book

Copyright 2015 by Linda S. Vanden Heuvel. All rights reserved. No part of this publication may be reproduced, stored in a retrieval system, or transmitted in any form or by any means, electronic, mechanical, photocopied, recorded, or otherwise, without the prior written permission of the publisher. For information, write Addicus Books, Inc., P.O. Box 45327, Omaha, Nebraska 68145.

ISBN 978-1-940495-13-2

Typography Jack Kusler

Library of Congress Cataloging-in-Publication Data

Vanden Heuvel, Linda S., - author.
Divorce in Wisconsin : the legal process, your rights, and what to expect / Linda S. Vanden Heuvel.
pages cm
Includes bibliographical references and index.
ISBN 978-1-940495-13-2 (alk. paper)
1. Divorce—Law and legislation—Wisconsin. I. Title.
KFW2500.V36 2014
346.77501'66—dc23
2014034287

Addicus Books, Inc.
P.O. Box 45327
Omaha, Nebraska 68145
www.AddicusBooks.com
Printed in the United States of America
10 9 8 7 6 5 4 3 2 1

To Vanden Heuvel & Dineen, S.C. clients—
past, present, and future.
For their loyalty, trust, and resiliency.

Contents

Acknowledgments

My first acknowledgment goes to the clients of Vanden Heuvel & Dineen, S.C. Each day, divorce clients trust the attorneys of Vanden Heuvel & Dineen, S.C., to guide them through this confusing and uncertain time in their lives. They continually remind us that divorce is personal and unique to each individual client.

In contrast, the legal system is predictable and must be applied consistently and in conformance with Wisconsin law. As a result, it is important to acknowledge the judiciary and attorneys who each day balance the unique facts and circumstances of each case with the mandates of the law.

The staff at Vanden Heuvel & Dineen, S.C. is dedicated to making the process of divorce, legal separation, custody/ placement disputes, and other family law matters easier for its clients. Each attorney at Vanden Heuvel & Dineen, S.C. works diligently to provide comprehensive and tenacious legal representation. A special thank you must be given to the legal assistants of Vanden Heuvel & Dineen, S.C., particularly Barbara A. Schwind, who worked side by side with me to write *Divorce in Wisconsin.*

I also thank my publisher, Rod Colvin of Addicus Books. His knowledgeable and patient support has guided me in writing this first edition of *Divorce in Wisconsin.* He has helped me provide understandable, nontechnical answers to important divorce questions by Wisconsin residents.

If this edition eases any person's journey through the divorce process, it is because of the generosity and knowledge of many, for which I extend my heartfelt gratitude and appreciation.

Attorney Linda S. Vanden Heuvel
www.vhdlaw.com

Introduction

Every day I meet with men and women trying to decide whether to file for divorce. It is a difficult time for almost all involved. I am hopeful that this book will help remove some of the uncertainty that results from divorce, which is a life-changing experience.

Whether you initiate or respond to a divorce, you are facing change in many aspects of your life. Parenting, family relationships, finances, social networks, personal belongings, residence, job performance—each is impacted by the divorce process. My purpose in writing *Divorce in Wisconsin* is to help you navigate through this uncertain and often unpredictable experience. The more control and clarity you feel over the process, the better you will be able to make sound decisions regarding very challenging choices.

I understand, from providing legal representation to thousands of clients, that in order to move through the legal and emotional phases of divorce, a tremendous amount of support is needed from family, friends, and legal counsel. *Divorce in Wisconsin* was written to be part of that support network. It is not intended to be a substitute for advice from your own attorney or financial advisor. Rather, it is designed to assist you in partnering with your attorney to reach your goals in the resolution of your divorce.

I have been a successful family law attorney for over thirty years. I hope that the product of this experience and background, *Divorce in Wisconsin,* will aid you in reaching a successful resolution of your divorce. Remember, during your divorce, you may have hard, grief-filled days and you may face mountains of uncertainty, but your divorce will resolve, and you will move forward in a new and different direction with new possibilities for the future.

Best wishes on your journey.

Attorney Linda S. Vanden Heuvel
www.vhdlaw.com

1

Understanding the Divorce Process

The process of ending a marriage often creates feelings of anxiety and fear of the unknown. However, understanding divorce procedure can bring some predictability which, in turn, will provide you with a greater sense of confidence and comfort, and a footprint for the steps to reaching a successful resolution of your divorce.

It is important to develop a basic understanding of the divorce process. This knowledge will lower your anxiety if your attorney or the court starts using words or phrases you do not understand. It will help reduce your frustration about the length of the process because you will be equipped to recognize the reasons supporting each step and procedure. Sometimes just realizing that you are completing the steps of the divorce process can bring reassurance that progress is being made toward the final resolution of your divorce.

It is also important to note that your emotions, as well as the emotions of your spouse, may also drive the process. You are strongly encouraged to use good sense and reasoning to make divorce decisions and to refrain from letting the hurt and pain that follows the end of a relationship be the guide to your decision making. You are encouraged to seek guidance and therapy if needed.

Making decisions based on common sense and factual information, not anger and emotion, will speed the resolution of your divorce and will make Wisconsin's no-fault divorce process easier.

The purpose of *Divorce in Wisconsin* is to provide you with an understanding of the divorce process and procedure, to reduce frustration with the length of the divorce process, and to increase your awareness of the steps necessary to conclude your divorce in a successful manner.

1.1 What steps are taken during the divorce process?

If you are initiating the divorce, the divorce process in Wisconsin typically involves the steps listed below:

- Obtain a referral for a family law or divorce attorney. Ask for specific referrals to attorneys who are experienced and knowledgeable in divorce law.

- Schedule an appointment with a divorce attorney. You may want to interview more than one attorney to determine which attorney will best meet your divorce needs.

- Prepare questions and gather basic documents for your initial consultation (more about these documents later).

- Meet with an attorney for an initial consultation.

- When you decide to retain a particular attorney, you will pay a retainer to your attorney and sign a written retainer or legal services agreement.

- Provide any additional requested information and documents to your attorney. Take other actions, as advised by your attorney.

- Your attorney will prepare a *summons* and *petition for divorce.* The petition will require your signature.

- After discussion with your attorney, a determination will be made whether a temporary hearing is necessary in your case. A *temporary hearing* is a hearing before a family court commissioner to decide temporary issues until the divorce is finalized. Issues that may be addressed at the temporary hearing include child support, maintenance, placement, allocation of debt, and/or attorney fee contribution. If it is determined that a temporary hearing is needed in your case, your attorney will prepare the necessary documents to schedule the hearing. Those documents will

2

then be filed with the clerk of court in the county where your divorce is filed, along with the summons and petition for divorce.

- After pleadings, formal written documents, have been filed and a temporary hearing date scheduled, the pleadings must be served on your spouse.

- There are different ways to accomplish service. Your attorney will discuss your service options with you. You have ninety days after the filing of the summons and petition to serve the pleadings on your spouse. One sixty-day service extension may be granted by the court. If either party receives public assistance, a copy of the summons and petition must also be served on the county child-support agency.

- If you are the spouse served with divorce papers, the foregoing process will also apply to your situation. However, rather than filing a summons and petition for divorce, your attorney will prepare a *response* and *counterclaim* to the summons and petition, which is due twenty days after the service of the summons and petition. You may also request a temporary hearing if necessary in your case.

- Financial information must be provided to your attorney in advance of any temporary hearing. Information to be provided includes, but is not limited to, W-2s, tax returns, recent payroll stubs, your budget, a listing of all assets and liabilities, life insurance, and inherited and gifted property.

- Negotiations are generally conducted relative to the proposed terms of the *temporary order* on matters such as custody, placement, support, maintenance, payment of debts, and temporary possession of the family home. If you can reach a temporary agreement with your spouse, a stipulation setting forth the terms of your agreement will be drafted. If settlement cannot be reached on temporary issues, your attorney will likely prepare financial statements, maintenance and child-support calculations, and budgets for presentation at the temporary hearing.

- A temporary hearing is held if you and your spouse cannot reach agreement.
- A temporary order is prepared by the family court commissioner, court, or one of the attorneys, approved as to form by the other attorney, and submitted to the court for filing.
- If you have minor children, you and your spouse must attend a parent education class, develop a parenting plan (if custody or placement is in dispute), and participate in mediation. Generally, in Wisconsin the issues of custody and placement must be resolved before the court will address financial issues.
- Both parties will conduct discovery to obtain information regarding all relevant facts. *Discovery* is the obtaining of information from the other party which is necessary to settle or try a case. Discovery includes formal requests for information, as well as informal discovery, which is merely a request from one attorney to the other for documents and information.
- Valuations of all assets will be obtained, including real estate, retirement accounts, vehicles, investments, and business valuations. Sometimes it is necessary to hire appraisers and/or experts.
- You will confer with your attorney to review facts, identify issues, and assess the strengths and weaknesses of your case. With the assistance of your attorney, you will review strategy and develop a proposal for settlement.
- You and your spouse, with the support of your attorneys, will attempt to reach agreement through written proposals, mediation, settlement conferences, or other alternative dispute resolution.
- If you and your spouse reach an agreement on all issues, one of the attorneys will prepare a *marital settlement agreement,* which is signed and approved by you and your spouse and your children's guardian *ad litem,* if applicable. A *guardian ad litem* is an attorney appointed to represent the best interests of your

children if custody or placement is contested during the divorce.

- The marital settlement agreement and updated *financial disclosure statements* are filed with the court.

- The court holds a brief, final hearing called a *default hearing*. You and your spouse will testify that you understand and agree with the terms of the marital settlement agreement; state that the marriage is irretrievably broken; testify that your financial statement correctly identifies all income, assets, and liabilities; and provide the court with basic information about the marriage.

- Judgment is entered, and divorce is granted. Each party is advised that he or she cannot remarry for a period of six months subsequent to the granting of the divorce.

- Your attorney completes necessary orders and drafts documents to implement the terms of the divorce. These orders and documents will address transfer of real estate, retirement accounts, vehicles, implementation of child support, and more.

- If your case is not resolved by a default divorce, your case will proceed to further litigation and potentially trial.

- Additional discovery will probably be completed by the attorneys, including depositions, experts' analyses, valuations, vocational rehabilitation examinations, and more.

- At this stage, because your case is in a trial posture, you may be compelled to pay your attorney an additional retainer to fund the work needed to prepare for trial and trial itself. You will be charged for costs, such as any transcript fees, witness fees, service fees, and expert-witness fees.

- If agreement has been reached on some issues, but not all, one of the attorneys will prepare a *partial marital settlement agreement* on agreed issues. All disputed issues are set for trial.

- You will work hand-in-hand with your attorney to prepare your case for trial.

5

- Your attorney prepares witnesses, drafts trial exhibits, conducts legal research on contested issues, drafts pretrial motions with supporting affidavits, prepares direct and cross-examination of witnesses, prepares an opening statement, drafts subpoenas of witnesses, prepares a closing argument and suggestions to the court, and more.
- Prior to trial, you will meet with your attorney on one or more occasions to prepare for trial and your trial testimony.
- The court may order mediation or arbitration in an attempt to resolve all differences prior to your trial actually taking place. Alternative dispute resolution can take place at any time during the divorce process.
- Either pre- or posttrial, the court may order each party to file a brief to address the law relative to disputed issues.
- Trial is held. Each party provides testimony and exhibits setting forth his or her position relative to any disputed issues. Attorneys also generally make opening and closing statements. There are no jury trials in divorce actions in Wisconsin.
- The judge renders his or her decision.
- One attorney, generally the petitioner's attorney, prepares the *findings of fact, conclusions of law,* and *judgment of divorce* and submits it to the other attorney for approval as to form.
- The findings of fact, conclusions of law, and judgment of divorce is then submitted to the court for its signature. This is the pleading that sets forth all of the terms of your divorce.
- Your attorney completes necessary orders and documents to implement the terms of the divorce. These orders and documents cover transfers of real estate, retirement accounts, closing of credit cards, transfer of title, child support, maintenance payments, and more.

In the event you wish to appeal the divorce decision, your posttrial rights are discussed in chapter 16.

Ten Divorce Mistakes to Avoid

1. Failing to understand the divorce process

2. Confusing your emotional needs with the business decisions of divorce

3. Forgetting to weigh the cost vs. the benefit of each contested issue

4. Putting too much emphasis on "winning"

5. Failing to be truthful

6. Believing that the award of custody and placement means the children lose the other parent

7. Deciding to fight every issue. The greater the fight the more costly the divorce. Fighting over every issue will probably result in the sale of some assets to pay for the cost of litigation.

8. Prolonging the divorce. Failing to divide your assets in a timely manner often means sharing the increased value of that asset with your spouse.

9. Getting divorce advice from family and friends

10. Not following your attorney's advice

1.2   Am I required to be represented by an attorney in order to obtain a divorce in Wisconsin?

No. You are not required to retain an attorney to obtain a divorce in Wisconsin. However, if your case involves child-custody or child-placement issues, maintenance, or significant property or debts, you should carefully consider whether or not it is in your best interest to proceed without an attorney.

If your divorce does not involve any major issues, if you cannot afford a retainer, or if you simply want to proceed without legal representation, you can represent yourself *pro se*. A person who proceeds in a legal matter without a lawyer is referred to as acting *pro se*, or on one's own. *Pro se* divorce forms are available at www.wicourts.gov/forms1/circuit. You can also contact your local county clerk of court's office to ask what services are available to assist self-represented litigants. There may also be low-cost legal service programs available in your area. Check online for potential references. Some attorneys also offer payment plans or work *pro bono*. Contact your local bar association for other potential options for free or low-cost legal services.

If you are considering proceeding without an attorney, at a minimum, schedule an initial consultation with an attorney to discuss your rights and responsibilities according to Wisconsin divorce law. Meeting with an experienced family law attorney may help you determine whether it is cost-effective and legally smart to represent yourself in your divorce action. If you and your spouse reach a marital settlement agreement, you may want an attorney to review the document before you sign and file it with the court. Even if you begin the divorce unrepresented, you may decide you need an attorney during the divorce process if you become overwhelmed or unsatisfied appearing *pro se*.

1.3 What is my first step if I decide to retain an attorney to start my divorce?

If you decide to retain an attorney, locate a law firm that regularly handles family law issues as part of its law practice. Your divorce is important. You do not want to choose a lawyer who is unfamiliar with divorce trends, procedures, and divorce laws in Wisconsin.

The best recommendations generally are received from former clients and other people who have knowledge of a lawyer's experience and reputation. You can also search online for client reviews, although these reviews are not always reliable. Lawyers are also rated by Avvo, Inc. (www.Avvo.com) and Martindale-Hubbell (www.Martindale.com). These organizations provide a forum for people to share information about particular lawyers and law firms.

If you are only considering divorce and have not yet made a final decision, it is nevertheless wise to schedule an appointment with a family law attorney to obtain information about the divorce process and to obtain guidance about the issues in your case. Be able to identify your most important goals in seeking a divorce. Is custody and placement the biggest issue? Maintenance? Keeping the family home? It is important that you and your divorce attorney are on the same page when determining the goals for your divorce.

When you make your initial appointment, ask the lawyer or his or her legal staff what documents you should take with you to your initial consultation. This will help make your consultation more enlightening and cost-effective, and will provide the lawyer with necessary information to evaluate your case. If you have already been served with divorce or legal separation pleadings, provide these pleadings to the attorney at the initial consultation. Bring any prior divorce judgments, as well as any temporary restraining orders or permanent injunctions. Be prepared with any prenuptial or premarital agreements between you and your spouse.

Also, make a list of questions to ask the attorney at your first meeting. Some of these questions should include the following:

- How long have you practiced law in Wisconsin?
- What percentage of your practice is devoted to family law and divorce?
- If you are not available to answer my questions during my divorce, who will answer my questions? Will anyone other than you be assigned to my case?
- What is your hourly rate?
- What is your retainer? Will you provide me with a written legal services agreement in advance for my review?

1.4 Is Wisconsin a no-fault state, or do I need grounds for a divorce?

Wisconsin is a no-fault divorce state. This means that neither you nor your spouse are required to prove that the other is "at fault" in order to be granted a divorce. Proof of factors such as infidelity, cruelty, or desertion are not necessary to obtain a divorce in Wisconsin. The only requirement is that the marriage is irretrievably broken.

If either party testifies that the marriage is irretrievably broken, that testimony is generally sufficient for the court to grant the divorce. If one party testifies that the marriage is not irretrievably broken, the court will generally nevertheless grant the divorce, based on the premise that a marriage cannot continue if one party wants out of the marriage.

9

1.5 My spouse has told me she will never "give" me a divorce. Does that stop me from obtaining a divorce in Wisconsin?

No. Wisconsin does not require that your spouse agree to a divorce. The judge, not your spouse, grants your divorce. Under Wisconsin law, to obtain a divorce you must state under oath that your marriage is "irretrievably broken." This is a legal term meaning that there is no possibility of reconciliation between you and your spouse. Nor do you have to prove that you participated in marital counseling to establish that your marriage is "irretrievably broken."

1.6 How will a judge view my infidelity or my spouse's infidelity?

Because Wisconsin is a no-fault divorce state, there will rarely be testimony or evidence introduced about either spouse's infidelity, with one potential exception. The court may hear testimony regarding an extramarital affair if child custody or child placement is an issue and the affair impacts the best interest of the minor children.

1.7 Do I have to get divorced in the same state in which I was married?

No. You do not have to get divorced in the same state in which you were married. You may file for divorce in Wisconsin if you or your spouse meet the residency requirements. However, Wisconsin may be limited in its ability to address custody and placement as part of the divorce process unless additional factors are addressed. Be sure to talk to your attorney about this issue if your children reside or have resided in another state prior to the filing of the divorce action.

1.8 How long must I reside in Wisconsin in order to obtain a Wisconsin divorce?

Either you or your spouse, not both, must have been a resident of Wisconsin for at least six months prior to the filing of the divorce in order to meet the jurisdictional residency requirement for a divorce in Wisconsin. One party must also reside in the county where the divorce is filed for a period of thirty days prior to filing. In the event the six-month requirement is not met, a party may file for legal separation if that party has been a resident of a Wisconsin county for the preceding thirty days. There is no requirement that a party actually remain in Wisconsin during the divorce. The jurisdictional requirements must only be met on the date of filing.

1.9 May I obtain a divorce in Wisconsin even though I don't know my spouse's current location or address?

Wisconsin law allows you to proceed with a divorce even if you do not know the current address of your spouse. First, take action to attempt to locate your spouse. Contact family members, friends, neighbors, coworkers, former coworkers, or anyone else who might know the whereabouts of your spouse. Utilize resources on the Internet that are designed to help locate people.

Let your attorney know of your efforts to find your spouse. Inform your lawyer of the last known address of your spouse, as well as any work address or other address where your spouse may be located. In the event your attorney unsuccessfully attempts service on your spouse, the next step is to provide notice through publication in the newspaper serving his or her last known address.

Although your divorce may be granted following service of notice by publication in a newspaper, you may not be able to get other court orders such as those for child support or custody/placement without obtaining personal service on your spouse. Talk to your attorney about your options and rights if you don't know where your spouse is living.

1.10 I just moved to a different county in Wisconsin. Do I have to file in the county where my spouse lives?

You may file your petition for divorce either in the county where you reside or in the county where your spouse resides, so long as you or your spouse have resided in that county for thirty days.

1.11   I immigrated to Wisconsin. Will my immigration status stop me from getting a divorce?

If you meet the residency requirements for divorce in Wisconsin, you may obtain a divorce in Wisconsin no matter what your immigration status. *Immigrant status* is a term defining the status of people who live permanently in the United States but are not United State citizens. Immigrant status includes the status of permanent resident, immigrant, green card holder, or resident alien. It is imperative that you talk to an experienced immigration attorney about the impact of divorce on your immigration status. These are two different concepts. While you may get divorced in Wisconsin, that divorce may have an impact on your immigration status. It is important to retain knowledgeable legal counsel before proceeding with divorce if your immigration status may be impacted as a result of your divorce.

1.12   I want to get divorced in my Indian tribal court. What do I need to know?

Each tribal court has its own laws governing divorce. Requirements for residency, grounds for divorce, laws regarding property, maintenance, and children may vary substantially from Wisconsin law. Some tribes have very different laws governing placement, removal of children from the marital home, and cohabitation with a third party. Contact an attorney who is knowledgeable about Indian tribal law before filing for divorce in tribal court.

1.13   Is there a waiting period for a divorce in Wisconsin?

Yes. Wisconsin has a mandatory 120-day waiting period. This waiting period begins on the day that the respondent, the person who did not initiate the divorce process, is given legal notice of the divorce. This date is either the day that the respondent is personally served with the divorce pleadings or the day that the respondent signs an admission of service acknowledging that he or she has received the filed divorce pleadings.

The 120-day waiting period can be waived for the protection of the health or safety of either of the parties or of the children of the marriage. In order for this emergency contingency to be granted, specific grounds must be identified on the record and approved by the court.

1.14   What is a *petition for divorce*?

A *petition for divorce* is a document signed by the person filing for divorce and filed with the clerk of court to initiate the divorce process. The petition sets forth the vital statistics of each of the parties, including name, address, date of birth, employment information, names and dates of birth of children, and date and place of marriage, as well as the issues in the divorce. A sample petition for divorce is listed in the appendix.

1.15   My spouse said she filed for divorce last week, but my lawyer said there's nothing on file at the courthouse. What does it mean to *file for divorce*?

When lawyers use the term "filing" they are ordinarily referring to filing a legal document at the courthouse, such as delivering a petition for divorce to the clerk of court. Sometimes a person who has hired a lawyer to begin a divorce action uses the phrase "I've filed for divorce," although no pleadings have actually been filed with the clerk of court in the county where the person resides. In that instance, you can probably assume that your spouse has signed all the necessary paperwork to commence the divorce. To be sure, you can check Wisconsin Circuit Court Access website (WCCA) http://wcca.wicourts.gov to determine whether and when the divorce has been filed.

1.16   If we both want a divorce, does it matter who files?

Generally, no. In the eyes of the court, the petitioner (the party who files the petition initiating the divorce process) and the respondent (the other spouse) are not seen differently by virtue of which party filed. The court, as a neutral decision maker, will not give preference to either party.

1.17   Are there advantages to filing first?

Discuss with your attorney whether there are any advantages to your filing first. Your attorney may advise you to file first or to wait until your spouse files, depending on the overall strategy for your case and your circumstances. For example, if there is a concern that your spouse will begin to transfer assets after learning about your plans for divorce, your attorney might advise you to file for divorce immediately and to seek a temporary order to protect against any transfer of assets. However, if you are separated from your spouse but have a beneficial temporary arrangement, your attorney may advise you to wait for your spouse to file.

Ask your attorney to assist you in making the decision whether and when to initiate the legal process.

1.18 Am I able to stop the newspaper from publishing notice of the filing or granting of my divorce?

Documents filed with the court, such as a *petition for divorce* or a *judgment of divorce*, are matters of public record. Newspapers have a right to access this information, and many newspapers publish this information as a matter of routine. Contact your local newspaper to learn more.

In some cases, however, on the court's order, portions of a divorce file, such as documents containing financial information, may be "sealed" or "under seal."

Check the Wisconsin Circuit Court Access website (WCCA) http://wcca.wicourts.gov/, which provides access to most Wisconsin circuit courts records. The court information found in WCCA is a matter of public record and available on the Internet.

1.19 I do not want to serve the divorce pleadings on my spouse at his or her office or workplace. Are there alternative ways to serve the divorce pleadings?

It is not necessary to serve your spouse at his or her place of employment. Your spouse may stop at your attorney's office to pick up the pleadings and to sign an *admission of service,* which acknowledges his or her receipt of the summons and petition for divorce and any additional pleadings. The pleadings and an admission of service may also be forwarded to your spouse by mail, but then it is your spouse's obligation to return the signed admission of service to your attorney. If there is cooperation between the parties, I suggest initially using these last methods of service. The use of an admission of service is not appropriate for all cases, so discuss with your attorney the best choice for your case. If your spouse is not cooperative with these methods, then it may be necessary to serve the divorce pleadings by a process server or law enforcement. A sample service letter to your spouse and a sample admission of service are listed in the appendix.

1.20 Should I sign an admission of service even if I don't agree with the contents of the summons and petition for divorce?

Signing the admission of service does not mean that you agree to the content of the petition for divorce or other pleadings. You are simply advising the court that you received a copy of the pleadings.

Voluntarily signing the admission of service avoids the need for formal service by a process server or law enforcement. By signing the admission of service, you are not waiving any rights that you have relative to the divorce process itself. Follow your attorney's advice on whether and when to sign an admission of service.

1.21 Should I contact an attorney immediately on receipt of divorce pleadings?

Yes. Contact your attorney or obtain an attorney immediately on receipt of divorce pleadings. It is important that you obtain legal advice as soon as possible. Even if you and your spouse are working together on the divorce, having independent legal counsel can help you make decisions now that will ultimately impact your divorce and your life after divorce. For example, the decision whether to vacate the residence may be a major determinant in custody and placement decisions, but the decision to vacate is often made early in the divorce process, without an understanding of its impact on other issues.

Your initial divorce filings sometimes include a request for a temporary hearing. It is possible you will receive only a short notice of the temporary hearing date. While temporary hearings provide "temporary" orders, more often than not these temporary orders are a precursor of the final marital settlement agreement. It is imperative that you are fully prepared for the temporary hearing with sufficient documents to support your position.

1.22   What is an *ex parte court order*?

An *ex parte court order* is obtained by one party from the court without giving prior notice of the request to the other party and his or her attorney.

With the exception of restraining orders and emergency situations, judges are reluctant to sign *ex parte* orders. Ordinarily the court will require a party to give notice to the other side of any requests for court orders, and a hearing before the judge or court commissioner will generally be held before any decisions are made. An *affidavit,* which is a written statement sworn under oath, is usually required before a judge will sign an *ex parte* order. When an *ex parte* order is granted, the party who did not request the order will have an opportunity to have a subsequent hearing before the judge to determine whether the temporary *ex parte* order should become permanent or whether it should be dismissed.

1.23   What is a *motion*?

A *motion* is a request that the judge enter a court order of some type. For example, your attorney may file a written motion asking for an order related to temporary custody, child support, placement, or financial matters, such as payment of debts.

Motions may also be procedural, for example, a motion for an adjournment of your case or a motion to extend time to file a brief.

1.24   Once my petition for divorce is filed, how soon will a temporary hearing be scheduled?

In most cases a temporary hearing can be held within thirty to sixty days of the divorce filing, assuming your spouse can be served with the pleadings in a timely manner. There are exceptions to every rule. In some cases the court will set an emergency hearing within a matter of days; in some cases, because of scheduling issues, the time for the temporary hearing will be extended.

1.25 How much notice will I get if my spouse seeks a temporary order?

Wisconsin law requires that you receive reasonable notice of any court hearings. In the case of a motion for a temporary hearing, notice generally requires a minimum of five days, excluding holidays and weekends.

1.26 During my divorce, what are my responsibilities?

Your attorney will explain what actions you should take during each step of the divorce process. These steps may include the following:

- Keep in regular contact with your attorney.
- Update your attorney regarding any changes in your contact information, such as address, phone numbers, and e-mail address.
- Provide your attorney with all requested documents and information in a timely manner.
- Complete forms and questionnaires in a timely manner.
- Appear in court on time and dressed appropriately.
- Be direct about asking any questions you might have.
- Make sure your attorney is aware of your settlement objectives, so that you are both on the same page in the negotiation process.
- Remain respectful toward your spouse throughout the process.
- Do not discuss the divorce with your children.
- Comply with any temporary court orders, such as restraining or support orders.
- Advise your attorney of any significant developments in your case.
- Pay attorney fees and costs in a timely manner or make alternative arrangements with your attorney.

Do your part in the divorce process. This will enable your attorney to partner with you to obtain a positive divorce result while at the same time maintaining or lowering your attorney's fees and costs.

1.27 I'm worried that I won't remember to ask my lawyer about all of the issues in my case. How can I be sure I don't miss anything?

Write down all of the topics you want to address with your attorney, including your goals for the divorce and the priority of those goals. Your lawyer will also help you in identifying the issues in your case. The following checklist will also provide guidance in determining what issues are applicable to your unique divorce.

Divorce Issues Checklist

Issue	Notes
Divorce	
Legal separation	
Annulment	
Custody of minor children	
Placement of minor children	
Removal of children from jurisdiction	
Parenting plan	
Child support	
Deviation from child-support guidelines	
Variable expenses	
Wage assignment	
Cost of living adjustment	
Parental alienation	
Grandparents' rights	
Automatic withholding for support	
Child-support arrearage from temporary order	
Child-care expenses	
Child-care credit	
Terms of child support	
Health insurance for minor children	

Divorce Issues Checklist (Continued)

Issue	Notes
Uninsured medical expenses for minor children	
Qualified medical support order	
Private school tuition for children	
College expenses for children	
College saving accounts	
Health insurance	
Real property: marital residence	
Real property: such as rentals, cabins, and commercial property	
Time-shares	
Retirement accounts	
Federal or military pensions	
Business interests	
Business valuation	
Checking accounts	
Savings accounts	
Money market accounts	
Anticipated tax refunds or tax liability	
Investments	
Stock options	
Stock purchase plans	
Life insurance policies	
Frequent flyer miles	
Credit card points	
Season tickets to events	
Premarital or nonmarital assets	
Premarital or nonmarital debts	

Divorce Issues Checklist (Continued)

Issue	Notes
Pets	
Personal property division: including motor vehicles, recreational vehicles, campers, airplanes, collections, furniture, electronics, tools, and household goods	
Inherited items	
Exchange date for personal property	
Division of marital debt	
Mortgages	
Home equity loans	
Motor vehicle loans	
Bank loans	
Tax liens	
Personal loans	
Student loans	
Credit card balances	
Property settlement	
Maintenance	
Life insurance to fund unpaid maintenance	
Arrearage of maintenance from temporary order	
Tax exemptions for minor children	
Tax consequences	
IRS Form 8332 and allocation of tax credits	
Filing status for tax returns for last/current year	
Former name restoration	
Attorney fees	

1.28   What is a *marital settlement agreement*?

A *marital settlement agreement* is a written document that includes all of the agreements you and your spouse have reached in your divorce. The marital settlement agreement will contain provisions setting the terms of each specific agreement between you and your spouse.

The marital settlement agreement is a separate pleading and is incorporated into the judgment of divorce, which is the final court order dissolving your marriage.

1.29   What happens after my spouse and I sign the marital settlement agreement? Do we still have to go to court?

Yes. After you and your spouse approve and sign the marital settlement agreement, it must still be approved by the court. A default divorce hearing will be scheduled after the passing of the 120-day mandatory waiting period under Wisconsin law.

1.30   If my spouse and I think our marital settlement agreement is fair, why does the court have to approve it?

The court has a duty to make sure that your marital settlement agreement is fair and reasonable under Wisconsin law. The court has to make sure neither party was coerced into signing the agreement. For those reasons, the court must review your agreement. The court must consider the facts and circumstances of your case when reviewing the agreement. Not every case will result in an equal division of the assets and debts from the marriage. However, if either party agrees to a lopsided marital settlement agreement, the court will confirm that the party is fully informed of his or her rights before approving that party's decision.

1.31   Wisconsin is a *marital property state*. What does this mean to a couple who is divorcing?

This term refers to you and your spouse's equal, undivided interest in your marital property. All property accumulated by either spouse to the date of divorce is generally considered joint marital property, with two exceptions. Inheritances and gifts are not considered a part of the marital estate unless the gifts are given from one spouse to the other. It is critical that your attorney speak with you in detail about the acquisition and source of all assets that exist at the time of your divorce filing.

1.32 My spouse has all our financial information. How will I be able to prepare for my divorce if I don't know the facts or have these documents?

Once your divorce has been filed, your attorney will proceed with a process known as *discovery*.

Through discovery, your attorney will ask your spouse to provide documents and information needed to prepare your case. Your attorney can also subpoena information directly from a third-party source to obtain the requested documentation.

1.33 My spouse and I want our divorce to be amicable. How can we keep it that way?

You and your spouse are to be commended for your willingness to cooperate with each other while proceeding with your divorce. This will make your lives easier and save you money in attorney's fees and costs. It is also more likely to result in a mutually agreeable final resolution of your divorce.

Find a lawyer who understands your goal to reach an amicable settlement. Encourage your spouse to do the same. Cooperate with the prompt exchange of necessary information, then ask your attorney about the options of mediation, arbitration, and negotiation to assist in reaching an agreement. Even if you are not able to settle all of the issues in your divorce, these actions will increase the likelihood of agreement on many of the terms of your divorce. You may also want to consider collaborative divorce.

1.34 What is *collaborative divorce*?

Collaborative divorce is a type of divorce based on five principles:

- Each party has an attorney specifically trained to work cooperatively and who agrees to try to settle your case without litigation.
- The parties sign a written agreement not to litigate in court.

- The parties voluntarily exchange information. There is no formal discovery.
- The parties work corroboratively until they reach a mutually agreeable resolution.
- If either party decides to reject the collaborative divorce process and proceed to litigation, each party must retain a new attorney to represent his or her interests.

Collaborative divorce involves a team approach and includes each party, his or her attorney, and other professionals such as mental health and financial experts, with the shared goal of a negotiated settlement.

Talk to your lawyer about whether your case would be well suited for the collaborative divorce process.

1.35 May I choose the judge who will decide my case?

You have some limited ability to determine the judge assigned to your case through the right of substitution. If you do not want to proceed with the judge originally assigned to your case, you may file one substitution of judge. Hopefully that substitution will result in the assignment of the judge of your choosing, but that may not be the case because the next judge is selected in the usual court rotation.

1.36 I have a same-sex marriage. Is the divorce process any different for me?

Wisconsin recognizes same-sex marriages. A Wisconsin citizen may marry an individual of his or her choosing, whether of the same or opposite sex. Wisconsin's marriage and divorce laws are applied uniformly, no matter what each person's sexual orientation.

1.37 How long will it take to get my divorce?

The sooner you and your spouse reach agreement of all issues, the faster your divorce will conclude. Assuming all outstanding issues, such as custody, support, property division, and allocation of debts, are settled between you and your spouse, a final default hearing may be scheduled any time after the 120-day waiting period, subject to the restrictions of the court's calendar.

1.38 What is the significance of my divorce being final?

The finality of your divorce is important for many reasons. The date of the judgment of divorce can affect many life decisions, including your right to remarry, your eligibility for health insurance, and your filing status for income taxes.

1.39 When does my divorce become final?

A judgment of divorce is effective the date it is granted by the court. A divorce is generally granted by the court on the date of default divorce or the final date of trial, but there are exceptions to this rule, which your attorney can address with you.

1.40 How do I get my former name legally restored?

If you want your former name restored, let your attorney know so that this provision can be included in your judgment of divorce. If you want to change your legal name after the divorce and did not provide for the change at the time of your divorce, it will be necessary to file a separate legal action for a name change.

2

Coping with Stress during the Divorce Process

It may have been a few years ago. It may have been many years ago. It may have been two months ago. But when you said "I do" you meant "until death do us part." Like most people, you planned to be happily married for life.

But things change. Life happens. People do not live up to expectations. Whatever the circumstances, you now find yourself considering divorce. The emotions of divorce can range from one extreme to another as you proceed through the process. You may feel relief and excitement at the possibility of moving forward with your life. On the other hand, you may feel pain and anger and helplessness at the thought of what lies ahead. You may experience fear, sorrow, and a deep sense of loss or failure. It is important to find support for coping with all of these strong emotions.

Because going through a divorce can be an emotional time, having a clear understanding of the divorce process and what to expect during the process will help you make better decisions. And, when it comes to decision making, educate yourself so that you can make reasoned, well-thought-out decisions relative to your future goals.

2.1 My spouse left home weeks ago. I don't want a divorce because I feel our marriage can be saved. Should I still see an attorney?

It's a good idea to consult an attorney. Whether you want a divorce or not, there may be important actions to take now to protect your assets, credit, home, children, and future right

25

to support. In Wisconsin, if one spouse wants a divorce, the court will, with very few exceptions, grant the divorce to the petitioning party. The court reasons that if one person wants out of the marriage and wants a divorce, there has been an irretrievable breakdown of the marriage—and the divorce will be granted no matter what the objections of the other party. If the court finds no reasonable prospect of reconciliation, it will make a finding that the marriage is irretrievably broken for purposes of divorce.

2.2 The thought of going to a lawyer's office to talk about divorce is more than I can bear. I canceled my first appointment because I just couldn't do it. What should I do?

Many people contemplating a divorce may be meeting with a lawyer for the first time. They feel anxious about the experience.

Ask a trusted friend or family member to attend the initial consultation with you if that will help you to feel more comfortable and secure. Be aware, however, that before allowing your friend or family member to actually participate in the initial consultation, the attorney will want to confirm that you are willing to waive the confidentiality of your meeting by inclusion of a third party in the consultation.

If you decide to allow your friend or family member to actually participate in the initial consultation, that friend or family member can help you identify questions that are particular to your case, take notes during the initial consultation, and may help you remember any advice provided by the attorney. If having someone attend the consultation is not an option for any reason, simply express your concerns and fears to the attorney during your first meeting. The attorney will understand your fear and uncertainty at the prospect of divorce and will attempt to put you at ease and provide information that will leave you better equipped to address the divorce process.

It is far easier to go through divorce with an attorney by your side than to participate in the process unrepresented.

2.3 There is some information about my marriage that I think my attorney needs to know, but I'm too embarrassed to discuss it. Should I tell my attorney anyway?

Your attorney has an ethical duty and obligation to keep anything you discuss about your marriage confidential according to *Wisconsin's Rules of Professional Responsibility.*

Attorneys who practice divorce law are accustomed to hearing intimate and private information about clients and their families. Although this information may be deeply personal and embarrassing to you, it is unlikely that anything you tell your lawyer will be a shock to him or her. It is far better to arm your attorney with information so that he or she can make reasoned, intelligent decisions about your case. It serves no useful purpose to keep information from your attorney, who needs all relevant facts in order to fully protect your legal interests. If talking to your attorney doesn't work for you, consider sending the attorney a private and confidential e-mail from your personal e-mail account or a letter that fully expresses the facts. The best option is to talk personally with your attorney.

2.4 I've decided to file for divorce. How do I tell my spouse about my decision?

Once you've made the decision to divorce, set a private time to discuss your decision with your spouse (unless you fear for your safety or the safety of your children). In all likelihood your marriage has had problems for some time and your spouse will not be totally surprised by your decision to file for divorce.

Don't let your spouse be the last to know. If you want to have a workable negotiated divorce, the time to start that process is with a respectful conversation about your decision to file for divorce.

Also remember that when you file for divorce, the filing is listed on the Wisconsin Circuit Court Access website at http://wcca.wicourts.gov, so the information will immediately become available to your spouse. Don't let your spouse hear the news from another person.

2.5   I'm unsure how to tell our children about the divorce. I am worried I'll say the wrong thing. What's the best way to tell our children about the divorce?

There is no best way. Only you know your children. One of your children may react totally different than another one. Think about it in advance. Talk to your spouse about how to talk to the children about divorce. It's important that the two of you talk to the children together, if at all possible. Your goal is to convey to your children that they are loved. Even though mom and dad are divorcing, that does not mean that you are divorcing the children. Let them know that although things are going to be different, one thing will remain the same—the fact that you love them and that no divorce is going to change that love.

How you talk to your children about the divorce will depend on their ages, maturity, development, and need to know. Simpler answers are best for young children. Avoid giving them more information than they need. Changes in your children's everyday lives, such as a change of residence or one parent leaving the home, are important to children. They, too, will feel scared and anxious and will need the reassurance that both parents remain committed to them. Don't talk to children about legal proceedings and meetings with lawyers. This is adult information that should not be shared with children except under the most limited and exceptional circumstances.

After the initial discussion, keep the door open for further discussion. Let your children know that you are available to talk if questions arise. Assure them that it is okay to feel hurt and angry and upset. Acknowledge their feelings and offer support. Consider talking to school counselors, and consider getting your children counseling if you and your spouse believe that option will be helpful for the children.

2.6   My youngest child seems very depressed about the divorce, the middle one is angry, and my teenager is skipping school. How do we cope?

Don't ignore your children's difficulties in coping with the divorce. A child's reaction to divorce can vary depending on his or her age and other factors. Some may cry and beg for a reconciliation, and others may behave inappropriately.

Reducing conflict with your spouse, being a consistent and nurturing parent, and making sure both of you remain involved in the children's activities and education will provide security and a foundation that some parts of their lives will remain unchanged and positive.

Support groups for children whose parents are divorcing are also available at many schools and religious communities. A school counselor can provide support. Talk to the school counselor and ask him or her to immediately advise you if he or she can identify red flags relative to your child's behavior. If more help is needed, confer with a therapist experienced in working with children. Include your spouse in the discussions. Although you may sever your husband-and-wife relationship, you will continue to be parents.

2.7   I am so frustrated by my spouse's "Disneyland" parent behavior. Is there anything I can do to stop this?

Feelings of guilt, competition, or remorse sometimes lead a parent to be tempted to spend parenting time in trips to the toy store and special activities. Other times these feelings can result in an absence of discipline in an effort to become the favored parent or to make the time "special."

Shift your focus from the other parent's behavior to your own. Do your best to continue to be a supportive, reliable, loving parent during this time. This includes maintaining your children's routines relative to meals, bedtimes, chores, and homework. When possible, encourage family activities, as well as individual time with each child. Don't bad-mouth the other parent. If you have a foundation of love and support for your children, the actions of your spouse will not destroy that foundation.

Relative to your spouse's "Disneyland" efforts, make a list of how he or she is attempting to buy your children's allegiance. Don't share the list with your children. Just be prepared to have this documentation available in the event custody and placement become an issue.

Try to keep an open mind that your spouse's newfound involvement with the children may have some positive impact on the children because it will improve the relationship between parent and child. Remember, the issue is the best interest of your children, not how you feel about the other parent's conduct.

2.8 Between requests for information from my spouse's lawyer and my own lawyer, I am totally overwhelmed. How do I manage gathering all this detailed information by the deadlines imposed?

First, simply get started. Don't put off the task because many of these requests take time to obtain information from third parties. Ask your attorney any questions you may have. Make sure you are following instructions and not going off on a tangent. Provide only the information requested by your attorney.

Second, for some people it is easier to break down the obligation into smaller parts. Perhaps one evening gather your tax returns, and on the weekend work on preparing your monthly living expenses.

Another option is to ask a member of your family or a friend to assist you in drafting the necessary documents. Remember, you are probably providing your attorney with no more than a good rough draft. Very rarely will it be the final product because your attorney will want the opportunity to review the information that you have submitted. Do your best. Be thorough. Be clear. Be concise. Don't put it off. Provide the information to your attorney for final editing and approval.

2.9 I am so depressed about my divorce that I'm having difficulty getting out of bed in the morning. What should I do?

See a doctor now. Follow his or her recommendations for a psychologist, psychiatrist, or therapist. Join the YMCA. Get some exercise. Feelings of depression are common during a divorce. You want to make sure that you acknowledge and treat any psychological or physical problems. Going through a divorce is difficult. If you are having a problem with the process, realize you are not alone. Get help. Doing nothing and failing to admit that you need some assistance to get through the divorce may negatively impact issues in your divorce, including placement of your children. There is help available.

Take advantage of that help to address your state of mind and need for professional help.

Your health and your ability to care for your children are both essential. Follow the recommendations made by your health care professionals for therapy, medication, or other measures to improve your wellness. Remember, you are not alone. Help is available.

2.10   Will taking prescribed medication to help treat my insomnia and depression hurt my case?

Generally, no. Talk to your health care professional and follow his or her recommendations. Taking care of your health is of the utmost importance during this difficult time and will serve your best interest as well as the best interest of your children. Inform your attorney of any medications you are taking or treatment you are seeking. The court will look favorably on the fact that you identified a problem and addressed it. It is far worse to ignore the problem and to sink deeper into depression or sleeplessness or both.

2.11   I know I need help to cope with the stress of the divorce, but I can't afford counseling. What should I do?

You cannot afford not to get assistance. There are a number of options available in Wisconsin to address the need for help to deal with the stress of divorce. These options include meeting with a member of the clergy, joining a divorce support group, turning to friends and family members, or going to a therapist or psychologist.

If your budget is a concern, contact a social services agency that offers counseling services on a sliding-fee scale. In Wisconsin, outpatient services are provided by the Wisconsin Community Mental Health Counseling Centers, Inc. (www. communitymhccenters.com), www.HelpPRO.com, the Department of Health Services (www.dhs.wisconsin.gov/mental-health), and more. Contact the clerk of court in the county where you are located in order to obtain further referrals.

Additionally, there are several resources identified in the appendix of this book that will help determine if free or reduced fee counseling is available to you. If none of these options are available, review your budget and prioritize the need for counseling.

2.12   I'm the one who filed for divorce, but I still have loving feelings toward my spouse. I feel sad about divorcing. Does this mean I should dismiss my divorce?

Maybe, but a better option may be placing your divorce on a ninety-day suspension. In Wisconsin, you can place your divorce on a ninety-day suspension in order to explore the possibility of reconciliation. During the suspension period, you and your spouse may resume living together as husband and wife. If there are temporary orders in effect, they will be suspended. If there is any possibility that your marriage can be saved during this ninety-day suspension, you will have the opportunity to explore marriage counseling to address the problems in your marriage. If counseling fails, the ninety-day suspension can be lifted and your divorce will proceed through the process. If you and your spouse decide to reconcile permanently, the divorce will be dismissed.

So how do you decide if counseling is a viable option if your marriage appears to be on the rocks, but you continue to have positive feelings for your spouse? Ask yourself these questions: Have you and your spouse already participated in marriage counseling? Has marriage counseling helped in any way? Does your spouse actively participate or complain all the way to the counseling session? Does your spouse suffer from alcoholism? Drug addiction? Sex addiction? Gambling addiction? Is your spouse facing these addictions head-on or denying their existence? Has your spouse sought treatment for any addiction? Are you the victim of domestic abuse? Are you worried about your safety or the safety of your children if you remain in the marriage? Is your spouse involved in another relationship? Is your spouse willing to terminate that relationship and move forward with you? The answers to these questions should point you in a decisive direction.

Every case is different. My best advice is to work hard toward reconciliation, but if reconciliation is not successful, you should seriously consider whether proceeding with the divorce action is the best option for your future. Talk to your therapist or social worker or spiritual advisor to help determine the right path for you and your children.

2.13 Will my lawyer charge me for the time I spend talking to him about my feelings about my spouse?

Yes. Your attorney generally gets paid by the hour, and if you are using that time to discuss your feelings and emotional concerns, your attorney is still paid his or her hourly rate. However, if your attorney is being paid a flat rate for handling your divorce, the time spent talking with you will be included in that flat fee. Remember, however, that your lawyer is not a therapist, and your money may be better spent in actual therapy or counseling.

2.14 My lawyer doesn't seem to realize how difficult my divorce is for me. How can I get her to understand?

Any divorce client wants support and understanding from his or her attorney. That's why you selected your attorney in the first place. Speak frankly to your attorney about your concerns. It may be that your lawyer does not see the significance of your issues. So communicate. Talk personally to your attorney. Send your attorney an e-mail advising him or her of the issues you believe are significant. Your willingness to improve communication will assist your lawyer in understanding how best to support and communicate with you.

2.15 I've been told not to speak ill of my spouse in front of our children, but I know my wife routinely trashes me to the children. Why can't I just speak the truth?

Don't copy the negative actions of your spouse. Your children need you. Your children need to know that they can rely on you to be a steady force in their lives. If your spouse is bad-mouthing you, write down and verify any such speech so that it can be brought to the attention of the court or the guardian *ad litem* or your spouse's attorney. Keep your children out of your divorce. Divorce is hard enough on children. You do not want to play any part in making the process more difficult for your children.

2.16 Nobody in our family has ever been divorced, and I feel really ashamed. Will my children feel the same way?

Being the first person in your family to go through a divorce is a difficult burden to bear, even outside the divorce process. Families have expectations and goals, and divorce is not included in those goals and expectations. But times change and needs require action. If your marriage puts you and your children in an untenable situation, having the fortitude to file for divorce is a sign of strength, independence, and responsibility. You are to be commended rather than criticized. Recognize that families come in different identities and formations. Your goal now is not to maintain your marriage, but to restructure your family so that you and your children are happy and whole.

Your children will have an opportunity to witness you overcoming obstacles, demonstrating independence, and moving forward in your life. You can be a great teacher to your children during this time by demonstrating pride in your family and in yourself.

2.17 I am terrified of having my deposition taken. My spouse's lawyer is very aggressive, and I'm afraid I will say something that will hurt my case.

A deposition is an opportunity for your spouse's attorney to gather information and to assess the type of witness you will be if your case proceeds to trial. Feeling anxious about your deposition is normal, but remember that most divorce depositions are quite uneventful.

Your attorney will meet with you in advance to prepare you for the deposition and to give you fair warning of the questions opposing counsel will ask. The attorney will offer you guidance and instruction on how to respond to questions. The goal is to prepare for your deposition in advance so you have the confidence and information you need to successfully participate in the deposition. Once the deposition starts, your attorney will be sitting next to you the entire time.

2.18   I am still angry at my spouse. How can I be expected to sit in the same room during a settlement conference?

Talk to your attorney about your options and his or her recommendations. One option may be "shuttle" negotiations. With this method, you and your attorney remain in one room while your spouse and his or her attorney are in another room. Settlement offers are then relayed between the attorneys throughout the negotiation process. By shifting your focus from your angry feelings to your goal of settlement, it may be easier to proceed through the process with this method.

Four-way, face-to-face meetings are very common in the divorce process. More can be accomplished across the negotiating table than in trial. Your attorney will assist you in preparation for the settlement conference, and your attorney can act as spokesperson. If questions arise, ask to speak to your attorney outside the negotiation session. In this situation, downplay your anger. Being angry during the settlement negotiations may render the negotiation process fruitless—wasting time, energy, and money. Have a game plan. Stick to it. Rely on your attorney to be the quarterback of the negotiation session. The fastest way to get over your anger is to settle the divorce and proceed with your future.

2.19   I'm afraid I can't make it through trial without having an emotional breakdown. How do I prepare?

A divorce trial can be a highly emotional time, requiring a great deal of support. Some of these ideas may help you through the process:

- Meet with your lawyer in advance of your court date to prepare for trial.

- Ask your lawyer whether there are any documents you should review in preparation for trial, such as a transcript of your prior deposition, your interrogatory answers, and your financial disclosure statement.

- Visit the courtroom in advance to get comfortable with the surroundings.

- Ask your lawyer about having a member of your family or friend available in the courtroom to lend support. That person should not be your significant other whose presence may escalate already raw emotions.

- Avoid alcohol, eat appropriately, dress for success, exercise, and get plenty of rest during the days leading to trial. Each of these will help you prepare for the emotions of the day.

- Visualize a successful divorce trial. Picture yourself sitting in the witness chair, giving clear, confident, and truthful answers to any questions you are asked.

- Arrive early at the courthouse so that you can participate in any last-minute negotiations.

- Take slow, deep breaths. Breathing deeply will steady your voice, calm your nerves, and improve your focus.

By taking the above steps, you can increase the likelihood of a successful trial experience. Your attorney will be prepared to support you throughout the proceedings.

2.20 I am really confused. One day I think the divorce is a mistake, the next day I know I can't go back, and a few minutes later I can hardly wait to be single again. Some days I just don't believe I'm getting divorced. What's happening?

Denial, transition, and acceptance are common feelings for a person going through a divorce. One moment you might feel excited about your future and a few hours later you might think your life is ruined.

Remember that you will go through different stages as you proceed with the divorce process. You may not pass from one stage to the next in a direct line. Feelings of anger or sadness may suddenly appear, even years after you are divorced. Divorce is hard. It is not a happy time and you should feel free to grieve over the loss of your marriage. On the other hand, your mood might feel bright when you think about future plans, even while you are mourning the loss of your marriage and your life as it used to exist.

Taking good care of yourself is essential during this period of your life. Your vacillating emotions require a tremendous amount of energy. Allow yourself to experience your emotions, but also continue moving forward with your life.

3

Working with Your Attorney

If there is one thing on which you can rely in your divorce, it is that you will be given plenty of advice from friends and family. Well-intentioned neighbors, cousins, and complete strangers will be happy to tell you war stories about their ex-spouse or about their sister, brother, or cousin who got divorced many years ago. Some people will insist that they know exactly what steps you should take, even though they know little, if anything, about the individual circumstances of your case or the laws in Wisconsin.

But there is one person whose advice will be important to you: your attorney's. Your lawyer should be your trusted and supportive advocate at all times throughout your divorce. The advice of your attorney may affect your life for years to come. You will never regret taking the time and energy to choose the right attorney for you and your individual circumstances.

Consider your relationship with your attorney as a partnership. With clear and open attorney-client communication, you will have the best opportunity for a positive outcome of your divorce, and the divorce process itself will prove less stressful.

By working effectively with the right attorney, you will be able to rely on the attorney's professional advice and simply thank those family, friends, and neighbors for sharing their divorce experiences and horror stories with you.

3.1 Where do I begin looking for an attorney for my divorce?

There are many ways to find a divorce lawyer. Ask for a recommendation from people you trust who have already gone through a divorce and had a successful relationship with their divorce attorney. If you know other professionals, such as accountants, doctors, or therapists, who regularly work with attorneys, ask for a referral to an attorney who is experienced in divorce, custody and placement disputes, and/or family law. Sometimes you will receive a referral from a person who is very disappointed in the results of his or her divorce, but thought opposing counsel did a masterful job. You may want to put that opposing counsel on your list of potential attorneys to represent your interests.

Consult your local bar association or the Wisconsin Bar Association at www.wisbar.org/forpublic/ineedalawyer/pages/lris.aspx, to utilize their referral services. Be sure to specify that you are looking for an attorney in your local area who handles divorces and is experienced in family law. It is important to obtain an attorney who is knowledgeable in the areas of divorce and family law to represent your interests in your divorce. You may also want to select an attorney who is familiar with the judges, clerks, and attorneys in the county where your divorce is filed.

Check with the law schools at Marquette University and the University of Wisconsin-Madison. A faculty member may be able to recommend a family law attorney in your area.

Options are also available online. Most attorneys have websites that provide information on their practice areas, professional associations, experience, and philosophy. The following sites also provide referral information and lawyer reviews: www.Avvo.com and www.Martindale.com.

3.2 How do I choose the right attorney?

The most important step in filing for divorce is to select an experienced divorce attorney. Your divorce is important. You do not want to retain an attorney who is unfamiliar with Wisconsin divorce trends, procedures, and laws. Although many attorneys handle divorce, it is likely you will have more effective representation from a family law attorney with experience and recognized credentials in the areas of Wisconsin divorce, custody and placement disputes, property division, and support.

Before meeting with a divorce lawyer, identify the issues that are most important to you and the questions that should be addressed in your initial consultation. The most important question an attorney asks a potential client is about his or her goals in seeking the divorce. Is custody and placement the biggest issue? Maintenance? Keeping the family home? It is important that you and your divorce attorney are on the same page. Your attorney should be a trusted professional with whom you feel comfortable sharing information openly. He or she should be a zealous advocate for your interests who will help you make many strategic and procedural decisions throughout your divorce.

Your initial divorce consultation may be your first meeting with an attorney. Most attorneys want to be supportive and provide you with useful information about divorce law and procedures. Feel free to seek all of the information you need to help you determine that you have made the right choice in selecting an attorney.

It is important that you have confidence in the attorney you hire. If you're unsure whether the lawyer is really listening to you or understanding your concerns, keep looking until you find one who meets your requirements. Consider the qualities in an attorney that are important to you. Even the most experienced and skilled attorney is not right for every person.

The following are questions you might ask before selecting a divorce attorney to represent your interests:

- How long have you practiced law in Wisconsin?
- What percentage of your practice is devoted to family law and divorce?
- Have you previously represented people in situations like mine?
- What is your Martindale-Hubbell rating? What is your Avvo rating?
- How will I be able to reach you in an emergency?

- If you're away from the office, will someone in your office know about my case if I need help in your absence?
- Will you discuss my case with me over the telephone?
- If you do not practice in this area of the law, will you provide me with other attorney recommendations?
- Who else in your law firm will work on my case?
- What percentage of your divorce cases actually go to trial?
- Are you familiar with the judges, clerks, and attorneys in the county where my divorce will be filed?

The attorney-client relationship is based on trust and good communication. Make sure you are comfortable with the lawyer's style and method of practice.

3.3   Should I hire a "bulldog"—a very aggressive attorney?

Again, consider the qualities in an attorney that are important to you. A "bulldog" may promise to be overly aggressive and take your spouse for everything he or she is worth. However, it is important to create a mutually respectful relationship with your spouse during and after the divorce, especially if you have minor children. Hiring an attorney with a reputation as a fierce litigator is often a good idea if it appears that your case may proceed to trial on custody and placement, maintenance, child support, or other significant issues. An attorney with a reputation as a tenacious trial attorney is always someone you want to have in your "back pocket," but there is no need, generally, to start a divorce with aggressive, intimidating tactics. A worthy goal in your divorce is the ability of you and your spouse to jointly appear as parents in your children's wedding photos or graduation pictures, even after your divorce is long finalized. This is one of those times when "walk softly, but carry a big stick" is a good plan of action.

Additionally, expect the cost of your divorce to be more if there is substantial, continuing litigation and high-conflict communication between the attorneys and between you and your spouse. The right attorney will be able to negotiate a reasonable settlement, as well as litigate tenaciously if settlement efforts fail.

3.4 Should I interview more than one attorney?

Be willing to interview more than one attorney. Every lawyer has different strengths, and it is important that you find the one who is right for you. Sometimes it is only by meeting face to face with more than one attorney that you can balance competing strengths and weaknesses in the attorney's representation. That being said, sometimes you immediately know after the first interview that you have met the attorney who will best represent your interests. Follow your intuition, as well as your research relative to the selection of an attorney. The best divorce attorneys are busy, and you may rest assured that if you believe an attorney is good and will well represent your interests, the likelihood is that your spouse and your spouse's attorney will think your attorney is excellent, too. That respect is a good start to the divorce process.

Remember that changing lawyers in the middle of litigation can be stressful and costly. It is wise to invest energy at the commencement of the divorce in selecting the divorce attorney who is right for you. But times change, issues change, judges change, and circumstances in general change. If you find during the divorce that the attorney you selected is not meeting your needs, it is far better to substitute attorneys than to proceed with an attorney who is not protecting your interests or with whom you do not feel compatible.

3.5 My spouse says because we're still friends we should use the same attorney for the divorce. Is this a good idea?

No. It is not a good idea to use the same attorney as your spouse. Even in the most amicable of divorces, the parties have differing interests and expectations. Lawyers owe a duty of confidentiality and loyalty to a client, so a lawyer cannot represent both you and your spouse in the divorce.

However, it is not uncommon for one party to retain an attorney while the other party does not. That does not mean that the attorney represents the interests of both parties, but rather that one party goes unrepresented, sometimes incorrectly believing his or her interests are represented. That is not the case. The attorney who drafts the marital settlement agreement is one-sided and adverse to the unrepresented spouse because the attorney singularly represents the interests of his or her client. The unrepresented spouse's interests are not protected, nor has the unrepresented spouse been provided with any advice relative to legal rights and responsibilities.

If your spouse has filed for divorce and you have decided not to retain legal counsel, you should nevertheless consult with an attorney for initial advice about the divorce process. Also consider retaining an attorney for the purpose of reviewing the proposed marital settlement agreement. The Wisconsin Supreme Court allows limited-scope representation. *Limited-scope representation* allows an attorney's role in a divorce to be limited to one or individual proceedings or issues. Specific procedures will apply to limited-scope representation, so make sure any lawyer you retain on this basis is familiar with this new Wisconsin representation option. Although limited scope representation is better than no representation, it is not better than legal representation from start to finish.

3.6   What information should I take with me to the initial consultation with an attorney?

If you have already been served with divorce pleadings, provide these pleadings to the attorney to review at the initial consultation. You should also provide any prior judgments of divorce, restraining orders, and prenuptial or postnuptial agreements between you and your spouse. Paternity and adoption orders may also be of importance to the attorney at the initial consultation. The attorney will also ask you for the dates of birth and Social Security numbers of all members of your family, so be prepared with that information.

One of the most important financial tools in any divorce action is your income tax return. The income tax return not only provides information regarding income from all sources, but also information such as pensions, investments, business write-offs, and business expenses. Try to provide at least the last two years of any personal and business income tax returns for review at your initial consultation. If available, you should also provide current payroll stubs for you and your spouse.

If your situation is urgent or you do not have access to these documents, don't let that fact stop you from scheduling an initial consultation with an attorney. Reliable, accurate, legal advice is more important than obtaining detailed financial information at the beginning of the divorce process. Your attorney can explain to you the options for obtaining these financial records if they are not readily available to you.

3.7 What unfamiliar words might an attorney use at the first meeting?

Law has a language all its own, and attorneys sometimes lapse into "legalese," forgetting that nonlawyers may not recognize words used daily in the practice of law. Some words and phrases you might hear at your initial consultation include the following:

- *Summons*—The summons is used to begin the divorce action. It must be personally served on the respondent. If the respondent cannot be located, the action is started by publishing the summons in the local newspaper.

- *Petition*—The petition sets forth statistical facts about the marriage and the parties and also states that the marriage is irretrievably broken. The petition is served with the summons.

- *Petitioner*—The petitioner is the person who files the divorce petition.

- *Respondent*—The respondent is the person who did not file the divorce petition.

- *Jurisdiction*—The jurisdiction is the authority of a court to make rulings affecting a party.

- *Service*—The process of notifying a party about a legal filing.

- *Motion*—A motion is a written request that the court enter a particular order. A hearing will generally be held to determine whether or not the motion should be granted.

- *Affidavit*—An affidavit is a statement of facts that is verified by the writer and submitted to the court in support of a pleading.

- *Temporary order*—This is an order of the court or by the family court commissioner setting forth temporary orders in effect prior to the final divorce. It usually covers such items as custody, visitation, support, attorney's fees, temporary use of the home and other property of the parties, payments of bills and mortgages, and more.

- *Response and counterclaim*—The response and counterclaim is a pleading that the respondent will file in response to the petition. The response will set forth any areas of disagreement with the allegations and requests contained in the petition. For example, the respondent may allege that the marriage is not irretrievably broken or may allege that the petitioner is not a fit parent for custody and placement. A counterclaim sets forth the respondent's divorce requests.

- *Discovery*—The process during which each side provides information to the other party, either formally or informally.

- *Stipulation*—A formal, written agreement between the parties and/or their attorneys. It can cover any subject relevant to the divorce process.

- *Default divorce*—If there is a stipulation or agreement regarding all terms of the final judgment, the divorce is considered to be a "default" divorce.

- *Contested divorce*—A contested divorce is one in which the parties cannot agree about one or more of the terms of the divorce, such as division of assets, allocation of debts, maintenance, child support, custody or placement, and more.

- *Findings of fact, conclusions of law,* and *judgment of divorce*—This is a formal, written document usually prepared by the petitioner's attorney and approved by opposing counsel. The judgment is signed by the judge who makes formal findings of fact and conclusions of the law. This document sets forth the facts of the divorce, as well as the terms of the divorce resolution on all issues.

Never hesitate to ask your attorney the meaning of a term. Your complete understanding of your lawyer's advice is essential. For additional information, see the glossary at the end of this book.

3.8   What can I expect at my initial consultation with an attorney?

Most attorneys will ask that you complete a questionnaire prior to the meeting so the attorney is aware of your basic demographic and financial circumstances and can offer advice tailored to your individual needs.

The nature of the advice you get from an attorney during an initial consultation will depend on whether you are still deciding to file for divorce or if you are ready to file for divorce immediately. Your attorney's advice will also depend on whether you have decided to move from the residence, whether custody and placement are issues, your financial circumstances, and whether there is a prenuptial agreement. Each set of circumstances is different and guides an attorney's time and attention in the initial consultation.

During the initial consultation, you can expect to discuss the following issues with your attorney:

- A brief history of your marriage
- Background information regarding yourself, your spouse, and your children
- Basic income and employment information
- The circumstances supporting your decision to file for divorce
- Your intentions and goals regarding a successful resolution of your divorce
- Your specific questions and concerns about the divorce process and procedure

You can expect the attorney to provide you with the following information:

- The basic procedure for divorce in Wisconsin
- Identification of potential issues in divorce
- Background information regarding the firm
- Information about attorney fees, retainers, and court costs

Although some questions may be impossible for the attorney to answer at the initial consultation, the initial consultation is an opportunity to weigh whether you and the attorney will work well together as partners in your divorce action.

3.9 Will the communication with my attorney be confidential?

Yes. Your lawyer has an ethical duty to maintain your confidentiality. This duty of confidentiality also extends to the legal staff working with your attorney. The privileged information that you share with your attorney will remain private and confidential unless this privilege is waived by you alone.

3.10 How can I make sure the facts of my divorce are not made public?

Your attorney cannot disclose information about your divorce because of the existence of attorney-client privilege. But sometimes information about your divorce becomes public because of your own actions. To ensure that communications between you and your attorney remain confidential, and to ensure that the facts and circumstances of your divorce do not become public, consider the following suggestions to maintain privacy:

- Do not disclose the content of your communications with your attorney to third parties. Third parties include friends and family members.

- Social media provides the potential for waiving the attorney-client privilege by publicly disclosing confidential information. Do not post information or send messages relating to your case on Facebook, Twitter, or other social media websites.

- Do not post information relating to your case or communications with your attorney on a personal blog, video blog, online chat rooms, or online message boards.

- Do not use your work-related e-mail to communicate with your attorney or to discuss your case. Depending on your employer's policy relating to electronic communication, the attorney-client privilege may be waived by communicating with your attorney or by discussing your case through your personal e-mail account (such as Gmail, Yahoo, or Hotmail) on a work computer. To ensure your communications remain confidential, it is best to limit communication via e-mail to your private e-mail address from your home computer.

You may actually want to waive your attorney-client privilege in some instances, for example if you want your attorney to consult with an expert or to talk to a member of your family about your divorce. In that event, you will generally sign an attorney-client waiver in which you specifically waive the attorney-client privilege.

3.11 May I take a friend or family member to my initial consultation?

Yes, but you will waive your attorney-client privilege if you include another person in your initial consultation. You should address this issue with the attorney prior to simply walking into the initial consultation with another person. That being said, having another person present during your initial consultation may be a source of support and additional information. That person may be able to take notes on your behalf so that you can focus on the attorney's advice and can ask questions relevant to your particular circumstances.

3.12 What exactly is my attorney's role at the onset of the divorce process?

Your attorney will play a critical role in helping you obtain a successful divorce. That's why it is important that both you and your attorney get off to a good start at the onset of the divorce.

Here are the first steps your attorney will likely take on your behalf at the beginning of the attorney-client relationship:

- Check for any conflict of interest.
- Determine whether the court has jurisdiction of your divorce or whether a different court has concurrent jurisdiction. For example, if your spouse files in Milwaukee County and you file in Kenosha County, both you and your spouse will have filed correctly, assuming you meet the time requirements for jurisdiction. A determination will have to be made as to the proper venue.

- Develop a strategy and philosophy for your divorce. Prioritize those issues of most importance to you. Advise you of your rights and responsibilities.
- Listen to your concerns and know the facts and circumstances of your particular case.
- Prepare a comprehensive financial disclosure statement with your assistance. A sample financial disclosure statement can be found in the appendix.
- Explain Wisconsin's divorce law and what you can expect relative to the court's decision making. Identify what factors the court addresses in rendering its decision.
- Explain and maintain attorney-client privilege.

As your advocate, your attorney represents your interests from the date of engagement and payment of the retainer to the filing of the judgment of divorce.

3.13   What other professionals will work with my attorney on my divorce case?

Depending on the issues identified by your attorney, you can expect to work with a number of different professionals, including appraisers, financial planners, real estate agents, child psychologists, and more.

Additionally, in some cases where custody or placement is disputed, the court may appoint a guardian *ad litem* to act as an attorney advocate for the minor child/children. This attorney has the duty to represent the best interest of your child/children.

3.14   I've been divorced before, and I don't think I need an attorney this time. However, my spouse is hiring an attorney. Is it wise for me to be unrepresented?

Having gone through a prior divorce, you may have learned a great deal about the divorce process as well as your legal rights. However, you should be cautious about proceeding without legal representation.

Every divorce is different. The length of your marriage, whether custody and placement are in dispute, whether you signed a prenuptial agreement, whether a business and other assets have to be appraised, the amount of your financial estate, the disparity of incomes between you and your spouse, and your age and health are some factors that impact whether or not you should be represented by an attorney.

In addition, divorce law is complex and ever-changing. Only an attorney can recognize legal issues and determine creative, legal solutions to those issues. While *pro se* ("on one's own") assistance may be available if you represent yourself, generic *pro se* forms do not take into account your individual circumstances. Of course, your financial well-being is also a factor in determining if you can afford legal representation. You will have to balance these factors to determine whether to retain an attorney or to represent yourself in your divorce action.

At a minimum, you may wish to obtain an initial consultation with an attorney to discuss your rights and responsibilities in your divorce. Armed with this additional information, your decision whether or not to retain legal counsel should be clearer.

3.15   May I take my children to meetings with my attorney?

Generally, the answer is no. You want the ability to speak candidly with your attorney about the facts and circumstances of your case and to speak freely about significant issues in your marriage. This is not information for the ears of children. In addition, it is important that you give your attorney your full attention, which you cannot do if children are in the office during the consultation with your attorney.

Most law offices are not designed to accommodate young children and are ordinarily not "child-proof." For both your child's well-being and your own peace of mind, do not include your children in meetings with your attorney. Get a babysitter or explore other arrangements for your children during that time.

It's also recommended that you take every measure to keep information about the divorce from your children. They should not be in the middle of the divorce proceedings. Knowledge that you are seeing an attorney can add to your child's anxiety. It can also make your child a target for questioning by the other parent.

3.16 What is the role of the *legal assistant* or *paralegal* in my attorney's office?

A *legal assistant* or *paralegal* is a trained legal professional whose duties include providing legal support for you and your lawyer. Legal assistants assist in the development of discovery, preparation of financial documents, receipt of information required in the divorce process, scheduling, document review, case updates, and more. Working with a legal assistant can make your divorce easier because a legal assistant is likely to be available and knowledgeable about your case. If your attorney is not available, the legal assistant or paralegal may be able to answer your basic questions or provide information regarding the scheduling of your case. Remember, however, a legal assistant is prohibited from giving legal advice. It is important that you respect the limits of the role of the legal assistant if he or she is unable to answer your questions because the answers may require legal advice.

3.17 My attorney is not returning my phone calls. What should I do?

You have a right to expect your phone calls to be returned by your attorney in a reasonable time frame. You may, however, obtain a quicker response by e-mail, so explore that option with your attorney. Remember, most divorce attorneys are litigators as well, so much of their time is often spent in the courtroom. It is unrealistic to expect an attorney to answer his or her phone calls within a few minutes or a few hours under those circumstances. Be patient.

Here are some other options to consider:

- Ask to speak to a legal assistant or another attorney in the office.
- Send an e-mail or fax telling your lawyer that you have been trying to reach him or her by phone, and explain the reason why it is important that you receive a call.
- Ask the receptionist to schedule a phone conference for you to speak with your attorney at a specific date and time.

- Schedule an appointment with your attorney to discuss both the issue needing attention as well as your concerns about communication.

Your attorney wants to provide good service to you. If your calls are not being returned, take action to get the communication with your lawyer back on track, but also remember that phone calls to your attorney incur fees. Be judicious in the number of phone calls you make to your attorney and consider other communication options, such as e-mail or fax, which may be quicker and less expensive.

3.18   How do I know when it's time to change lawyers?

Changing lawyers is costly. You will incur legal fees for your new attorney to review information that is already familiar to your current attorney. You will spend time giving much of the same information to your new lawyer that you provided to your original attorney. A change in lawyers may also result in adjournments in your case.

Your answers to the following questions will provide insight into the decision whether to seek substitute counsel:

- Have I spoken directly to my attorney about my concerns?
- When I expressed concerns, did my lawyer take action accordingly?
- Is my lawyer open and receptive to what I have to say?
- Am I blaming my lawyer for the bad behavior of my spouse or opposing counsel?
- Have I provided my lawyer with all requested information so the lawyer may take necessary action in my divorce?
- Is my dissatisfaction based on the conduct of my attorney, or am I disillusioned by the laws of the State of Wisconsin or the actions of the judge?
- Do I trust my lawyer to act in my best interest?
- What would be the advantages of changing lawyers when compared to the cost?

- Do I believe my lawyer will support me in achieving the outcome I'm seeking in my divorce?

Every effort should be made to resolve concerns with your attorney. If you have made this effort and the situation remains unchanged, it may be time to substitute lawyers. Remember, however, that the lawyer you are terminating usually is entitled to be paid his or her attorney's fees in full before the substitution of attorney takes place. Also be aware that any substitution of attorney must be approved by the court. Substitution is not automatic, particularly if a trial is scheduled within a short time frame. As a result, the best alternative is to identify any problems with your attorney and give your attorney sufficient time to address those issues.

3.19 What should I expect when working with my attorney during the divorce process?

Your attorney will provide you with legal support and guidance during the divorce process. Each case is different. Each attorney has his or her own methods and procedures. Each law firm has different resources, staff, communication skills, and relationships with other attorneys and judges. But generally you may expect the following attorney-client involvement in any divorce:

- *Meet with your attorney before court appearances.* You can expect your attorney to meet with you prior to any significant court appearances. A "meeting" may include an office appointment, a telephone conference, communication via e-mail, or communication between you and legal assistants. It depends on the importance and difficulty of the court appearance.

- *Discuss the importance of the temporary hearing.* You can expect your attorney to discuss with you the importance of obtaining temporary orders during the divorce process to protect your interests and the interests of your children. Temporary orders are sometimes needed to spell out each party's rights and responsibilities while the divorce is pending.

- *Explain the divorce process.* You can expect your attorney to explain the legal process if you have questions regarding any step of your divorce. Understanding the legal process reduces the stress of your divorce.

- *Listen to your questions and concerns.* You can expect your attorney to listen to your questions and to address any of your concerns about the divorce process.

- *Advise you of your divorce rights.* You can expect your attorney to advise you relative to your divorce rights and responsibilities and to project reasonable outcomes in your case. Your attorney does not have a crystal ball and cannot guarantee a particular result in your divorce case, but your attorney should understand the facts and circumstances of your case and apply those facts and circumstances to Wisconsin divorce law.

- *Assist in the completion of discovery.* You can expect your attorney and his or her staff to assist you in the completion of discovery responses and to provide you with guidance relative to your deposition and trial testimony.

- *Communicate and negotiate with opposing counsel.* You can expect your attorney to communicate with opposing counsel and to attempt to negotiate a reasonable settlement on your behalf. Although your attorney cannot control the actions of your spouse and his or her attorney, your attorney is able to initiate communication and to act as your advocate relative to all divorce issues.

- *Create solutions.* You can expect your attorney to think creatively regarding issues in your case and to provide options for your consideration. But remember, Wisconsin law controls. Although you may want your attorney to set legal precedent on your behalf, an attorney is bound by the laws of the State of Wisconsin, as well as the financial circumstances of your case.

- *Facilitate the negotiation process.* Although your attorney can't force your spouse to settle the divorce, your attorney may take action to promote settlement, including drafting settlement proposals, or scheduling mediation, or four-way settlement conferences.

- *Be prepared.* You can expect your attorney to be prepared to try your case with the knowledge, preparation, and expertise necessary to obtain a realistic result on your behalf. Before going to trial, you can expect your attorney to provide you with his or her analysis of the potential outcome, again recognizing that no attorney can guarantee a particular result.

3.20 Are there certain things my attorney cannot or will not do on my behalf?

Yes. Although there are many things your attorney can successfully accomplish during your divorce, there are some things your attorney cannot accomplish, no matter what the circumstances:

- *Change your spouse's actions.* An attorney cannot force your spouse to exercise placement with your children. However, be mindful that failure to follow a placement order may result in an increase in child support because one party is supporting the children 24/7. It may also be a basis for modification of the placement order. Keep your attorney advised of the status of placement.

- *Make opposing counsel or your spouse respond to settlement offers.* An attorney cannot force the other party to respond to a settlement proposal. Your attorney may send settlement proposals to your spouse or opposing counsel if your spouse is represented by an attorney. However, your attorney cannot make the other party respond or accept a settlement proposal. Both parties must agree on all terms of a settlement proposal before the court incorporates the settlement into a court order or judgment of divorce. If one party rejects the settlement proposal or any part of it and makes the decision to proceed to trial, a trial will occur, even if the party's position is unreasonable.

- *Control opposing counsel's communication.* An attorney cannot control the tone of communication from opposing counsel or communications from the other party or the other party's family members. Unfortunately, communication from the opposing attorney may sometimes appear rude, condescending, abusive, or controlling. Your attorney cannot control the actions of opposing counsel, your spouse, or your spouse's family.

- *Relive your life.* Your attorney cannot remedy poor financial decisions made during your marriage. With few exceptions, Wisconsin law requires division of the marital estate at the time of divorce. Neither your attorney nor the court can remedy prior poor financial decision making, such as overspending or poor investments by your spouse.

- *Demand an accounting of how support payments are spent.* Absent extraordinary circumstances, Wisconsin law does not require the parent receiving child support to provide an accounting of the use of child support.

- *Guarantee timely payment of support.* Enforcement of payment of support is possible only when it is court ordered. In most circumstances, Wisconsin law requires implementation of a wage assignment. However, even with a court order, you may experience inconsistent timing of payment due to job loss, refusal to pay, or underreporting of income, particularly in cases of self-employment. Keep your attorney advised of repeated missed payments.

- *Keep your expense and payment records.* Your attorney cannot help you collect child care and uninsured medical expenses if you do not keep records and receipts of payment. If your judgment of divorce requires you to provide documentation of payment of expenses to the other party and you fail to do so, in all likelihood you will be prohibited from collecting reimbursement for those expenses. Follow the court's orders regarding documentation to the other party, even if he or she doesn't pay the expenses. Always keep records of these expenses and the payments made by each parent. Note the date and time of payment and make copies of any communications with the other parent. It is much easier to keep these records contemporaneously rather than attempt to obtain copies of old checks, day care bills, medical bills, and insurance documents at a later time.

There are simply certain things your attorney cannot do. Your attorney cannot suddenly make your spouse act on matters in a timely fashion and become more organized. Remember why you're getting divorced, and do not expect your attorney to be able to control the actions of your spouse and his or her attorney.

4

Attorney Fees and Costs

Any time you make a major investment, you want to know the up-front cost, projected future costs, and whether the investment is going to reap benefits in the end. Investing in quality legal representation for your divorce is no different. You want to know what your legal counsel will be able to accomplish on your behalf.

The cost of divorce is a major concern for almost all divorce litigants. As a result, you want to make a reasoned, intelligent decision as a consumer of legal services. You want to retain an experienced, recognized, successful attorney, but you also want to pay reasonable attorney fees.

While the initial retainer or engagement fee is easily ascertainable, divorce fees depend on a number of factors and are not always predictable at the onset. In Wisconsin, these factors include the amount and character of services, responsibility and difficulty of the legal work involved, nature and importance of litigation, professional skills and experience of your attorney, value of your marital estate, expertise and reputation of the firm you select to represent you, results and benefits derived from the legal services, and more.

There are some steps you can take to control the cost of your divorce, the most important of which is insisting on a written retainer or legal services agreement. It is also important to develop a plan for payment of your attorney fees and any costs associated with the divorce. Discuss fees at your initial consultation. Speak openly about your concerns and your ability to pay. Ask the attorney how fees are charged and determined.

Make sure you review any retainer or legal services agreement in advance. Don't just sign the document the minute it is set in front of you. Read it before you sign!

4.1 May I get free legal advice from a lawyer over the phone?

An attorney will usually not provide free legal advice over the phone or by e-mail because insufficient facts are known about the specific circumstances of your case. To give advice in a vacuum opens the door to misinformation, incorrect advice, and potential malpractice by the attorney. Prior to answering questions about your divorce, an attorney must review the basic facts, circumstances, and background of your marriage. Lawyers will, however, usually answer general questions about the divorce process over the phone.

4.2 Will I be charged for an initial consultation with a lawyer?

Each law firm has its own policy. Some attorneys provide a free initial consultation. Others charge an hourly fee for the consultation.

When scheduling your initial appointment, ask whether or not the consultation is free. If not, what is the cost? If a fee is charged for the initial consultation, you will be required to pay the fee at the time of the initial consultation.

4.3 If I decide to hire an attorney, when do I have to pay him or her?

Once you make the determination to retain an attorney, payment arrangements must be made. You are generally required to pay the retainer and sign the legal services agreement at the same time. The retainer is not necessarily the final fee you will pay for the divorce but is the initial, up-front, start-up fee for retention of the attorney or law firm. Generally, the attorney-client relationship does not begin until the retainer is paid in full or mutually agreeable payment arrangements are made.

4.4   What exactly is a *retainer*?

A *retainer* is a sum paid to your lawyer in advance for services to be performed and costs to be incurred in your divorce.

If your case is accepted by the law firm, expect the attorney to request a retainer following the initial consultation. The amount of the retainer may vary from hundreds of dollars to several thousand dollars, depending on the nature of your case. Contested custody or placement cases, or divorces involving businesses or interstate disputes, for example, are likely to require higher retainers.

4.5   Will my attorney accept my divorce case on a *contingency fee basis*?

No. A *contingency fee* is a percentage fee that is paid at the conclusion of successful case resolution. In Wisconsin, lawyers are prohibited from entering into a contingent fee contract for divorce representation.

4.6   How much does it cost to get a divorce?

The cost of your divorce will depend on many factors. Some attorneys handle divorces for a flat fee, but most charge an hourly rate. A *flat fee* is a fixed amount for the legal services provided. A flat fee is more likely to be used when there are no children of the marriage and the parties have agreed on the division of their property and debts. It is important that you discuss fees and costs during your initial consultation with the attorney.

Be sure to ask your attorney what portion of the retainer is refundable if you do not continue with the case or if you terminate your relationship with the attorney before the retainer payment is used in its entirety. Your retainer agreement should also identify a method for resolving fee disputes. In Wisconsin, the State Bar of Wisconsin provides a fee arbitration program at State Bar of Wisconsin, P.O. Box 7158, Madison, WI 53707-7158 or (800) 728-7788 (www.wisbar.org/forpublic/ihaveadisputewithmylawyer/pages/fee-arbitration-program.aspx).

Before proceeding to fee arbitration, talk to your attorney. Often, errors and misunderstandings can be quickly and satisfactorily addressed. Even if a genuine dispute occurs, most attorneys are willing to address the issue in order to maintain a positive attorney-client relationship. The worst thing either the client or the attorney can do is ignore the problem.

4.7   What are typical hourly rates for a divorce lawyer?

In Wisconsin, attorneys charge varying rates. Fees depend on the experience of the attorney, law firm rates, difficulty of the case, skills, reputation, location, and many more factors. Rates in Milwaukee can exceed $500 per hour. Rates in small communities are generally as low as $150 per hour. Currently, a reasonable, mid-range hourly rate is $250 to $300. Rates may increase and decrease as the economy rises and falls.

Larger law firms charge different rates for different attorneys, so make sure you know your options and which attorney will be assigned to your case and at what hourly rate. Remember, experience and reputation count, so rate is not the only factor in determining which attorney to retain to represent you in your divorce.

4.8   If I can't afford to pay the full amount of the retainer, will I be able to make monthly payments to my attorney?

Every law firm has its own policies regarding payment arrangements for divorce clients. Often these arrangements are tailored to the specific client. Most attorneys will require a substantial retainer to be paid at the beginning of the case. Some attorneys may accept monthly payments in lieu of the retainer. Some attorneys may require an additional retainer as your original retainer is used and your case progresses. Ask your attorney frank questions to make sure you know your exact responsibility for payment of legal fees.

4.9   I agreed to pay my attorney a substantial retainer to begin my case. Will I have to make monthly payments in addition to the retainer?

Maybe yes, maybe no. Each attorney and law firm has different practices and procedures. Generally, the retainer is depleted by subtracting the hourly rate for legal services performed, and as the retainer is depleted, an additional retainer may be required. Alternatively, the retainer agreement may have a provision that requires any unpaid legal fees to be paid within thirty days of receipt. Remember, some attorneys charge interest on unpaid balances, so the best way to keep costs down and maintain a positive attorney-client relationship is to pay your attorney fees on time. If you are unable to do so, communicate with your attorney and make other specific payment arrangements mutually agreeable to both of you.

4.10 My lawyer gave me an estimate of the cost of my divorce and it sounds reasonable. Do I still need a written fee agreement?

Absolutely. You need a written fee agreement. In order to define the scope of legal services and to ensure specificity regarding hourly rate and payment of costs, a retainer agreement is necessary. Costs generally include costs of experts, transcripts, filing fees, appraisers, and more. Some attorneys include costs of postage and copying, some do not. That issue should be addressed in your retainer agreement.

A clear fee agreement reduces the risk of misunderstandings between you and your lawyer. It will also help maintain a good attorney-client relationship focused on legal representation and not on a dispute over fees and costs.

A retainer or legal services agreement is a contract between you and your attorney and will usually include the following:

- How much the attorney is going to charge, including the hourly rate and initial retainer fee
- Whether you will be responsible for costs such as filing fees, service fees, deposition fees, long-distance calls, copying, and expert-witness fees
- The scope of the legal representation
- The minimum fees for various services
- Accounting methods and options in the event of a payment dispute

4.11 How will I know how the fees and charges are accumulating?

Your retainer agreement should spell out how payment of attorney fees and costs will be determined. Even if your attorney agrees to handle your divorce for a "flat fee," your fee agreement should clearly state what legal services are included in the flat fee.

At the outset of your case, be sure your written fee agreement includes a provision that your attorney will provide you with regular statements of your account or on request. Review each statement promptly after you receive it. Check to make sure there are no errors, such as duplicate billing entries. If you have questions regarding any legal service performed or costs charged, contact your attorney or his or her staff to address the issue. Your attorney's office should welcome any questions you have about services provided.

If you do not regularly receive an account statement from your attorney, call your attorney's office to request an updated statement. Legal fees and costs can mount quickly. It is important that you stay aware of the status of your legal expenses.

4.12 What expenses are related to the divorce litigation in addition to lawyer fees?

Talk to your attorney about other fees and costs that may be incurred as part of your divorce. These fees and costs may include filing fees, court reporter expenses, subpoenas, expert-witness fees, vocational evaluation costs, and mediation or parenting class fees. Expert-witness fees may be a substantial expense, ranging from hundreds to thousands of dollars, depending on the type of expert and the extent to which the expert is involved in your case. In a custody/placement case, there may be fees for the guardian *ad litem,* psychological evaluations, social services investigations, and more.

Your attorney should talk to you in advance of incurring any major expenses so you can make appropriate arrangements for payment and can advise your attorney of your position on incurrence of these costs. However, some costs, such as filing fees, transcript costs, and more, are not discretionary. Arrangements must be made for payment of these expenses even if you did not approve them in advance.

4.13 Who pays for the experts such as appraisers, accountants, psychologists, and mediators?

Costs for the services of experts, whether appointed by the court or hired by the parties, are ordinarily paid by the parties.

In the case of a guardian *ad litem,* an attorney who is appointed by the court to represent the best interest of your children, the total guardian *ad litem* fees depend on the amount of time spent by the guardian *ad litem* and at what hourly rate. Guardian *ad litem* fees are generally split 50/50. However, depending on the circumstances, such as great disparity of income or over-trial, one party may be ordered to pay the entire fee, or one party may be required to advance the fee. (Over-trial occurs when one party extends the litigation process even though there is little or no chance of success on the merits. Sometimes the cost of this extended litigation must be borne by the party who caused the "over-trial.") If you can demonstrate a very low income and inability to pay, the county may be ordered to pay your share of the guardian *ad litem* fee, or a payment schedule may be set up to give you time and opportunity to make regular payments.

Psychologists either charge by the hour or set a flat fee for their evaluations. Again, the court may order one party to pay the fee or both parties to share the expense. It is not uncommon for a psychologist to request payment in advance and hold the release of an expert report until fees are paid.

Mediators may charge a flat fee or an hourly rate. Generally, each party will pay one-half of the mediator's fee.

The fees for many experts, including appraisers and accountants, will vary depending on whether the expert performs one isolated service such as an appraisal, or the expert is called to testify as a witness in a deposition or at trial.

Some fees are exclusively the responsibility of the party incurring the cost. For example, one party may require a vocation rehabilitation expert to support his or her position that his or her spouse is able to work at a higher level. In that event, the fee for the vocational rehabilitation expert will be paid by the party who called him or her as a witness.

Fees and costs vary from case to case and from attorney to attorney. Again, the best way to keep fees and costs within your expectations is to have a specific written retainer agreement that spells out how fees and costs are determined.

4.14 What factors will impact how much my divorce will cost?

Although it is difficult to predict the total amount of your legal fees, the following are some of the factors that impact the total cost:

- Whether custody and placement are in dispute
- Whether your divorce presents any novel legal questions
- Whether a pension plan(s) is subject to division
- Whether there is a prenuptial or postnuptial agreement between the parties
- Whether either of the parties have received gifted or inherited property, and whether or not that property has been commingled
- Whether you and/or your spouse have a premarital interest in property or debt
- The nature and number of the issues contested
- The cooperation of your spouse and opposing counsel
- The frequency of your communication with your attorney
- The ability of you and your spouse to communicate with each other
- The promptness with which information is provided and/or exchanged between both you and your spouse and the attorneys
- Whether there are litigation costs, such as fees for expert witnesses or court reporters
- The extent of discovery
- The hourly rate of the attorney

Reviewing regular invoices from your attorney and communicating with your attorney about any questions or concerns will help keep you on track with the overall cost of your divorce.

4.15 Will my attorney charge for phone calls and e-mails?

Unless your case is handled on a flat-fee basis, you should expect to be billed for any communication with your attorney. Your attorney will provide much of his or her representation by phone or e-mail.

Make sure, when you call your attorney for advice, that you plan your phone call in advance to reduce any wasted time. Organize the information you want to discuss. Review in advance your questions and any concerns. This will keep your attorney-client phone call or e-mail communication to a minimum while at the same time addressing each of your questions and concerns.

4.16 Will I be charged for talking to the staff at my lawyer's office?

It depends. Check the terms of your fee agreement with your lawyer. Whether you are charged fees for talking to law firm members other than your attorney depends on the firm procedure. Most law firms charge for the services of legal assistants, paralegals, and law clerks.

Remember that nonlawyers cannot give legal advice, so it is important to respect their roles. Don't expect the receptionist to give you an opinion whether you will be awarded primary placement of your children or whether you will receive sufficient maintenance.

4.17 What is a *litigation budget,* and how do I know if I need one?

If your case is complex and you are anticipating substantial legal fees, ask your attorney to prepare a *litigation budget* for your review. This may help you understand the nature of the services projected, the time that may be spent on your case, and the overall amount of attorney fees and costs you can expect to pay if your divorce is going to include substantial litigation. This information may also be helpful for budgeting and planning for additional retainers. Knowing the anticipated costs of litigation may help you make meaningful decisions about the benefits of trial versus the benefits of settlement.

4.18   What is a *trial retainer,* and will I have to pay one?

The purpose of a *trial retainer* is to fund the additional, time-intensive legal services needed to prepare for trial and for trial itself. A trial retainer is a sum of money paid in advance to your attorney when it becomes necessary to start the trial preparation process.

Confirm with your attorney that any unearned portion of your trial retainer will be refunded if your case settles in advance of trial. Remember, however, many cases settle on the courthouse steps the day of trial, after days and hours of costly trial preparation. Ask your lawyer whether and when a trial retainer might be required in your case so that you can avoid surprises and plan your budget accordingly.

4.19   How do I know whether it is cost-effective to go to trial?

Deciding whether or not to take a case to trial is a challenging decision that requires the expertise, experience, and knowledge of your attorney to weigh and determine. Although the decision is ultimately yours, your attorney will be able to provide you with his or her opinion of the likelihood of success on various trial issues.

When issues in dispute are primarily financial issues, settlement is easier because you are able to balance the financial cost of trial with the financial benefit of a negotiated settlement. Your attorney, in most instances, will be able to provide you with a range of expectations, in the event your case goes to trial. Operating with this information, you can generally decide whether there is a cost benefit to a potential win at trial versus a specific, clear, negotiated settlement.

If your decision whether to proceed to trial involves a child-custody/placement issue, your decision is more difficult. You ultimately have to decide what is in the best interest of your children, taking into consideration the recommendations of the guardian *ad litem,* social worker, psychologist, and others. The cost of litigation or trial may or may not play a role in this decision making depending on your financial circumstances.

4.20 Is there any way I can reduce some of the legal expenses of divorce?

Litigation of any kind may be expensive, and divorces are no exception. There are some things you can do to control costs, including the following:

- *Put it in writing.* Instead of calling your attorney with a question, consider providing it to your attorney by mail, fax, or e-mail. This will create an accurate record and it may take less time for your attorney to answer than playing telephone tag.

- *Keep your attorney informed.* Your attorney should keep you up to date on the status of your case. You should do the same with your attorney. Advise your lawyer about any significant developments in your life including a change of address, change of employment, change of income, or purchase or sale of property. During your divorce, if your contact information changes, be sure to notify your attorney. Your attorney may need to reach you with information, and reaching you in a timely manner may help avoid more costly fees later.

- *Obtain copies of documents.* An important part of divorce discovery includes the collection of documents, such as tax returns, account statements, credit card statements, and medical records. These records may be available at your fingertips. It is far easier and less costly for you to obtain the information than for your attorney to do so.

- *Review your attorney's website.* The answers to commonly asked questions about the divorce process may often be found on your attorney's website. Check www.vhdlaw.com for valuable divorce information.

- *Get to know the support staff at your lawyer's office.* Although not able to provide legal advice, the receptionist, legal assistant, paralegal, legal secretary, or law clerk may be able to answer your questions regarding the status of your case. All communication with your attorney's staff is required to be kept strictly confidential.

- *Consider working with an associate attorney.* You may find that working with an associate attorney is a good option. Hourly rates for an associate attorney are typically lower than those charged by a more experienced attorney. Frequently, the associate attorney has trained under the more experienced lawyer and has developed good trial skills, legal knowledge, and divorce litigation experience.

- *Leave a detailed message.* If your attorney knows in advance why you are calling, your attorney can be prepared to answer your question when he or she talks to you. This not only gets your answer faster, but it also reduces costs.

- *Discuss more than one matter during a call or e-mail.* If your question is not urgent, consider waiting to call until you have more than one question. Whenever possible, provide information requested by your lawyer in a timely manner. This avoids the cost of follow-up by your lawyer and the additional expense of extending litigation.

- *Carefully review your attorney statements.* Scrutinize your billing. If you believe an error has been made, contact your lawyer's office to discuss your concerns.

- *Remain open to settlement.* Trial costs money and can polarize relationships. Although a trial is sometimes inevitable, there are circumstances when a negotiated settlement is in the best interest of all involved.

4.21 I don't have any money and I need a divorce. What are my options?

If you have a low income and few assets, you may be eligible to obtain divorce representation at no cost or minimal cost through one of the following organizations:

- Legal Aid Society of Milwaukee at http://lasmilwaukee.com
- University of Wisconsin Family Court Clinic at http://law.wisc.edu/eji/familycourt/index.html
- Legal Action of Wisconsin at www.legalaction.org

- State Bar of Wisconsin Modest Means Program (www.wisbar.org/forPublic/INeedaLawyer/Pages/Modest-Means.aspx)
- Community Justice, Inc. (www.communityjusticeinc.org)
- Northern Wisconsin Legal Advice Project (www.nwlap.org/client.php)
- Wisconsin Judicare, Inc. (www.judicare.org)

These organizations have a screening process for potential clients, as well as limits on the number and nature of cases accepted. The demand for services is usually greater than the number of attorneys available to handle such cases. Consequently, if you are eligible for legal services from one of these programs you may end up on a waiting list. If you believe you might be eligible for participation in one of these programs, inquire early to increase your opportunity to get the legal help you need.

Filing your divorce *pro se* ("on one's own") is also an option. You may obtain *pro se* pleadings for completion at https://myforms.wicourts.gov. Also, many Wisconsin counties have assistance programs to provide procedural direction to *pro se* litigants. Check with your local clerk of courts for more information.

4.22 I don't have much money, but I want an attorney to represent me. Where do I get the funds for a retainer?

If you have some money but not enough to retain an attorney, consider some of these financial options:

- Borrow the legal fees from friends or family. Often those close to you are concerned about your future and will support you in your divorce. If the retainer is too much money to request from a single individual, consider whether a group of friends and/or family would each contribute a lesser amount to help pay for your attorney.
- Charge the legal fees on a low-interest credit card or consider taking out a loan.

- Start saving. If your case is not urgent, consider developing a plan for saving the money you need to proceed with a divorce.
- Talk to your attorney about using money held in a joint account with your spouse.
- Find an attorney who will work with you on a monthly payment basis.
- Ask your attorney to bring a motion to request that your spouse contribute to your attorney's fees, especially if there is a substantial disparity in income between you and your spouse.
- If you and your spouse have acquired substantial assets during the marriage, you may be able to find an attorney who will agree to be paid when the assets are divided at the conclusion of the divorce.

Closely examine all sources of funds readily available to you. Consider contacting the State Bar of Wisconsin's Lawyer Referral and Information Service (LRIS) at (800) 362-9082. Let them know you have some ability to pay and ask for help finding a lawyer who will take your case for a reduced fee.

4.23 Is there anything I can do on my own to get child support if I don't have money for a divorce/paternity lawyer?

Yes. If you need child support for your children, contact the Wisconsin Department of Children and Families (http://dcf. wisconsin.gov), the Wisconsin Child Support Program (http:// dcf.wisconsin.gov/bcs/), or the child-support agency (http:// dcf.wisconsin.gov/bcs/agencylist.htm) in your county for help in obtaining a child-support order. These agencies can pursue support from the noncustodial parent of your children.

4.24 If my mother pays my legal fees, will my lawyer be able to tell her private information about my divorce?

Without your permission, your attorney cannot ethically disclose information about your case to another person even if that person is paying your attorney fees. No matter what the opinion and recommendation of the person paying your attorney fees, your lawyer's duty is to remain your zealous advocate. The attorney's loyalty is to you and you alone.

4.25 Can I ask the court to order my spouse to pay my attorney fees?

Yes. If you want the court to order your spouse to pay your legal fees, discuss this possible option with your attorney at the first opportunity. However, your attorney's fees are ultimately your personal obligation no matter who is ordered to contribute to them.

If there is a substantial disparity in income between you and your spouse, the court may order your spouse to advance fees, but generally because of the 50/50 property division presumption in Wisconsin, each party is ultimately ordered to pay his or her own fees and costs. You may be ordered to reimburse your spouse for fees advanced on your behalf.

4.26 What happens if I don't pay my attorney fees?

Your attorney may withdraw from representation if you do not comply with your fee agreement. Your attorney may also request a judgment against you for the amount of any outstanding attorney's fees plus interest and costs.

If you are having difficulty paying your attorney's fees, talk with your attorney about payment options. Consider borrowing the funds, using your credit card, or asking for financial help from friends and family.

Above all, do not avoid communication with your attorney if you are having challenges making payment. Keeping in touch with your attorney is essential to keeping a positive attorney-client relationship.

5

The Discovery Process

Discovery is one of the least understood steps in divorce, but it is often one of the most important. *Discovery* is a pretrial phase of divorce during which each party may obtain information from the opposing party or relevant third parties. The purpose of discovery is to ensure that both you and your spouse have access to the information needed to make necessary decisions in your divorce. Discovery includes the generation of all financial resources so the requesting party has sufficient information to negotiate a fair and reasonable agreement.

In some cases, one party handles most of the financial information in the marriage. If information is not voluntarily produced by that party during the divorce process, discovery allows the spouse without access to information to acquire that information by discovery.

Discovery may also include depositions of significant witnesses, both experts and laypersons, who can provide insight and information relative to issues in dispute, including custody, placement, expert valuations, and more.

The discovery process may seem tedious at times because of the need to obtain and provide detailed and copious information. Completing discovery, however, may help clarify the issues in divorce. The discovery process may also be costly, but not as costly as proceeding to trial without accurate and complete information.

5.1 What might be included in the discovery process?

Discovery includes the following:

- *Interrogatories*—A list of written questions one spouse sends to another as part of the discovery process. The recipient must answer the questions under oath and within a certain period of time, generally thirty days. The number of questions included in a set of interrogatories is usually limited by court rules.

- *Requests for production of documents*—A written document request to your spouse that relates to issues in your divorce. The request for production of documents must state the specific items requested. These items may include written reports of expert witnesses, statements of any party, financial records, loan applications, report cards, performance reviews, and many more.

- *Requests for admissions*—A written request that allows one party to request that another party admit or deny the truth of a statement under oath. If admitted, the statement is considered to be true for all purposes of the divorce. Requests for admissions are generally used to settle uncontested issues or to specifically determine the areas of dispute.

- *Depositions*—The out-of-court, under-oath testimony of a witness that is transcribed for potential later use in court or for discovery purposes. Depositions take place in a lawyer's office, not in court.

- *Releases*—Documents that authorize the release of confidential documents or records

- *E-discovery*—Discovery of electronically stored information. The parties should meet and confer as soon as possible to discuss the identification of potential subjects of *electronically stored information (ESI)*. These discussions should include the preservation of such information and the form in which the ESI discovery should be produced.

- *Physical and mental examination of parties; inspection of medical documents*—When the mental or physical condition of a party is an issue, the court may order the party to submit to a physical, mental, or vocational examination.

Talk to your lawyer about the nature and extent of discovery anticipated in your case.

5.2 How long does the discovery process take?

Discovery may take anywhere from a few weeks to many months, depending on factors such as the complexity of the case, the cooperation between you and your spouse, whether any expert witnesses are necessary, and the scheduling orders of the court.

Interrogatories, requests for production of documents, and requests for admissions must be answered, generally, within thirty days from receipt. Other time frames are less restrictive and are determined by the lawyers or by the scheduling order of the court.

5.3 My lawyer insists that we conduct discovery, but I don't want to spend the time and money on discovery. Is discovery really necessary?

The discovery process may be critical to a successful outcome of your case for the following reasons:

- It increases the likelihood that any agreements reached are based on accurate information.
- It provides necessary information for deciding whether to settle an issue or whether to proceed to trial.
- It assists in providing an accurate and complete defense to the position of your spouse.
- It avoids surprises at trial, such as unexpected layperson or expert-witness testimony.
- It helps make sure all potential issues are identified and addressed by your attorney.

Discuss with your attorney the reason a certain type of discovery is recommended to make sure discovery is consistent with your goals and a meaningful investment of your legal fees.

5.4   I just received interrogatories and a request for production of documents from my spouse's attorney. My lawyer wants me to respond with a rough draft within two weeks. I'll never make the deadline. What do I do?

Answering your discovery promptly will help move your case forward and help control your legal fees. There are steps you can take to make this task easier:

- First, look at all the questions. Many of them will not apply to your case or may be answered with a simple "yes" or "no."

- Ask someone you trust to help you. This may help make the process less difficult.

- Break it down into smaller tasks. If you answer just a few questions a day, the job will not be so overwhelming.

- Call your lawyer and ask whether a paralegal in the office is available to help you organize the needed information.

Delay in the discovery process often leads to frustration by clients and lawyers, as well as increased legal fees. Do your best to provide the information in a timely manner.

5.5   I don't have access to my documents, and my spouse is being uncooperative in providing my lawyer with information. Is my lawyer able to request information directly from an employer or financial institution?

Yes. Your attorney may ask your spouse to sign an authorization allowing the release of information to your attorney. This authorization is directed to the source of the information, such as an employer or financial institution. Your attorney may also decide to take the deposition of an officer of the financial institution or of the employer or to subpoena information to be provided to the attorney by a specific date and time.

5.6   My spouse's lawyer intends to subpoena my medical records. Aren't these private?

Whether your medical records are released in your case will depend on your spouse's and the court's need to know versus your right to privacy. You have patient-doctor and patient-psychologist privilege, which must be applied to the discovery process. This is a complex area of the law that must be discussed and researched by your attorney. There is no one answer that fits every person or situation.

5.7   I own my business. Will I have to disclose my business records?

Yes. You may be required to provide extensive records of your business in the discovery process. These records may include some or all of the following information:

Entity Records:

- Corporate minutes book
- Articles of incorporation and bylaws, including amendments, and corporate minutes if a corporation, or similar documents if a partnership or LLC
- List of the officers and directors
- Documents detailing any issues of stock, and details of any prior equity transactions involving the entity

Financial Statements and Supporting Documents:

- Corporate journals, ledgers, and trial balances
- Financial statements for the last three fiscal years ended and the most current financial statements available
- Accounts payable list as of the latest fiscal year-end and available quarters of the current year
- Accounts receivable list as of the latest fiscal year-end and available quarters of the current year
- Explanation of significant nonrecurring and/or non-operating items appearing on financial statements, if any
- Information regarding any contingent assets or liabilities
- Depreciation schedules showing original cost and accumulated depreciation by named item

Assets/Debts:

- A current list of all assets and debts concerning your business, including a list of all inventory, where it is located, the individual value of all inventory, and all notes or other accounts payable owed by the business

- All notes and mortgages owed by your business to third parties, together with amortization schedules regarding such payments

Banking Records:

- Monthly statements from all accounts in any bank, credit union, savings and loan association, or other financial institution in which your business has had any interest in the last eighteen months and all checks and check registers for the same period
- All net-worth statements filed with any financial institution within the last twenty-four months
- All notes and debts to banking institutions

Taxes:

- State and federal tax returns for the last three fiscal years ended
- Internal Revenue Service or other government agency audits or reports, including all adjustments, received during the last three years

Evidence of Property Values:

- Appraisals of real estate, equipment, collectibles, and any other business appraisals that may exist
- Insurance policies in force and amounts of coverage at the valuation date
- Real and/or personal property tax bills for the last two years
- Most recent personal property tax form

Contractual Agreements and Obligations:

- Copies of significant leases in effect for equipment and property
- Copies of any buy-sell agreements, options to purchase stock or rights of first refusal, trust agreements,

or other documents affecting the ownership rights of the owners of your business

- Information regarding prior sales or offers to buy control or other interests in the entity being valued
- Covenants not to compete
- Other significant contracts

Management and Operation of the Entity:

- Compensation statements for owners, directors, partners, officers, and managers, including benefits received for the last three fiscal years and available quarters of the current year

Sales and Marketing:

- Budgets, projections, sales forecasts, and profit-and-loss forecasts for the last two years and future years, if available
- Copies of marketing literature, including catalogs, brochures, or advertisements

Sale of/Transfer of Ownership of Business:

- If your interest has been sold or transferred in any manner, produce an accounting of all transfer papers and consideration received.

Personal Investment in Business Interests:

- Any documents relating to the investment of moneys or other assets by you to date including, but not limited to, copies of canceled checks, subscription agreements, and any financial statements furnished in connection with the acquisition of your interest
- Any documents relating to any indebtedness incurred by you in connection with your acquisition of such interest including, but not limited to, copies of canceled checks, purchase agreements and notes, subscription agreements, and any financial statements furnished in connection with the acquisition

- Any documents of loans you personally made to the business or any other business entity or any loans the aforementioned made to you, personally
- Any financial statements or credit applications prepared on behalf of you, personally, or on behalf of the business or any other business or entity you have an interest in, furnished to any bank or lending institution

Provisions for Disposition of Business on Death of Owner:
- Any documentation or information relating or pertaining to you, referring to or dealing with the disposition of your interests on the death, disability, or other reason for cessation of any entity in which you hold/held an economic interest

Employee Compensation and Benefits:
- List of all employees and all documentation relating to payroll including your salary and benefits
- Summary plan description for shareholders, partners, and/or participation in profit sharing, pension plans, and health insurance plans for shareholders, partners, and employees. Include any policies regarding payment or reimbursement for participants in each plan
- All life insurance policies that accumulate any cash value

No matter which business document you provide, consider asking the court to sign an order keeping the information private and confidential, except for access by the attorneys, business valuators, and parties in your divorce.

5.8   It's been two months since my lawyer sent interrogatories to my spouse, and we still don't have my spouse's answers. I answered my interrogatories on time. Is there anything that can be done to speed up the process?

The failure or refusal of a spouse to follow the rules of discovery may add to both the frustration and expense of the divorce process. Talk with your attorney about filing a *motion to compel* seeking a court order that your spouse be compelled to provide the requested information by a certain date. A request for attorney fees may also be part of the motion to compel because of your spouse's failure to timely respond to discovery.

Your attorney should determine whether different options to obtain the documents may produce a more positive result, such as a *subpoena duces tecum* and/or *notice of deposition* to an employer or financial institution if your spouse does not comply with discovery.

5.9 What is a *deposition*?

A *deposition* is the asking and answering of questions under oath outside of court in the presence of a court reporter. The person being deposed may not ask any questions. It is only the attorney who asks questions of the person being deposed. A deposition may be taken of you, your spouse, or potential witnesses in your divorce case, including experts. Both attorneys will be present. You and your spouse also have the right to be present during depositions of any witnesses in your case. A deposition may be videotaped or transcribed by a court reporter. A deposition, which is usually conducted in a lawyer's office, may last fifteen minutes or may take days.

5.10 What is the purpose of a deposition?

A deposition may serve a number of purposes, including the following:

- Obtaining necessary information and background relative to a witness
- Assessing the credibility of a witness and his or her demeanor as a witness
- Helping your attorney determine what witnesses to subpoena for trial
- Helping to avoid surprises at trial by determining the testimony of a witness in advance of trial
- Preserving testimony in the event the witness becomes unavailable for trial

Depositions may be essential tools in a divorce, especially when a case is likely to proceed to trial.

5.11 Will what I say in my deposition be used against me when we go to court?

If you testify at trial and give testimony contrary to your deposition, your deposition may be used to impeach you, or call into question your integrity or truthfulness, by showing the inconsistency in your statements. It is important to review your deposition prior to your trial testimony to make sure you are consistent and knowledgeable about the facts of your case.

5.12 Will the judge read the depositions?

Unless a witness becomes unavailable for trial or gives conflicting testimony at trial, it is unlikely that the judge will ever read the depositions.

5.13 How should I prepare for my deposition?

To prepare for your deposition, review the important documents in your case, such as the petition for divorce, any answers to interrogatories or request for production of documents you have previously submitted, your financial statement, and any temporary hearing affidavits.

Gather all documents you've been asked to provide for your divorce and deliver them to your attorney in advance of your deposition for copying and review. Talk to your attorney about the type of questions you will be asked. Discuss with him or her any questions you are concerned about answering.

5.14 What will I be asked? May I refuse to answer questions? Are there rules to follow during a deposition?

Questions in a deposition may cover a broad range of topics including your education, work, income, and family. The attorney is allowed to ask anything that is reasonably calculated to lead to the discovery of admissible evidence, even if the answer may ultimately be inadmissible at trial. If you are unsure whether or not to answer a question, look to your attorney for advice.

Your attorney may object to inappropriate questions. If there is an objection, say nothing until the attorneys discuss the objection. You will be directed whether to answer.

Remember the following advice when answering questions during your deposition:

- Never state facts that you do not know. If you do not know an answer to a question, say so.
- Never attempt to explain or justify your answer. You are there to give the facts as you know them. You are not supposed to apologize or attempt to justify those facts.
- Only give the information that you have readily at hand. Do not promise to get information that you don't have readily at hand, unless your attorney advises it.
- Do not, without your counsel's request, reach into your pocket for a driver's license, Social Security card, or other documents. The discovery deposition purpose is to elicit facts that you know. Unless you have been served with a subpoena that directs you to bring certain documents to the deposition, you are not required to bring or produce anything while you are testifying.
- Do not let the opposing attorney get you angry or excited. Under no circumstances should you argue with the opposing attorney.
- If your attorney begins to speak, stop whatever answer you may be giving and allow your attorney to make his or her statement. If your attorney tells you not to answer a question, then you should refuse to do so.
- You may take your time in answering a question. Remember, the deposition does not show the length of time you took to answer a question.
- Do not joke during a deposition. The humor may not be apparent in the transcript.
- Do not volunteer any facts not requested by a question.
- Answer truthfully.
- After the deposition is over, do not chat with your spouse or your spouse's attorney. Remember, the other attorney does not represent your interests. Do not let a friendly manner cause you to drop your guard.

The bottom line is to be prepared and to follow your attorney's instructions to the letter. The above guidelines are just that, guidelines. Your attorney knows the specifics of your case, and you should follow his or her direction prior to and during the deposition.

5.15 What if I give incorrect information in my deposition?

You will be under oath during your deposition, so it is very important that you be truthful. If you give incorrect information by mistake, contact your attorney as soon as you realize the error. If you lie during your deposition, you risk being impeached by the other lawyer during your divorce trial. This could cause you to lose credibility with the court, making your testimony less valuable. Make sure you read the transcript of your deposition once you receive it from your attorney. If there are any areas that are untruthful or that may require further information, consult your attorney at once.

5.16 What if I don't know or can't remember the answer to a question?

You may be asked questions of which you have no knowledge. It is always acceptable to say "I don't know" if you do not know the answer. Similarly, if you cannot remember, simply say so.

5.17 What else do I need to know about having my deposition taken?

The following suggestions will help you give a successful deposition:

- Prepare for your deposition by reviewing and providing necessary documents.
- Get a good night's sleep the night before. Eat before you have your deposition taken or at least have something in your pocket to eat in case the deposition lasts longer than you originally expect.
- Arrive early for your deposition so that you have time to get comfortable with your surroundings, but do not talk to opposing counsel. Wait for your attorney to arrive.

- Relax as much as possible. Your attorney is there to protect your interests and to guide you during this process.
- Remember your spouse's attorney will be judging your credibility and demeanor.
- Listen carefully to the entire question. Do not try to anticipate questions or start thinking about your answer before the attorney has finished asking the question.
- If you don't understand a question, say so.
- Take your time and carefully consider the question before answering. There is no need to hurry.
- If your answer is an estimate or approximation, say so. Do not let an attorney pin you down to anything if you are not exactly sure. Don't guess.
- If an attorney mischaracterizes something you said earlier, say so or ask to talk with your attorney.
- Speak clearly and loudly enough for everyone to hear you.
- Answer all questions with words, rather than gestures or sounds. "Uh-huh" is difficult for the court reporter to distinguish from "unh-unh" and may result in inaccuracies in the transcript.
- If you need a break at any point in the deposition, request one.

Remember that the purpose of your deposition is to support a good outcome in your divorce.

5.18 Are depositions always necessary? Does every witness have to be deposed?

Depositions are less likely to be scheduled if you and your spouse are reaching agreement on most of the issues in your case and you are moving toward a settlement. Depositions are more likely to be required in cases where there are significant issues between the parties. Although depositions of all witnesses are usually unnecessary, it is common to take depositions of expert witnesses.

5.19   Will I get a copy of the depositions in my case?

Ask your attorney for copies of the depositions taken in your case. It will be important for you to carefully review your deposition if your case proceeds to trial.

6

Mediation and Negotiation

If your marriage is difficult, you probably expect your divorce to be difficult. You picture yourself retaining a lawyer with a reputation as a "barracuda" because you have an angry spouse and there is increasing animosity between the two of you. You wonder if there is any way out of this nightmare.

Alternatively, perhaps you and your spouse are parting ways amicably. Although you don't necessarily agree on all the terms and conditions of your divorce, each of you is hopeful that the divorce will be a reasonable and respectful process. You want to spend your hard-earned money moving forward rather than paying high attorney fees, expert-witness fees, and other costs.

In either case, trial before a judge is not the only option available to you. In fact, most Wisconsin divorce cases settle without a trial. Mediation and/or settlement negotiations may help resolve any disputed issues without the necessity of trial before a judge.

Resolving your divorce through mediation or a negotiated settlement has many advantages. You have the ability to achieve a mutually determined agreement with a known and predictable outcome, reduced attorney fees, and little, if any, risk of appeal. Despite the circumstances that led to the end of your marriage, it may be possible for your divorce to conclude on a cooperative note through the use of mediation or other settlement options.

6.1 What is the difference between *mediation* and *negotiation*?

Both mediation and negotiation are methods used to avoid contentious litigation and to give you and your spouse the ability to make decisions about your divorce and about your future without the intervention of a judge.

Mediation utilizes the skills of a trained mediator who acts as an independent, neutral third party who assists you and your spouse in the settlement process. Mediation is often referred to as *alternative dispute resolution* or *ADR. Mediation is defined as a cooperative process involving the parties and a mediator, the purpose of which is to help the parties resolve their disagreements by applying communication and dispute resolution skills.

Negotiation is a fact of life in any divorce and involves the attorneys and parties working toward a final resolution of all divorce issues without the necessity of court intervention.

6.2 What types of issues may be mediated or negotiated?

Any issue in your case can be mediated or negotiated. However, you may also decide that certain issues are non-negotiable, although it is always best to keep an open mind. In advance of mediation or negotiation, determine if any issue is nonnegotiable so you can advise your spouse of that fact before or at the commencement of negotiations. For example, a nonnegotiable issue may be the children's attendance in the same school district where they currently reside. By advising all parties of this position, you can move forward within that parameter rather than wasting time on alternative proposals. If there is no agreement and the parties remain entrenched in different positions, trial is the answer.

6.3 Are there different types of mediation? How does mediation work?

Generally, in a Wisconsin divorce there are two times when mediation is implemented. Initially, if custody or placement is in dispute, the court will order the parties to mediation. In custody/placement mediation, you and your spouse will meet with a trained mediator to attempt to resolve nonfinancial issues involving your children. Your attorney is not present during custody/placement mediation.

Mediation is also used to resolve other divorce issues, such as property division and support. In this type of mediation, you and your spouse, as well as your attorneys, meet with the mediator to attempt to reach resolution. It is your responsibility to participate in mediation with an open mind.

There is no hard-and-fast procedure for mediation. Generally, in final divorce mediation, the parties convene together and the mediator advises the parties of his or her role. The facts are reviewed jointly to make sure there is an agreement to the facts of the marriage and the issues in dispute. At that point, each party and his or her attorney generally sit in a separate room and the mediator participates in shuttle diplomacy from one room to the other, exchanging proposals and information, as necessary, until resolution or impasse is reached.

How long the process of mediation continues depends on many of the same factors that affect how long your divorce will take. These include how many issues are in disagreement, the complexity of these issues, and the willingness of each of you to work toward an agreement. Your case could settle after one mediation session or it might require a series of meetings. Mediation may last an hour or may last the entire day into the night. If resolution is reached, the agreement is immediately reduced to writing by one of the attorneys. If mediation fails, the court is advised so that the case can proceed to trial.

6.4   My lawyer said that mediation and negotiation may reduce delays in completing my divorce. Is this accurate?

When the issues in your divorce are decided by a judge there are many opportunities for delay. Reasons for adjournment and delay may be:

- Waiting for the trial date
- Having to return to court on a later, second date if your trial is not completed on the day it is scheduled
- Waiting for the judge's ruling on your case
- Scheduling additional court hearings after your trial to resolve disputes about the intention of your judge's

rulings, issues that were overlooked, or issues disputing the language of the judgment of divorce

Each one of these factors could delay your divorce by days, weeks, or even months. Mediating or negotiating the terms of your divorce judgment can help eliminate these delays.

6.5 How will mediation and negotiation lower the costs of my divorce?

If your case is not settled by agreement, you will go to trial. If there are many issues in your divorce and these issues are complex, such as custody, placement, and valuation issues, your attorney's fees and costs have the potential of skyrocketing.

By settling your case without the necessity of trial, you may be able to save thousands of dollars in legal fees and much emotional distress. You should know in advance the potential cost of divorce litigation so you can balance the costs of litigation with any negotiated settlement.

6.6 Are there other benefits to mediating or negotiating a settlement?

Yes. A divorce resolved by a mediated or negotiated agreement may have these additional benefits:

- *Allow for brainstorming.* Mediation and negotiating settlement allow brainstorming between the parties and lawyers. Looking at all possible options invites creative solutions to common goals.

- *Find solutions unique to you.* Rather than using a one-size-fits-all approach, a negotiated settlement allows you and your spouse to consider the unique circumstances of your situation to reach a positive outcome.

- *Open communication.* Mediation and negotiation provide each party an opportunity to be heard.

- *Take control of decisions impacting your children.* Your children will be better served if you and your spouse jointly determine your children's placement schedule rather than letting the judge decide. The judge does not know, love, or understand your children.

- *Eliminate risk.* If a judge decides the outcome of your divorce, you give up control over the terms of the settlement. The decisions are left in the hands of the judge. If you and your spouse reach agreement, however, you have the power to eliminate the risk of an uncertain outcome.

- *Decrease conflict.* If your case goes to trial, it is likely that you and your spouse will give testimony that will be upsetting to the other. As the conflict increases, the relationship between you and your spouse deteriorates. This may be harmful to your children and family. Contrast this with mediation or settlement negotiations, in which you open communication. It is not unusual for the relationship between parents to improve after mediation and resolution of the divorce by a negotiated settlement.

- *Utilize experts.* Using trained professionals, such as mediators, retired judges, and lawyers, may help you reach a settlement that at one time seemed impossible. These professionals have skills to help you focus on what is most important to you and shifts your attention away from irrelevant facts. Mediators and attorneys can help you understand the legal implications of any decision and can project the outcome if your case goes to trial.

- *Focus on resolution.* The process of trial is stressful. Your energy is better spent focusing on your children, your finances, and the emotions of resolving your divorce rather than litigating it.

- *Move forward.* When you are going through a divorce, the process may feel like it's taking an eternity. By reaching an agreement, you and your spouse are better able to put the divorce in the past and move forward to a better future.

6.7   Is mediation mandatory in custody and placement disputes?

With few exceptions, mediation is mandatory if custody or placement is an issue. Wisconsin law provides that in any case in which it appears that legal custody or physical placement is contested, the parties shall attend at least one session with a mediator. If the parties and the mediator determine that continued mediation is appropriate, no Wisconsin court may hold a trial or a final hearing on legal custody or physical placement until after mediation is completed or terminated.

Prior to mediation, if you and your spouse are able to reach an agreement regarding custody and placement, that agreement can be reduced to writing and incorporated into the judgment of divorce without the necessity of mediation. Without such an agreement, however, mediation is mandatory.

6.8   My spouse abused me, and I am afraid to participate in mediation. Should I participate anyway?

You may be able to participate in mediation by the use of separate rooms, different locations, different times, or mediation via Skype or phone. Talk to your attorney about your mediation concerns. The mediator must be advised of the specific circumstances of your case in order to make appropriate arrangements in exceptional circumstances.

In addition, the court may waive mediation in some limited situations. A court may waive mediation if it finds that attending mediation will cause undue hardship or will endanger the health or safety of one of the parties. In reaching its decision, the court considers whether one of the parties engaged in abuse of the child or other party and whether either party has a significant problem with alcohol or drug abuse. Additional criteria may be considered if the requesting party can prove that a party's health or safety will be endangered by attending the session.

Prior to starting mediation, the mediator will ask you to complete forms that address the issue of domestic abuse and drug or alcohol abuse, among other factors. Accurate completion of this information is essential in order for the mediator to assess safety issues and to evaluate the balance of power between the parties if mediation in fact occurs.

Talk with your attorney if you have experienced domestic violence or if you feel threatened or intimidated by your spouse. Even if mediation is not waived, you will likely be assigned an experienced mediator trained in high-conflict situations.

6.9   What training and credentials do mediators have?

The background of mediators varies. Some are attorneys. Many are retired judges. Many come from other backgrounds such as social work or psychology. Some mediators received their training through the state of Wisconsin, others were trained out of state. Any custody and placement mediator in Wisconsin must have twenty-five hours of mediation training or three years of professional experience in dispute resolution. Every mediator must have training in the dynamics of domestic violence and the effects of domestic violence on victims of domestic violence and on children.

Your attorney can check the credentials of your mediator. In Wisconsin, mediation is generally provided through family court services that supervise and perform mediation and any legal custody and physical placement study services. Mediation is provided in every county in the state. In addition, the parties to any action affecting the family may, at their own expense, receive services from a private mediator.

6.10   How do I prepare for mediation?

Prior to attending a mediation session with your spouse, discuss with your attorney what issues remain on the table for resolution in mediation. Know your settlement range and prioritize the issues of most significance. It is sometimes a good idea to have a specific, written proposal to take to mediation so that you can make your position known and you have a specific proposal at your fingertips. Oftentimes a mediator will ask for proposals and other relevant documents in advance of mediation so that the mediator can be fully prepared to assist the parties in reaching settlement.

6.11   Do children attend the mediation sessions?

No.

6.12 I want my attorney to look over the agreements my spouse and I discussed in mediation before I give my final approval. Is this possible?

Yes. Not only is this possible, it is unconditionally recommended. Before giving your written or final approval to any agreements reached in mediation, it is critical that your attorney review the agreements. This is necessary to make sure that you understand the terms of the mediated settlement and that its terms are correctly incorporated into the final judgment. It is important that the terms of the final judgment and the terms of the mediated agreement do not in any way conflict.

6.13 Who pays for mediation?

The cost of mediation must be paid by you and/or your spouse. Often it is a shared expense. Expect your mediator to address the matter of fees in advance of mediation.

6.14 What if mediation fails?

Mediation is not always successful. Sometimes it takes a number of attempts. Sometimes issues must be left to determination by the court. Sometimes mediation provides insight and cause for reflection, enabling a negotiated settlement at a later date. Mediation can be used to educate either party, so its value is not only measured by whether an agreement is signed on the day of mediation.

6.15 What is a *settlement conference*?

A *settlement conference* may be a powerful tool for the resolution of your case. It is often called a *four-way meeting* because it includes you and your attorney, as well as your spouse and his or her attorney. Sometimes the guardian *ad litem*, social worker, financial advisor, or other experts may be included in the settlement conference. That is a determination made by the attorneys involved. The goal is to negotiate a resolution of your case without the necessity of trial. Settlement conferences are most effective when both parties and their attorneys see the potential for a negotiated resolution and are fully prepared at the settlement conference to negotiate.

6.16 Why should I consider a settlement conference when the attorneys are able to negotiate through letters, e-mails, and phone calls?

A settlement conference may eliminate the delays that often occur when negotiations take place through correspondence, e-mails, and calls between the attorneys. Rather than waiting days or weeks for a response, you may receive a response on a proposal in a matter of minutes because you are together in the same location with the same priority of settlement.

A settlement conference also enables you and your spouse, if you choose, to fully explain to the other the exact reasoning behind any request or proposal. Supporting documents can be immediately provided. A settlement conference is an opportunity for eye-to-eye contact to resolve issues then and there with the assistance of attorneys and other professionals.

6.17 How do I prepare for my settlement conference?

Being well prepared for the settlement conference will help you make the most of this opportunity to resolve your case without the necessity of trial. To prepare for any settlement conference, talk to your attorney about what you should bring to the conference. In most instances, the information will already be accessible at your attorney's office because of prior discovery and informal exchange of information. Here are some additional ideas that will make your settlement conference more productive:

- Provide in advance any additional, requested information. This will generally include updated payroll stubs, most recent tax returns, updated debt amounts, most recent asset valuations, or other documentation.
- Know in advance the issues to be addressed at the settlement conference.
- Go with a positive attitude, a listening ear, and an open mind to any settlement conference. Go with the attitude that your case will settle. Be willing to listen to your spouse and his or her attorney. Be willing to share and explain your position. Resist the urge to

interrupt. Ask to talk to your attorney in private if you believe misinformation has been provided or if you want to update your lawyer on any significant issues.

Few cases settle without each side demonstrating some flexibility and a willingness to compromise.

6.18   What will happen at my settlement conference?

Typically the conference will be held at the office of one of the attorneys, with both parties and lawyers present. If there are a number of issues to be discussed, an agenda may be used to keep the focus on relevant topics. From time to time throughout the conference, you and your attorney may meet alone to consult as needed. If additional information is needed to reach agreement, some issues may be set aside for later discussion.

The length of the conference depends on the number of issues to be resolved, the complexity of the issues, and the willingness of the parties and lawyers to communicate effectively. An effort is made to confirm in writing which issues have been resolved and which issues remain disputed. A second settlement conference may be necessary, or the parties may decide to draft a *partial marital settlement agreement* setting forth any issues resolved at the settlement conference for submission to the court. This limits the number of issues to be decided at trial.

6.19   What is the role of my attorney in the settlement conference?

Your attorney is your advocate during the settlement conference. You may count on him or her to support you throughout the process, to make sure that all issues are addressed, and to counsel you privately outside the presence of your spouse and his or her lawyer.

6.20   Why is my lawyer appearing so friendly with my spouse's attorney?

Successful negotiations rely on building trust between the parties working toward agreement. Your lawyer may be respectful or pleasant toward your spouse or your spouse's lawyer to promote a good outcome for you. In addition, opposing lawyers often work together on a regular basis and see each other at the courthouse or attorney functions. It is a positive thing if your attorney has a good relationship with other attorneys, judges, and court staff. That can only work to your advantage.

6.21   If my spouse and I reach an agreement, how long will it take before it is finalized?

If a settlement is reached on all issues through negotiation or mediation, one of the attorneys will draft a marital settlement agreement that must be reviewed and signed by you, your spouse, and the guardian *ad litem,* if applicable. That document is then filed with the court and a final divorce date is set before the judge assigned to your case or the family court commissioner. Wisconsin has a 120-day waiting period, so the divorce date cannot be set prior to the expiration of 120 days from the date of service or signing of the admission of service. Timing of the divorce date is also dependent on the court and the attorneys' schedules.

7

Emergency: When You
Fear Your Spouse

Suddenly you are in a panic. Maybe your spouse was serious when he or she threatened to take your child and leave the state. What if your spouse changes the locks and kicks you out of your own home? Suppose all of the bank accounts are emptied? Your fear heightens as your mind spins with every horror story you've ever heard about divorce.

Facing an emergency situation in divorce may make you feel as though your entire life is at risk. You may not be able to concentrate on anything else. At the same time, you may be paralyzed with anxiety and have no idea how to protect yourself. No doubt you have countless worries about your future.

Remember that you have overcome many challenges in your life before this moment. There are people willing to help you. You have strength and wisdom you may not even know exist. Step by step, you will make it through this difficult time of your life.

When facing an emergency, stay focused on your immediate needs. Set aside your worries about the future. Reach out to others for support and guidance so that you can take any necessary action to address both the abuse and the divorce process.

7.1   I need to get divorced as quickly as possible to get away from my abusive spouse. What is my first step?
Your first step is to seek legal advice at your earliest opportunity. The earlier you get legal counsel to advise you of your rights, the better. Also call the nearest domestic abuse hotline for information and assistance.

7.2   I'm afraid my abusive spouse will try to hurt me and/ or our children if I say I want a divorce. What can I do to protect myself and my children?

In addition to meeting with an attorney at your first opportunity, develop a safety plan in the event you and your children need to escape your home. A good way to accomplish this goal is to get support from an agency that helps victims of domestic violence. Call the National Domestic Violence Hotline at (800) 799-7233 to get more information about the domestic violence program closest to you. The National Coalition Against Domestic Violence recommends that your safety plan include a list of safe people to contact, that you memorize the phone numbers of people and places to call for help, that you have sufficient cash on hand for emergencies, and that you have a code word prearranged for friends and family so you can advise them of trouble without alerting your spouse.

Find a lawyer who understands domestic violence. Often your local domestic violence agency will help with a referral. Talk to your lawyer about your safety concerns. Ask your lawyer about seeking a temporary restraining order, which is a court order that restrains an abuser from having any contact with you.

Although most instances of abuse involve women as the victim, this is not always the case, and men must follow the same steps as women in obtaining and providing a safe haven for themselves and their children.

7.3   I am afraid to meet with a lawyer because I am terrified my spouse will find out and get violent. What should I do?

Schedule an initial consultation with an attorney who is experienced in working with domestic violence victims. When you schedule the appointment, let the firm know your situation and instruct the law office not to place any calls to you that you think your spouse might discover. If there is a cost for the initial consultation, pay for your consultation in cash.

Consultations with your attorney are confidential. Your lawyer has an ethical duty not to disclose your meeting with anyone outside the law firm. Let your attorney know your concerns so that extra precautions can be taken by the law office to protect you and office staff while you are meeting with your attorney.

7.4 I want to give my attorney all the information needed so my children and I are safe from my spouse. What information does this include?

Provide your attorney with complete information about the history, background, and evidence of abuse:

- The types of abuse (for example, physical, sexual, verbal, financial, mental, and emotional)
- The dates, time frames, or occasions that the abuse occurred
- The locations where abuse occurred
- Medical records or hospital bills confirming your injuries
- Police reports identifying the abuse circumstances
- E-mails, letters, notes, or journal entries that confirm any abuse
- Any photographs taken of your injuries or destruction of personal property because of domestic violence
- Any witnesses to the abuse or evidence of the abuse
- Any statements made by your spouse admitting the abuse
- Evidence of alcohol or drug abuse by your spouse
- The presence of guns or other weapons in your home or your spouse's access to same

The more comprehensive and specific the information you provide to your lawyer, the easier it will be for your attorney to make a strong case for the protection and safety of you and your children.

7.5 I'm not ready to hire a lawyer for a divorce, but I am afraid my spouse is going to get violent with my children and me in the meantime. What can I do?

It is possible to seek a temporary restraining order from the court without representation from an attorney. There are a number of domestic abuse agencies in your area who will assist you in this effort. Call the National Domestic Violence

Hotline at (800) 799-7233 for information about the agency nearest you. It is possible for the judge to order your spouse out of your home and to order your spouse to refrain from any contact with you.

7.6   What are *restraining orders, temporary restraining orders,* and *domestic abuse temporary restraining orders*?

Restraining orders are court orders directing a person to refrain from engaging in certain behavior. A *temporary restraining order* may order your abusive spouse to stay away from you, move out of the house, or stop harassing you, among other things. Although a temporary restraining order may be obtained *ex parte,* without notice to the other party, a subsequent hearing date will be set within fourteen days to give the other party the opportunity to present his or her position. This hearing is called an *injunction hearing.* At the injunction hearing, a request will be made for a permanent injunction based on the facts and circumstances of the abuse. Each party and additional witnesses may be compelled to testify at the hearing, after which the court or commissioner will render its decision whether to grant the injunction. An injunction may be granted for up to four years for domestic abuse and harassment.

If a domestic abuse injunction is granted, the responsible party will be ordered to surrender any firearms. In a harassment injunction, you can request that the court order the harassing party to surrender his or her firearms, if you can prove to the court that the party may use firearms to cause physical harm or endanger public safety.

The *domestic abuse restraining order* and/or injunction does not address custody, placement, or support orders with the exception of specifically identifying the terms of exchange of placement of the minor children. A separate family court action must be filed in order to address custody, placement, and child support.

Talk to your attorney about obtaining a domestic abuse restraining order if you are concerned about your safety, your children's safety, or if there has been a history of domestic abuse.

7.7   I'm afraid my spouse is going to take all of the money out of the bank accounts and leave me with nothing. What can I do?

Talk to your attorney immediately. If you are worried about your spouse emptying financial accounts or selling marital assets, it is critical that you take action at once. Your attorney will advise you whether or not you should move certain assets to different accounts to protect those assets from being hidden or spent by your spouse.

You may also want to notify account holders that a divorce is pending and that assets may not be transferred or concealed. As part of your divorce action, both you and your spouse will be restrained from disposing of assets without mutual agreement or court order. You and your spouse will also be required to act in good faith with respect to the other spouse's property.

7.8   My spouse says that I am crazy, that I am a liar, and that no judge will ever believe me if I tell the truth about the abusive behavior. What can I do if I don't have any proof?

Most domestic violence is not witnessed by third parties. Judges do not live in a vacuum and are aware of this fact. However, even without physical evidence, a judge may enter orders to protect you and your children if you give truthful testimony about your abuse that the judge finds credible. If you have been a victim of abusive behavior by your spouse, or if you have witnessed your children as victims, your testimony is likely to be the most compelling evidence. But when you are a victim, call the police. Take pictures. Call a neighbor. Get medical help. This type of evidence will support your testimony in court.

Be sure to tell your attorney about anyone who may have either seen your spouse's behavior or spoken to you or your children after an abusive incident. They may be important witnesses in your custody and/or placement case.

Your attorney's skills and experience will support you in giving effective testimony to establish your case. Let your lawyer know your concerns so that a strong case may be presented to the judge based on your testimony.

7.9   My spouse told me that if I file for divorce, I'll never see my child again. Should I be worried about my child being abducted?

Your fear that your spouse will abduct your child is a common one. Parents kidnap their children to force continued interaction with the other parent, to spite the other parent, and from fear of losing custody or placement rights. The following are factors that appear to increase the risk that your spouse may kidnap your child. Your spouse:

- Has threatened abduction in the past
- Is suspected of abuse
- Has severe mental health issues
- Is a citizen of another country or a member of a different culture
- Has no strong ties to the location where the child resides
- Is not financially secure
- Is planning to get out of town fast and has obtained a passport, or your child's school and medical records

Talk to your lawyer to assess the risks in your particular situation. Together you may determine whether statements by your spouse are threats intended to control or intimidate you and/or whether legal action is needed to protect your children. To prepare for any unseen events, make sure you have your children's ID immediately available and teach your children their full name, address, and telephone number. Keep a list of contact information for your spouse and his or her relatives. If available, write down your spouse's passport, visa, and driver's license numbers. Have up-to-date photographs of you and your spouse and children on your phone or readily available. For more information, *see* U.S. Department of State, Office of Children's Issues, International Parental Child Abduction site: http://travel.state.gov/content/childabduction/english/about.html and Children's Passport Issuance Alert Program site: http://travel.state.gov/content/childabduction/english/preventing/passport-issuance-alert-program.html.

7.10 What legal steps may be taken to prevent my spouse from removing our child from the state?

If you are concerned about your child being removed from the state, ask your lawyer whether any of these options are available in your case:

- A court order giving you immediate custody until a temporary custody hearing can be held
- A court order directing your spouse to turn over passports for the child and your spouse to the court
- A court order requiring only supervised placement of your children by your spouse

Both state and federal laws are designed to provide protection from the removal of children from one state to another when a custody determination is sought and to protect children from kidnapping. *The Uniform Child-Custody Jurisdiction and Enforcement Act (UCCJEA)* (www.ncjrs.gov/pdffiles1/ojjdp/189181.pdf) was passed to encourage the custody of children to be decided in the state where they have been living most recently and where they have the most ties. Under the UCCJEA, the court in a custody and placement case must inquire whether the child has been a subject of litigation in any other state. If answered affirmatively, the issue of which state has jurisdiction will be determined.

The Parental Kidnapping Prevention Act (PKPA) makes it a federal crime for a parent to kidnap a child in violation of a valid custody order.

7.11 If I feel I am in harm's way, am I able to obtain a divorce more quickly in another state or country?

Wisconsin's 120-day waiting period may seem like a long time, but you may ask the court to waive that time requirement if you face immediate harm from your spouse.

If both you and your spouse define Wisconsin as your residence and you both intend to remain in the state, a divorce from another state or country will not be valid. You cannot obtain a divorce in another state or country, even if you reside there temporarily until you meet the residency requirement of that state or country.

7.12 My spouse says I have to move out now. Who decides who gets to live in the house while the divorce is pending?

If you and your spouse cannot reach an agreement regarding which of you will leave the residence during the divorce, the judge or family court commissioner will decide whether one of you should be granted exclusive possession of the home until the case is concluded. In some cases, judges have been known to refuse to order either party out of the house until the divorce is concluded or may order a nesting arrangement, where each party is designated exclusive use of the residence on specific days or weeks.

Abusive behavior by one party is one basis for seeking temporary possession of the home while the abusive spouse is ordered to vacate. If there are minor children, the party guilty of abuse will almost always be ordered to vacate the residence.

Other factors the judge may consider in determining allocation of the residence on a temporary basis include the following:

- Whether one party owned the home prior to the marriage
- After provisions are made for payment of temporary support, who can afford to remain in the home or obtain other housing?
- Who is most likely to be awarded the home as part of the final divorce?
- What options are available to each party for other temporary housing, including other homes or family members who live in the area?
- Special needs that would make a move unduly burdensome to one party, such as a health condition
- Self-employment from home, which could not be readily moved, such as a child-care business

If staying in the home is important to you or if you or the child is a victim of abuse, talk to your attorney so that a strong case is presented on your behalf at the temporary hearing or temporary restraining order.

8

Child Custody and Placement

When you and your spouse first began talking about the possibility of divorce, your top priority was probably your children. In fact, you or your spouse may have postponed the decision to file for divorce in order to protect your children from the potential effects of divorce. But now, having balanced all factors and having decided to file for divorce, you must address child custody, placement, and support issues as part of the divorce process.

Most of you who are reading this book have always tried to make wise, consistent, and loving decisions for your children. You have done your best to make sure that you act in the best interest of your children. That should not change now that you are involved in a divorce. You were a good parent before the divorce; in all likelihood you will be a good parent after the divorce. Your children's needs must be prioritized.

You will worry about the impact of custody and placement decisions on your children. How will these decisions impact your children individually since each child will react differently to the same set of circumstances? How will these decisions impact you? Your spouse? While you are attempting to answer these questions relative to your children, remember the answer should be determined jointly with your spouse. Only the two of you truly know which custody and placement schedule is in your children's best interest. It is likely that the final court order will give both you and your spouse placement with the children and an opportunity to be involved in the children's day-to-day lives.

105

8.1   What types of custody are awarded in Wisconsin?

Under Wisconsin law, there are three types of custody: joint legal custody, sole legal custody, and a mixture of the two. A person granted legal custody has the right and responsibility to make major decisions relative to the children. Major decisions include education, religious, and medical decisions, among others.

If custody is granted to both parents, it is defined as *joint legal custody*. In Wisconsin there is a presumption that joint legal custody is in the best interest of the child. Joint legal custody means that you and your former spouse will share equally in the fundamental decision making for your child. If you and the other parent are unable to reach an agreement on joint custody issues, you may be required to return to mediation or to court to allow the judge to break the impasse.

If legal custody is awarded to one parent, it is called *sole legal custody*. The court may grant sole legal custody if it finds that it is in the best interest of the children and that any of the following apply:

- Both parties agree to sole legal custody.
- The parties disagree over sole legal custody, but at least one party requests sole legal custody and the court finds any of the following:
    - One party is not capable of performing parental duties and responsibilities or does not wish to have an active role in raising the child.
    - One or more conditions exist at that time that would substantially interfere with the exercise of joint legal custody.
    - The parties will not be able to cooperate in future decision making as required under an award of joint legal custody.

There is also a hybrid of joint and sole custody. In this instance, the parties may be awarded joint legal custody with one party having decision-making authority if the parties cannot agree on an issue.

8.2 What is *physical placement* of a child?

Physical placement is the condition under which a party has the right to have a child physically placed with that party and has the right and responsibility to make, during that placement, routine daily decisions regarding the child's care. Physical placement is generally defined as where the child is living on a day-to-day basis.

8.3 What are the different types of physical placement?

In most cases each parent is awarded periods of physical placement of the children. The actual placement arrangement may take one of three basic forms:

- *Primary placement*—One parent has primary placement of the children. The other parent has periods of placement, which could take the form of every other weekend during the school year plus extra time in the summer. There is also usually an alternating of holidays. This is only an example and many other options can be applied.

- *Shared placement*—Under Wisconsin law, parents have a shared placement schedule if each parent has at least 25 percent or ninety-two days a year of physical placement with the minor children. The periods of physical placement are determined by calculating the number of overnights of each parent and dividing that number by 365. An example of a shared placement schedule is a 50/50 alternating week schedule.

- *Split custody*—Occasionally, and for a wide variety of reasons, children are split between the parents. With split custody, the placement schedules are usually set up to have the children together every weekend and for substantial times in the summer. There is a special split custody child-support rule that offsets and nets the child-support obligations of the parents.

8.4 What's the difference between *visitation* and *placement*?

Visitation generally occurs when a third party spends time with a minor child. Third parties include grandparents, significant others, or stepparents. *Placement* is the term used for parents when spending time with their children.

8.5 What factors does the court consider in awarding custody and physical placement?

The court considers all facts relevant to the best interest of the children. Some of the factors the court considers are:

- The wishes of the children's parent or parents as shown by an agreement between the parties, or a proposed parenting plan, or any other proposal submitted to the court at trial
- The wishes of the children, which may be communicated by the children or through the children's guardian *ad litem*
- The interaction and interrelationship of the children with his or her parent, parents, or siblings
- The amount and quality of time that each parent has spent with the child in the past
- The child's adjustment to the home, school, religion, and community
- Whether the mental or physical health of a party, minor child, or other person living in a proposed custodial household negatively affects the child's intellectual, physical, or emotional well-being
- The need for regularly occurring and meaningful periods of physical placement to provide predictability and stability for the child
- The availability of public or private child-care services
- The cooperation and communication between the parties and whether either party unreasonably refuses to cooperate or communicate with the other party
- Whether each party can support the other party's relationship with the child, or whether one party is likely to unreasonably interfere with the child's continuing relationship with the other party

- Whether there is evidence that a party engaged in abuse of the child
- Whether any of the following has a criminal record and whether there is evidence that any of the following has engaged in abuse of the child or any other child or neglected the child or any other child:
  - A person with whom a parent of the child has a dating relationship
  - A person who resides, has resided, or will reside regularly or intermittently in a proposed custodial household
- Whether there is any evidence of inter-spousal or domestic abuse
- Whether either party has or had a significant problem with alcohol or drug abuse
- Such other factors as the court may, in each individual case, determine to be relevant

8.6   How can I make sure I will be awarded primary placement of my children?

There are no guarantees that you will be awarded primary placement of your children in a divorce action, except in exceptional circumstances. The court weighs the factors addressed earlier in this chapter to make a determination relative to the allocation of placement. Although an attorney may give you his or her opinion relative to your likelihood of success in obtaining primary placement of your children, it is just an opinion. Any lawyer who guarantees a result in a custody and/or placement case is a lawyer who should be avoided.

8.7   How can I prove that I was the primary care provider?

One tool to assist you and your attorney in establishing your case as a primary care provider is a chart indicating the care you and your spouse have each provided for your children. The more information you provide about your history of parenting, the better argument your attorney can make in support of your placement position. A review of the activities noted in the following chart will help identify some activities that will support your role as primary provider of your children.

109

Parental Roles Chart

Activity	Mother	Father
Attended prenatal medical visits		
Attended prenatal class		
Took time off work after child born		
Got up with child for nighttime feedings		
Got up with child when sick at night		
Bathed child		
Helped child brush and floss teeth		
Cleaned child's bathroom, bedroom, and bedding		
Put child to sleep/bedtime rituals		
Woke child up in morning		
Put child down for naps		
Changed diapers/potty-trained child		
Helped child dress		
Combed/brushed/styled child's hair		
Cut/filed child's nails		
Planned, prepared, and fed meals to child		
Drove child to play dates		
Washed child's laundry		
Helped child learn numbers, letters, or colors		
Read to child		
Took child to museum/culture-related events		
Took child to library		
Helped child with arts and crafts projects		
Provided child with educational activities at home		
Helped child with practice for music, dance lessons, sports		

Parental Roles Chart (Continued)

Activity	Mother	Father
Took time off for child's appointments		
Stayed home from work with sick child		
Scheduled child's appointments		
Took child to doctor visits		
Went to pharmacy for child's medication		
Administered child's medication		
Administered first aid for child's minor injuries (cuts or stings)		
Called child's health-care providers		
Applied child's sunscreen/bug repellent		
Enforced child wearing bicycle helmet		
Took child to therapy		
Took child to optometrist/dentist		
Purchased clothing for child		
Purchased school supplies for child		
Purchased food for child's meals and snacks		
Packed child's lunches		
Taught child how to cook		
Transported child to school		
Picked up child after school		
Drove carpool for child's school		
Went to child's school activities		
Home-schooled child		
Helped child with homework and projects		
Offered explanations to child		
Attended parent-teacher conferences		
Helped in child's classroom		
Chaperoned child's school trips and activities		

Parental Roles Chart   (Continued)

Activity	Mother	Father
Arranged child's after-school care		
Transported child to day care		
Communicated with day care providers		
Transported child from day care		
Attended day care activities		
Signed child up for sports, dance, music		
Attended school functions		
Transported child to sports, dance, music		
Attended sports, dance, music practices		
Attended sports games, dance, music recitals		
Coached child's sports		
Transported child from sports, dance, music		
Transported child to driver's education		
Knows child's friends and friends' families		
Took child to religious education		
Obtained information and training about special needs of child		
Comforted child		
Participated in child's interest		
Nurtured child's self-esteem		
Set and enforced rules and limits		
Gave advice and talked to child		
Assisted child with pet care		
Bought and organized child's toys		
Planned child's parties		
Attended family vacations		
Played games with child		
Played sports with child		

Parental Roles Chart (Continued)

Activity	Mother	Father
Supervised child and friends at home		
Watched TV/DVDs with child		

8.8 If I am awarded shared physical placement, what are some examples of how the parenting might be shared?

In the event both parties have placement of ninety-two overnights or more, placement is considered shared. Although placement is generally awarded based on overnights, equivalent care is also considered. An example of equivalent care would be a parent who works third shift, but cares for the children each day.

In 50/50 shared placement arrangements, many parents follow a 2-2-5 schedule, or a variation thereof, where one parent has the children for two weekdays, the other parent has the children for the following two weekdays, and then the parties alternate weekends from Friday to Monday morning. Below is an example placement chart to demonstrate the 2-2-5 schedule.

	Monday	Tuesday	Wednesday	Thursday	Friday	Saturday	Sunday
Week 1	Mother	Mother	Father	Father	Mother	Mother	Mother
Week 2	Mother	Mother	Father	Father	Father	Father	Father

Another example illustrates a 9-5 schedule, which is sometimes flip-flopped during the summer so the schedule becomes 5-9 to the opposite parent.

	Monday	Tuesday	Wednesday	Thursday	Friday	Saturday	Sunday
Week 1	Father	Father	Mother	Father	Mother	Mother	Mother
Week 2	Father	Father	Mother	Father	Father	Father	Father

Parents can negotiate any type of schedule that works for them and the minor children. Sometimes the schedule is nothing more than an agreement to work together on a substantially 50/50 basis, leaving the actual dates and times flexible, based on the minor children's schedule and extracurricular activities. If the children are old enough, some parents prefer to have a one-week-on, one-week-off parenting schedule. Each family presents a different set of facts and circumstances to

113

be considered and weighed when determining the appropriate placement schedule.

8.9   What does it mean to have *split custody*?

Split custody refers to a custodial arrangement where each parent has sole physical custody of one or more of the children. Courts generally disfavor split custody because it separates the children from each other. However, in families with a disabled child or a child who is in need of additional health services, or in cases of child-on-child abuse, the use of split custody can provide for more attention and care focused on an individual child. Certainly other circumstances occur where split placement is ordered, but generally only under exceptional circumstances.

8.10   What is a *parenting plan*?

A *parenting plan* is a written document detailing what placement schedule each parent believes is in the best interest of the children. In a case where legal custody and/or physical placement is contested, a party seeking legal custody or periods of physical placement must file a parenting plan before any pretrial conference. A party required to file a parenting plan, who does not timely file a parenting plan, waives the right to object to the other party's parenting plan.

In Wisconsin, the court must set a placement schedule that allows the children to have "regularly occurring, meaningful periods of physical placement" with each parent that maximizes the amount of time the children will spend with each parent, taking into account geographic separation and accommodations for different households.

A parenting plan must provide the following information:
- What legal custody or physical placement the parent is seeking
- Where the parent currently lives and where the parent intends to live during the next two years
- Where the parent works and the hours of employment
- Who will provide any necessary child care when the parent cannot and who will pay for the child care
- Where the children will go to school

- What doctor or health care facility will provide medical care for the children
- How the children's medical expenses will be paid
- What the children's religious commitment will be, if any
- Who will make decisions about the children's education, medical care, choice of child-care providers, and extracurricular activities
- How the holidays will be divided
- What the children's summer schedule will be
- Whether and how the children will be able to contact the other parent when the children have physical placement with the parent providing the parenting plan
- How the parent proposes to resolve disagreements related to matters over which the court orders joint decision making
- What child support, family support, maintenance, or other income transfer there will be
- How the children will be transferred between the parties for the exercise of physical placement to ensure the safety of the children and the parties

A sample parenting plan form can be found in the appendix. The goal of the parenting plan is to resolve conflict without the need for extended litigation. It sets the parameters for each side's custody and placement proposal.

8.11 How much weight does the children's preference carry in determining placement?

The preference of your children is only one of many factors a court must consider in determining custody and placement. The age of your children and their ability to express the underlying reason for their preference to live with either parent will determine the amount of weight the judge will give to your children's preference. Although there is no age at which your children's preference determines custody and placement, most judges give more weight to the wishes of older children, as indicated to a guardian *ad litem* or social worker assigned to conduct a custody and placement evaluation.

The reasoning underlying your child's preference is a factor to contemplate. Consider the fifteen-year-old girl who wants to live with her mother because "Mom lets me stay out past curfew, I get a bigger allowance, and I don't have to do chores." Greater weight might be given to the preference of an eight-year-old who wants to live with his mother because "she helps me with my homework, reads me bedtime stories, and doesn't call me names like Dad does." There is not one steadfast rule relative to age as a preference indicator.

If you believe your child's placement preference may be a significant factor in the determination of custody and placement, bring that fact to the attention of your attorney so that he or she can best determine how to provide that information to the court or other custodial investigator.

8.12   At what age are the children able to talk to the judge about where they want to live?

Children do not generally speak directly with the court. If the children's voice must be heard, a guardian *ad litem* is generally appointed or a custodial investigation is ordered through the department of social services or related administrative agency.

8.13   What is a guardian *ad litem*? Why is one appointed?

As explained in an earlier chapter, a guardian *ad litem* in a custody and/or placement case is an attorney who is appointed by the court to represent the interest of your minor children who are not able to advocate for themselves during the court process. A guardian *ad litem* advocates for the best interest of the minor children. The guardian *ad litem* considers but is not bound by the wishes of the minor children.

The guardian *ad litem* will investigate the particular facts of your family, consult with other witnesses knowledgeable of your minor children and family, participate in negotiations, conduct formal and informal discovery, hire experts, participate in court proceedings, including trial, and make a recommendation on legal custody and/or placement of the minor children after his or her investigation. The guardian *ad litem's* role is to advocate for the best interest of the children, which may not be the same as advocating for what the children want custody and placement to be.

116

8.14   What does it mean to be an *unfit parent*?

Parental unfitness means that a person has a personal deficiency or incapacity that will likely prevent him or her from performing essential parental obligations, resulting in a failure to meet the best interest of a child. There is no one definition for unfitness. The following are some of the reasons a parent may face allegations of unfitness:

* physical, emotional, or sexual abuse
* excessive discipline
* failure to protect a child from abuse by another
* failure to report abuse or child neglect
* failure to provide food, clothing, proper hygiene, medical care, and education
* debilitating physical or mental illness
* substance abuse
* chronic alcoholism
* incarceration
* leaving a child unattended
* unsafe living conditions

These factors, as well as others, are applied on a case-by-case basis, taking into consideration the uniqueness of each situation. Make sure the existence of any of the above factors is reported to your attorney so that he or she can address these issues with you at the start of your divorce.

8.15   Do I have to allow my spouse to see the children before we are actually divorced?

Unless your children are at risk of harm by your spouse, your children should maintain regular contact with the other parent. It is important for children to experience the presence of both parents in their lives, regardless of the separation of the parents. Even if there is no temporary order for placement, co-operate with your spouse in making reasonable arrangements for placement with your children.

When safety is not an issue, if you deny contact with the other parent prior to trial, the judge or family court commissioner is likely to question whether you have the best interest of your children at heart. Talk to your spouse or your lawyer about what placement schedule would be best for your children on a temporary basis.

8.16 I am seeing a therapist. Will that hurt my chances of being awarded custody or placement?

The fact that you are seeing a therapist is generally considered positive recognition that you need assistance in some part of your life. Your well-being is important to your ability to be the best parent you can be. However, discuss your treatment with your lawyer. Your diagnosis may or may not affect your ability to parent effectively, and that issue must be addressed immediately by your attorney.

Your mental health records may be subpoenaed by the other parent's lawyer. For this reason it is important to discuss an action plan with your attorney for responding to any request to obtain your therapist's records. Ask your attorney to contact your therapist to alert him or her how to respond to a request for your mental health records. Do not sign any authorization from your therapist without approval and review by your attorney. Your right to privacy must be balanced against any request for the release of your mental health information for custody and/or placement determinations.

8.17 I am taking prescription medication to treat my depression. Will this hurt my chances of getting custody?

Feelings of depression, anxiety, and trouble sleeping are common during a divorce. Following through with the prescription recommendations made by your health care provider will almost always be considered favorably by the court. However, make sure your attorney is aware of your use of prescription medication so that he or she is prepared for any questions relative to the issues.

8.18 How is *abandonment* defined in Wisconsin? How does abandonment affect the outcome of a custody or placement case?

Criminal *abandonment* in Wisconsin is defined as follows: "Whoever, with intent to abandon the child, leaves any child in a place where the child may suffer because of neglect is guilty of a Class G felony." In addition, one of the factors the court must consider in awarding custody and/or physical placement is "the amount and quality of time that each parent has spent with the child in the past."

How abandonment affects the outcome of a custody or placement case is based on the exact facts of each individual divorce. There is no one answer. The intentional absence of a parent's presence, care, protection, or support are all considered. Also considered, in a potentially positive way, is a person's absence for health reasons, military service, or job requirements.

8.19   Will my children be present if we go to court?

In most instances, no. Judges make every effort to protect minor children from the conflict of their parents. For this reason, most judges will not allow children to be present in the courtroom to hear the testimony of witnesses.

Although the risk that your spouse may share information with your children cannot be eliminated, it would be highly unusual for a judge to allow children to hear such testimony in a courtroom.

8.20   Should I hire a private detective to prove my spouse is having an affair?

Because Wisconsin is a no-fault divorce state, hiring a detective to prove your spouse is having an affair will not be admissible in court unless you can show that the children are impacted by the affair. Your attorney will help you determine whether hiring a private investigator is a good idea in your particular case.

8.21   Will the fact that I had an affair during my marriage hurt my chances of getting custody?

An affair generally has no effect on most aspects of your divorce case, but could potentially impact custody or placement if your children were exposed to the affair, or if the affair has any provable negative impact on the best interest of the children.

In determining custody and placement, a court will generally not consider the existence of an affair, unless the children were actually exposed to a significant other when an order existed to the contrary; unless the children saw any sexual activity; or unless the children were negatively affected by the existence of the affair, such as teasing at school or common knowledge of the affair in the community.

If you are having an extramarital relationship, discuss this fact with your attorney so your attorney is prepared to address the circumstances. If you are involved in another relationship, do not involve your children in the relationship at least until your divorce is final, unless approved otherwise by your attorney, the court, or your children's therapist.

8.22   During the time my divorce is pending, is it okay to date or will it hurt my chances of getting custody or placement?

If custody or placement are disputed, talk with your attorney about your plans to begin dating. Your dating will probably not be significant if your children are not aware of it.

If your spouse is contesting custody or placement, it may be best to focus your energy on your children, the divorce itself, and taking care of yourself physically and emotionally. The only thing to truly avoid is your children's involvement in the dating process. If you do date, do so while your children are having placement with your spouse. Most judges frown on exposing your children to a new relationship when they are still adjusting to the separation of their parents. With limited exceptions, your children do not need to be exposed to your dates or a significant other until the divorce process is completed.

If you do date and become sexually involved with your new partner, it is imperative that your children be unaware of your sexual relationship. You want to make sure that you address the best interest of your children first and foremost, with your own needs a decided second in priority.

8.23   Will having a live-in partner hurt my chances of getting custody and/or placement?

If you are considering living with your significant other before your divorce is final, think again, and then discuss your decision with your divorce attorney. If you are already living with your significant other prior to starting the divorce, make sure your attorney is knowledgeable of this fact at the onset of the divorce. Your live-in significant other will automatically become a factor in any custody and placement determination, so it is important that your attorney be immediately made aware of his or her role in your life. Your attorney can assess the impact of your living situation and advise you accordingly.

Different judges have different views, and your attorney should have a good idea of the track record of the judge to whom your case is assigned. Your attorney will also want to know what kind of relationship, if any, there is between your spouse and your significant other. If there is friction, the existence of this animosity will certainly play a role in any decision regarding custody and/or placement.

Your attorney will also evaluate factors such as the length of your separation from your spouse, living arrangements within the home, the length of your relationship with your significant other, the children's relationship with your significant other, and your future plans such as engagement or marriage. But be aware, living with a significant other may put your custody and placement at risk.

Maintenance may also be impacted by the existence of a significant other who shares your expenses. This is a major dynamic decision in your divorce and in your life. The general rule is "Don't do it." The second general rule is "Don't do it until you talk to your attorney and get his or her input." Although there are exceptions to every rule, make sure you make this choice with your eyes wide open. Getting custody or placement of your children is at risk.

8.24   I am gay and came out to my spouse when I filed for divorce. What impact will my sexual orientation have on my case for custody and/or placement?

There are no laws in Wisconsin that limit your rights as a parent based on your sexual orientation. Be sure to choose a lawyer who will fully support you in your efforts as a parent without discrimination based on your sexual orientation. You will have to work together as a team with your attorney to accomplish your custody and placement goals. The specific factors the court must consider in awarding custody and placement are identified earlier in this chapter. Sexual orientation by itself is not one of those factors.

8.25   Are witnesses an important part of a custody and/or placement case?

Absolutely. Witnesses are critical in every custody and/or placement case. A witness can provide support for your position or can provide testimony to the contrary relative to your parenting ability.

Potential witnesses in a custody and/or placement case often include the following:

- family members
- family friends
- child-care providers
- neighbors
- teachers
- health care providers
- clergy members
- medical professionals

In considering which witnesses would best support your case, your attorney will weigh the following:

- Did this witness have substantial opportunity to observe you or the other parent, especially with your children?
- How frequently? How recently?
- How long has the witness known you or the other parent?

- What is the relationship of the witness to your children and your spouse?
- How valuable is the knowledge to which the witness would testify?
- Does this witness have knowledge more significant than other witnesses?
- Is the witness available and willing to testify?
- Is the witness clear in conveying information?
- Is the witness credible? Will the judge believe this witness?
- Does the witness have any biases or prejudices that could impact the testimony?
- Does the witness have particular experience and education that would aid the judge in determining the best interest of the children?

Provide your attorney with the phone numbers, addresses, and workplaces of each of your potential witnesses. This information can be critical to the role that the attorney has in interviewing the witnesses, assessing their presentation and credibility, and issuing subpoenas to compel their court attendance, if needed.

8.26   Will my attorney want to speak with my children?

In most cases your attorney won't ask to speak with your children. An exception might exist where custody is disputed or where either parent has made allegations of abuse or neglect, but your attorney will not do so without the input and approval of the guardian *ad litem* and the court.

The goal in any divorce action involving children is to shield the children from as many of the harmful effects of divorce as possible. That means moving carefully when considering, requesting, and conducting interviews of children.

8.27   What is a *child custody expert*? Why is one appointed?

If custody is disputed, the court may order a social services investigation by a social worker or another expert such as a psychologist, who can conduct an evaluation of the parties and minor children. In all but a few circumstances, the court relies on the recommendation of the guardian *ad litem* before ordering a social services investigation or retaining a psychologist or other expert to provide a recommendation in a custody and/or placement dispute.

These experts act as neutral evaluators whose roles are to determine the best interest of the children and to make recommendations to the court concerning custody and/or placement. Each expert will generally conduct a complete evaluation of the parties, which may include psychological testing, interviews of the parents and the children, home visits, and evaluation of the interaction between the children and each parent. The evaluator is also generally authorized to review and receive information, records, and reports concerning the parties involved. The evaluator will then submit a report to the court with his or her recommendation and may be called to testify at trial.

There usually is an agreement between the attorneys and court before a particular psychologist or evaluator is selected or appointed. In almost all circumstances, the court requests input into the selection process, and this is where it is imperative to have an attorney who is familiar with the reputations of child evaluators within Wisconsin and who can make a reasoned choice of evaluators on your behalf. The expert selected as a psychologist or evaluator is important, so make sure you consult with your attorney on this issue. Cost is sometimes a factor, and that must also be addressed in advance.

8.28 Would photographs or a video of my children help my placement case?

Photographs or a video depicting your children's day-to-day life can help the judge learn more about your children. It can demonstrate how your children interact with you, your spouse, siblings, and other important people in your family's life. The photographs or video can portray your children's rooms, home, and neighborhood, as well as show your children's participation in activities.

Talk to your lawyer about whether photographs or a video would be helpful in your case. Although photographs are more commonly used and are typically sufficient evidence, ask your lawyer if he or she recommends making a video, and if so, what scenes to include, the length of the video, and the editing process.

8.29 What impact does my use of social media and other technological devices have on custody and placement and other aspects of the divorce?

Whatever you place on social media is generally fair game for your spouse and his or her attorneys to include in any trial evidence. While your Facebook information may be funny and outrageous to your friends and family, a totally different spin can be placed on the same information by your spouse or the court. Act under the presumption that anything you place on social media will be accessible to the other party, either through discovery or otherwise.

Check your e-mail, Instagram, Facebook, Twitter, Linked-In, and other social media accounts. Make sure there is nothing on these accounts that can be used against you in the divorce. Remove or block anything potentially incriminating. Rest assured that if this information is on social media, it is accessible to your spouse and his or her attorney.

Also be extremely careful of the e-mails and texts you send to your spouse. They can be kept for years. E-mails can be printed. These communications are generally admissible in court.

Every now and then check your car. Make sure that your GPS data is erased. Make sure your car is not tagged with a GPS. Your I-PASS (Illinois electronic toll collection system) can be traced. It is possible to determine when your car has passed through tolls.

Dating websites are also a source of much information, including income and assets. Your web history is also subject to subpoena in some circumstances. Be aware of these factors before and during the divorce process and make sure to take any necessary precautions. If you wait, it may be too late.

8.30 I don't think it's safe for my children to have any contact with my spouse. How can I prove this to the judge?

Keeping your children safe is so important that this discussion with your attorney requires immediate attention. It is imperative that you select an attorney experienced in this type of specialized representation. Provide your attorney with all of the necessary facts and circumstances, including past and present allegations. Taking this type of action should not be based

125

on assumptions or unsubstantiated beliefs. Provide specific information about your spouse's history, including his or her use of alcohol or drugs, treatment for alcohol or drug abuse, arrest record, firearm registrations, and any other relevant facts. Check the WCCA website at http://wcca.wicourts.gov for additional information.

If you believe that your children are not safe with your spouse, plan for the protection of your children immediately. Try to obtain restrictions on your spouse's placement. Consider petitioning for a temporary restraining order, supervised placement, or certain restrictions on your spouse's placement, such as no overnight placement.

In this situation, expect extensive and costly litigation. It is rare that a court will provide no contact with the other parent unless facts are extreme and substantiated relative to the abuse or unfitness of your spouse. The appointment of a guardian *ad litem* will almost always be required.

8.31 How can I make sure my spouse's placement is supervised?

If you are concerned about the safety of your children when they have placement with your spouse, talk to your lawyer. You cannot unilaterally stop placement with your spouse, so you will have to file the appropriate motion to stop or compel supervised placement.

Ask your attorney whether, under the facts of your case, the judge would consider any of the following orders:

- Supervised placement
- Parenting classes for the other parent
- Anger-management or other rehabilitative program for the other parent
- A prohibition against drinking by the other parent before and during placement and perhaps random alcohol and drug testing

Judges have differing approaches to cases where children are at risk. Recognize that there are often practical considerations to consider, such as cost or the availability of people to supervise placement. Urge your attorney to advocate zealously for court orders to protect your children from harm by the other parent. There are generally additional support groups such as domestic abuse programs that will assist you in your efforts.

8.32 I want to talk to my spouse about our children, but all he wants to do is argue. How can I communicate without it always turning into a fight?

Because conflict is high between you and your spouse, consider the following:

- Ask your lawyer to help you obtain a court order that specifically addresses dates and times for custody and placement. This practice lowers the amount of necessary communication between you and your spouse.
- Put as much information in writing as possible.
- Consider using e-mail or text, especially for less urgent communication. Also consider using Our Family Wizard (www.OurFamilyWizard.com) as a communication option.
- Avoid face-to-face criticisms of your spouse's parenting.
- Avoid telling your spouse how to parent.
- Be factual and business-like.
- Acknowledge to your spouse the good parental qualities he displays, such as being concerned, attentive, or generous.
- Keep your children out of any conflicts. Do not share your emotions and anger with your children.
- Obtain a reference for a communications counselor in your area and schedule an appointment.

Talk to your attorney about developing a communication protocol to be used by you and your spouse. It is in everyone's best interest to lower the conflict between parents so that the children's needs are paramount.

8.33 What if the children are not returned from placement at the agreed time? Should I call the police?

Calling the police should be done only as a last resort if you feel that your children are at risk of abuse or neglect, or if you have been advised by your attorney that such a call is warranted. The involvement of law enforcement officials in parental conflict can result in far greater trauma to children than would a late return at the end of placement. Except in case of emergencies, contact your attorney first before calling the police.

The appropriate response to children not being returned according to a court order depends on the circumstances. If the problem is a recurring one, talk to your attorney regarding your options. It may be that a change in the schedule would be in the best interest of your children. If this situation happens on a regular basis, also consider bringing a contempt motion against your spouse to impose a penalty if your spouse continues to act contrary to existing orders.

Despite the behavior of the other parent, make every effort to keep your children out of any conflicts between you and your spouse.

8.34   I am considering moving out of state. What factors will the court consider in either granting or denying my request to move my child from Wisconsin?

If your relocation is contested, the court will decide whether to allow you to relocate. There are different standards that apply to relocation, depending on the facts of your case. If the parent proposing the move or removal has sole legal or joint legal custody of the child and the child resides with that parent for the greater period of time, the court may modify the legal custody or physical placement order if the modification is in the best interest of the children. There is a rebuttable presumption that continuing the children's placement with the primary placement parent is in the best interest of the children. This presumption may be overcome only by a showing that the move or removal is unreasonable. A change in the economic circumstances or marital status of either party alone is not sufficient to meet the standards for modification. The burden of proof is on the parent objecting to the move or removal. Some factors considered by the court in reaching its decision whether or not to allow relocation include the following:

- Whether the purpose of the proposed action is reasonable

- The nature and extent of the children's relationship with the other parent and the disruption to that relationship that the proposed action may cause
- The availability of alternative arrangements to foster and continue the children's relationship with and access to the other parent

If the parents have joint legal custody and have substantially equal periods of physical placement, the burden of proof shifts to the parent wanting to relocate. Generally, factors to be weighed include the reputation of the schools, the reason for the relocation, the anticipated standard of living of the children, periods of placement available to the other party, and location of relatives and friends.

If you are thinking about moving, talk to your attorney immediately. Your attorney can help you gather important information that may be needed in your removal case.

8.35 After the divorce, can my ex-spouse legally take our children out of the state during placement? Out of the country?

The answer to your question depends on the terms of your marital settlement agreement and your judgment of divorce. It is generally permissible to take children out of Wisconsin for a period up to ninety days. For example, if your ex-spouse wants to take the children to Disneyland on vacation, your ex-spouse can certainly do so. In order to take your children out of the country, you must give your permission. If these are particular areas of concern, address these issues in the marital settlement agreement. Some areas that you may want to address include the following factors. Remember that each case is different, and the following suggestions do not fit every situation:

- Limits on the duration or distance for out-of-state travel with the children
- Notice requirements
- Receipt of a complete itinerary including phone numbers, physical addresses, e-mail addresses, airline or other transportation data, and hotels
- Possession of the children's passport
- Posting of bond by the other parent prior to travel

- Requiring a court order for travel outside the country

Let your attorney know if you have special concerns about your children's travel or removal from the state.

8.36 If I am not given custody, what rights do I have regarding medical records and medical treatment for my children?

No matter which parent has custody, state law allows both parents to have access to the medical records of their children and to make emergency medical decisions. The only exception to this provision is a contrary order by the court.

8.37 If I'm not the primary caregiver, how will I know what's going on at my children's school? What rights to records do I have there?

Access to your children's school records is available to both parents unless there is a court order that specifically revokes those rights.

If you have limited placement of your minor children, it is especially important to develop a relationship with your children's teachers. Request to be placed on the school's e-mail or mailing list for all notices. Find out what is necessary to obtain copies of important school information and report cards.

You should communicate with your ex-spouse so you can both share and receive information about your children's progress in school. This will enable you both to support your children through any challenging periods in their education. It will also enable both parents to work together to share your children's successes and educational needs.

Generally, no matter which parent has custody or placement, your children will benefit by both parents' involvement in their education. Attend parent-teacher conferences and school events, help with school homework, and communicate positively with your ex-spouse for the benefit of the children.

8.38 If my spouse is awarded sole legal custody, may I still take my children to church during my placement?

The decision of your children's religious affiliation is a fundamental decision made by the parent with sole legal custody or together if the parents have joint legal custody. However, a noncustodial parent retains the authority to make day-to-day decisions for the children when the children are in his or her care. That may include taking the children to church, but that is an issue that should be addressed with your attorney and with the other parent.

8.39 What if my children do not want to have placement with my former spouse? Do I have to force my children to see my former spouse?

If your children are resisting placement with the other parent, try to determine the underlying reason for their recalcitrance. Try to figure out the answer to these questions:

- What is your children's stated reason for not wanting to visit their other parent?
- Do your children appear afraid, anxious, or sad?
- Do you have any concerns regarding your children's safety while with the other parent?
- Have you prepared your children for placement, speaking about the experience with enthusiasm and encouragement?
- Is it possible your children are perceiving your anxiety about the situation and are consequently having the same reaction?
- Have you provided support for your children's transition to the other home, such as completing fun activities in your home well in advance of the other parent's starting time for placement?
- Have you spoken to the other parent about your children's behavior?
- Are you able to provide anything that will make your children's time with the other parent more comfortable, such as a favorite toy, blanket, or book?
- Have you established clear routines in advance of your children's placement with the other parent such as packing a backpack, saying good-bye to a family pet, and/or inclusion of some favorite games?

The reason for children's reluctance to go with the other parent may be as simple as being sad about leaving you or as serious as being a victim of abuse in the other parent's home. It is important to look closely to determine the underlying reason and the best response to your children's behavior.

The court considers compliance with placement court orders a very serious matter. If one parent believes that the other parent is intentionally interfering with placement or is guilty of alienation of the parent-child relationship, it can result in further litigation and potentially a finding of contempt. Balanced against this potential situation is the possibility that your children feel unsafe or are victims of some sort of abuse. Weigh the facts and talk to your attorney about your available avenues of resolution. Except in emergency situations, a return to mediation may be your first avenue to address these problems.

8.40   What steps should I take to prevent my ex-spouse from being awarded placement of my children in the event of my death?

Unless the other parent is not fit to have custody and placement of your children, the other parent will be awarded placement of the minor children in almost all circumstances, in the event of your death. Every parent should have a will or trust naming a guardian for his or her children. If you do not intend to name the other parent as the guardian of your minor children in the event of your death, discuss this issue with your attorney to research possible alternatives.

In addition to your divorce attorney, talk to an estate planning attorney to determine how to best document and preserve any evidence that will prove that the other parent is not a good choice, or is unfit, to have custody and placement of your minor children in the event of your death. You may want to consider establishing a trust naming a person other than your ex-spouse as trustee so your former spouse does not control any inheritance left to your minor child. Remember, however, despite the terms of your will, trust, or guardianship, your spouse will likely receive placement of your children in the event of your death.

9

Child Support

Whether you are paying or receiving child support, the issue is often a subject of great concern and worry. Will there be enough child support to take care of the children? Will you have enough money to pay your bills and mortgage after you pay child support?

Today, because of child-support guidelines, parents have a better understanding and advance notice of the nature and extent of their potential child-support obligation. The mechanisms for both payment and receipt of child support are more clearly defined. Assistance is provided in the event child support has not been ordered, or in the event child support is not paid as required. The Wisconsin Child Support Program (www.dcf.wisconsin.gov/bcs) provides comprehensive information about the receipt and payment of child support.

9.1   What determines whether I will get child support?

Whether or not you will be entitled to child support depends on a number of factors. Factors that are significant in determining child support include the number of children; gross income of each parent; cost of health insurance; variable expenses; financial resources of the children; the needs of each party and the children; the standard of living the children would have enjoyed had the marriage not ended; the cost of child care; travel expenses; the amount of time the children spend in each parent's home; the physical, mental and emotional health of the children; tax consequences; and more.

133

9.2 May I request child support even if I do not meet the six-month residency requirement for a divorce in Wisconsin?

Yes, even though you may not have met the residency requirement to obtain a divorce in Wisconsin, you have a right to seek support for your children. Talk to your attorney or visit the Wisconsin Child Support Program website at www. dcf.wisconsin.gov/bcs for contact information and to apply for child-support services.

9.3 Am I entitled to temporary child support while the issue of custody and placement remains undecided on a permanent basis?

A judge or family court commissioner has authority to enter a temporary order for custody, placement, and child support. This order is given full force and effect until modified by another temporary order or a final decision is made relative to custody, placement, and child support. In most cases, a temporary hearing is scheduled as soon as the divorce process is started, and additional temporary hearings may be scheduled during the divorce process if circumstances change substantially.

9.4 What is *temporary support* and how soon can I get it?

If you or your children need financial assistance during the divorce process, bring that issue to the attention of your attorney at your first consultation. If you and your spouse are not able to agree on the amount of child support, maintenance, or family support to be paid, the issue is brought to the attention of the court by filing a *motion for temporary orders*. At the temporary hearing, each party will be able to present evidence in support of his or her position, and the court will render an order based on the facts determined at the hearing.

In the event the judge or family court commissioner orders child support, maintenance, or family support, an order will be entered and an *interim disbursement order* will be drafted. Your spouse's employer will be ordered to begin withholding support from his or her paychecks. Your spouse's employer will be required to send the support payment directly to the

Wisconsin Support Collections Trust Fund (WI SCTF) in Milwaukee, Wisconsin, which in turn will forward the child support to you via direct deposit or in the form of a child-support debit card.

9.5 How soon does my spouse start paying support for the children?

Your spouse may voluntarily pay child support at any time. It is in your and your children's best interest, however, to make sure that a temporary order is entered in order to identify the specific amount of child support due and when such payments are to be made. With an order in place you will also be able to enforce the order if your child's other parent stops paying child support outright or fails to pay the required amount.

9.6 How is the amount of child support I receive or pay determined if I have primary placement of the children?

The Wisconsin Department of Children and Families adopted and published a standard to be used by courts in determining child-support obligations. The standard is based on a percentage of the gross income of either or both parents. The definition of gross income is complex and should be determined by your attorney, taking into account all relevant factors. Once a parent's applicable gross monthly income is determined, the child-support guidelines as set forth below are payable to the parent who has primary placement of the children:

- 17 percent for one child
- 25 percent for two children
- 29 percent for three children
- 31 percent for four children
- 34 percent for five or more children

Child support that is higher or lower than the guidelines may be awarded in certain cases, for example:

- When either parent or child has extraordinary medical costs
- When a child is disabled with special needs
- For juveniles placed in foster care
- Whenever the application of the guidelines in an individual case would be unjust or inappropriate

When a judge orders an amount of support that is different from the guideline amount, it is referred to as a "deviation," and facts supporting the deviation must be placed on the record.

Due to the complexity of calculations under the guidelines, many attorneys use computer software to calculate child support. You may review the guidelines in greater detail at: http://dcf.wisconsin.gov/bcs/order/guidelines.htm.

9.7 Does the type and amount of placement I am awarded impact the amount of child support I will receive or pay?

This is a very complex question, totally dependent on the facts and circumstances of each individual case, but listed below are types of placement impacting the amount of child support received and paid. The following are just some of the factors that impact the determination of child support:

- *Serial family payment.* In the event the parent paying child support has another child-support obligation incurred as a result of a court order and the support obligation to be calculated is for children from a subsequent family or subsequent paternity judgment, special rules apply for the calculation of child support.

- *Shared placement.* If you are a shared-placement parent, special rules apply relative to the calculation of child support. A shared-placement parent means a parent who has a court-ordered period of placement of at least 25 percent (ninety-two overnights or more) and is ordered by the court to assume the child's basic support costs in proportion to the parent's placement time with the child. In addition to the shared-placement payor child-support obligation, the court also assigns responsibility for a payment of the child's variable costs in proportion to each parent's share of physical placement, with due consideration to a disparity in the parents' incomes.

- *Split-placement parents.* For parents who have two or more children and each parent has placement of one or more, but not all of the children, special provisions provide for the calculation of child support.

- *Low-income payor.* If a payor's monthly income available for child support is below the federal poverty guidelines, 75 percent to 150 percent of the current Federal Poverty Guidelines, there is a downward child-support deviation.
- *High-income payor.* A payor's full monthly income available for child support shall be considered in determining the payor's child-support obligation. The court applies reduced percentages to income at higher levels.
- *Special circumstances.* The court may apply any combination of special-circumstance provisions under the above provisions to determine a child-support obligation if the criteria apply and the combination of provisions is not specifically prohibited.

9.8   How does the court define *gross income* for child-support purposes?

Generally, a person's gross income is available for the payment of child support. *Gross income* under Wisconsin law includes all of the following:

- Salary and wages
- Interest and investment income
- Social Security disability and federal old-age insurance benefits
- Net proceeds resulting from worker's compensation or other personal-injury awards intended to replace income
- Unemployment insurance
- Income continuation benefits
- Voluntary deferred compensation, employee contributions to any employee benefit plan or profit-sharing, and voluntary employee contributions to any pension or retirement account whether or not the account provides for tax deferral or avoidance
- Military allowances and veteran's benefits
- Undistributed income of a corporation

Calculation of gross income is a complicated process. Make sure your attorney is aware of all sources of income so that child support can be correctly calculated.

9.9 What financial sources are not included in the calculation of gross income?
Gross income does not include any of the following:

- Child support
- Foster care payments
- Kinship care payments
- Public assistance benefits, except child-care subsidy payments shall be considered income to a child-care provider
- Food stamps
- Cash benefits paid by counties
- Supplemental security income and state supplemental security payments
- Payments made for social services or other public assistance benefits

9.10 I am receiving worker's compensation. May child support be taken out of these payments?
The portion of a worker's compensation lump sum benefits not intended to replace income is excluded from gross income in establishing a child-support order. However, your worker's compensation weekly benefits, which act as income replacement, are assignable for the collection of child support.

9.11 My spouse and I were ordered to pay variable expenses. What are *variable expenses*?
Variable expenses are the reasonable costs above basic support costs incurred by or on behalf of a child, including, but not limited to, the cost of child care, tuition, a child's special needs, and other activities that involve substantial cost. These costs may include extracurricular activities, music lessons, car insurance, uniforms, and/or dance lessons. The definition of what constitutes variable expenses should be explicitly included in your marital settlement agreement.

"Basic support costs" means food, shelter, clothing, transportation, personal care, and incidental recreational costs.

9.12 My spouse has a college degree but refuses to get a job. Will the court consider this factor in determining the amount of child support?

The earning capacity of your spouse may be considered in calculating child support. You and your attorney may want to consider hiring an expert to determine your spouse's earning capacity and to impute income to him or her, or your attorney may propose an earning capacity figure to the court for consideration.

Income imputed based on earning capacity means the amount of income that exceeds the parent's actual income and represents the parent's ability to earn, based on the parent's education, training, and recent work experience, earnings during previous periods, current physical and mental health, history of child-care responsibilities as the parent with primary placement, and the ability of work in or near the parent's community. The court reviews this criteria to determine whether or not income should be imputed to your spouse for child-support purposes.

If you believe your spouse is earning substantially less than the income she or he is capable of earning, express your concern to your attorney at the onset of your case. It takes time to research and establish the imputation of income to your spouse.

9.13 Will I receive child support directly from my spouse or from the state of Wisconsin?

Child support is generally withheld by wage assignment from the income of the payor. Employers routinely withhold child support from employee wages just as they withhold taxes or retirement.

If child support is not withheld by wage assignment from the parent's employer, that parent must make child-support payments directly to the Wisconsin Support Collections Trust Fund (WI SCTF) in Milwaukee. WI SCTF will then send the child support to the parent receiving support.

9.14   How will I receive my child-support payment?

The Wisconsin Support Collections Trust Fund has two methods of disbursing your child-support money: direct deposit or debit card. If you choose direct deposit, your child-support payment is automatically deposited into your bank account. Alternatively, your child support may be deposited directly onto a Wisconsin EPPIC Debit MasterCard. With the Wisconsin EPPIC Debit MasterCard, your child-support payments will be transferred electronically into your card account. You can use your card to pay for things you buy, or you can use your card to make cash withdrawals surcharge-free at MoneyPass ATM locations and at any financial institutions that display the MasterCard acceptance mark.

More information can be found on the Wisconsin Department of Children and Families website at http://dcf.wisconsin.gov/bcs/pay/pay_ways_cp.htm.

9.15   Is there any reason not to pay or receive payments directly to my spouse once the court has entered a child-support order?

Yes. Once a child-support order is entered by the court, the WI SCTF keeps a record of all support paid. If your payment is not made through WI SCTF, the state's records will show that you are behind in your child support.

Direct payments of child support may also result in misunderstandings between parents. You may have intended the money to pay a child-support payment, but your spouse may have thought the payment was extra money to help with your children's expenses or to pay a bill such as a tuition payment or dentist bill.

Payment of support through the WI SCTF protects both parents. However, if you ignore this information and a direct payment is made directly to your spouse, be sure a notarized receipt is signed and filed with the clerk of the circuit court of the county in which your child-support order was entered. This is important so that the state's records remain accurate. If no receipt is filed for a direct payment, it may later be considered a gift or payment for a non-child-support-related matter.

9.16 May I go to the courthouse to pick up my child-support payment?

No. In the past, payments for child support were made to the clerk of the circuit court in the county where the child-support order was entered. Today, all child-support payments in Wisconsin are processed through a central location, the WI SCTF.

9.17 How soon will my child-support payments start arriving?

A number of factors may affect the date on which you will begin receiving your child support. Here are the usual steps in the process:

- A child-support amount and start date for the support are decided either by agreement between you and your spouse or by order of the court.
- Either the court, your attorney, or your spouse's attorney prepares the court order.
- The attorney(s) who did not write the court order reviews and approves the proposed order.
- The court order is provided to the judge for signature.
- An interim disbursement order is implemented and provided to your spouse's employer, requiring that child support be withheld from future paychecks.
- Your spouse's employer withholds the support from the paycheck.
- The child support is transferred by the employer to the Wisconsin Child Support Payment Center.
- The Payment Center sends the money to you, either by direct deposit or in the form of a child-support debit card.

As you can see, there are a lot of steps in this process. Plan your budget knowing that the initial payment of child support might be delayed at any step of the process. If receipt of the payment of child support seems inordinately long in duration, contact your attorney to check on the reason for the delay.

9.18 Will some amount of child support be withheld from each of my spouse's paychecks?

It depends on the employer's policy and how your spouse is paid. If support is due on the first of the month, the employer has the full month to withhold the amount ordered to be paid. If an employer issues paychecks twice a month, it is possible that half of the support will be withheld from each check and paid to the WI SCTF at the end of the month or in two separate checks as the funds are withdrawn.

If an employer issues checks every other week, which is twenty-six pay periods per year, there will be some months in which a third paycheck is issued. Consequently, it is possible that no child support will be withheld from the wages paid in that third check of the month or that some checks will be for less than 50 percent of the monthly amount due.

Example: Suppose child support is $650 per month. Your spouse is paid every other Friday, or twenty-six times per year. The employer may withhold $300 per paycheck for child support ($300 x 26 = $7,800 ÷ 12 = $650). Although most months the support received will be $600, for a few months it will be $900. By the end of the year, however, your spouse will have paid the same amount as if $650 had been paid each month.

Over time, child-support payments typically fall into a routine schedule, which makes it easier for you and your spouse to plan your budgets.

9.19 If my spouse receives income outside of employment income, is that income accessible for child support?

Yes. Child support may be automatically withheld from most sources of income. These may include unemployment compensation, worker's compensation, investment income, self-employment, and more. Your attorney and the court will be familiar with child-support payment options. Talk to your attorney to address your concerns.

9.20 May I collect child support from both the biological parent and the adoptive parent of my child?

When your child was adopted, the biological parent's duty to support your child ended. However, it may be possible for you to collect past due child-support arrearages accrued before the adoption from your child's biological parent. Discuss this possibility with your attorney.

9.21 What happens with child support when our children go to the other parent's home for summer vacation? Is child support still due?

It depends. Whether child support is adjusted during extended placement with the noncustodial parent depends on the court order in your case. Generally, however, child support is awarded based on a twelve-month period taking into consideration the total number of placement days each party is allocated per year.

9.22 After the divorce, if I choose to live with my new partner rather than marry, may I still collect child support from my former spouse and my child's father?

Yes. Your new partner has no obligation to provide for the support of your child. That is the responsibility of your child's father.

9.23 May I still collect child support if I move to another state?

Yes. A move out of state will not end your right to receive child support. However, the amount of child support could be changed based on the additional costs of placement, such as airfare, hotels, or other travel expenses. A change in child support is not automatic. Your ex-spouse would have to file a motion to modify child support based on a substantial change in circumstances.

9.24 Can I expect to continue to receive child support if I remarry?

Yes, your child support will continue even if you remarry. The child-support obligation is your ex-spouse's obligation.

9.25 How long may I expect to receive child support?

Under Wisconsin law, child support is ordinarily ordered to be paid until the child is legally emancipated (becomes self-supporting), reaches the age of eighteen, or graduates from high school, whichever occurs later, but in no event after the child reaches the age of nineteen, if the child is pursuing an accredited course of instruction leading to the equivalent of a high school diploma.

9.26   Does interest accrue on past-due child support?

Yes, interest accrues on past-due child support. The amount of interest is determined by the state and is calculated by WI SCTF on any arrearages of record.

9.27   What action should I take if my ex-spouse refuses to pay child support?

Some counties have attorneys who are specifically designated to perform child-support enforcement services. Contact your local county child-support enforcement agency or your attorney to discuss your ex-spouse's failure to pay child support. Visit the website for the Wisconsin Department of Children and Families at ⟨http://dcf.wisconsin.gov/bcs/agencylist.htm⟩ for a listing of the offices and addresses of child-support agencies throughout Wisconsin who can help you.

In addition, if your former spouse is not paying child support, contact your attorney, who may file a contempt motion to address the issue of nonpayment, attorney's fees, and costs. The judge may order payment of both the current amount of support and an additional amount to be paid each month until the past due child support (referred to as "arrearages") is paid in full.

9.28   At what point will the state of Wisconsin help me collect back child support, and what methods do they use?

It depends. Whether and when the state of Wisconsin will help you collect back child support and the methods they will use depend on the amount of back child support owed. Each set of facts and circumstances is different, so there is not a rule that applies in every situation. Contact your local county corporation counsel's office to obtain specific information.

Driver's, recreational, and professional licenses may be suspended if more than three months of child support is owed. If more than $500 in back support is due, state or federal income tax refunds can be intercepted. When more than $2,500 is owed, a passport can be denied. In some cases, failure to pay child support can result in a jail sentence.

9.29 After the divorce, may my former spouse substitute buying sprees with the children instead of making child-support payments?
No. Purchases of gifts and clothing for a child do not relieve your former spouse from an obligation to pay court-ordered child support.

9.30 How does providing health insurance for my child affect my child-support obligation?
If you pay the health insurance premium for your child, the amount you pay may be taken into account when calculating child support. You may ask the court for a downward deviation from the child-support guidelines because you are paying the minor child's health insurance premium. Alternately, the court may order the health insurance premium for the minor child split on a 50/50 basis.

9.31 Am I required to pay for my child's uninsured medical expenses from the child support I receive?
Generally, the minor child's uninsured medical expenses are split between the parties on a 50/50 basis. However, the court must consider each party's ability to pay uninsured medical expenses when establishing the order.

9.32 My child receives BadgerCare Plus. Does my ex-spouse have any obligation to reimburse BadgerCare Plus?
Responsibility for a contribution to the cost of the other parent's premium for the BadgerCare Plus program (Wisconsin's health care program for children under nineteen years of age and families) may be ordered by the court. The court may incorporate responsibility for a contribution to the cost of the premium as an upward or downward adjustment to a payor's child-support obligation.

9.33   Can my spouse be required by the judgment of divorce to pay for our child's private elementary and high school education?

The answer to this question is complex and depends on the circumstances of your case. The court will look at factors such as the wishes of you and your spouse, the amount of child support being paid, the cost of private versus public education, your child's age and grade in school, and more. As a general rule, if your child attended a private school before the commencement of the divorce, the court is likely to continue your child's education in the same school if financially possible. Discuss this issue with your attorney and provide your lawyer with specific information about private school tuition, fees, uniforms, and other private education expenses.

9.34   Can my spouse be required by the judgment of divorce to contribute financially to our child's college education?

The legal duty of a parent to support a child does not include payment for college education. However, if your spouse voluntarily agrees to pay this expense, it may be included in the marital settlement agreement and findings of fact, conclusions of law, and judgment of divorce.

If your judgment includes such a provision, be sure the terms are specific. Terms to consider include:

- What expenses are included? For example, tuition, room and board, books, fees, and travel
- Is there a limit? For example, up to the level of the cost of attendance at the University of Wisconsin-Madison or a certain dollar amount
- When is the payment due?
- For what period of time does it continue?
- Are there any limits on the type of education paid?
- How many credits does my child have to be taking in order to receive this financial support?
- Do grades have an impact?

The greater the clarity in such a provision, the lower the risk for misunderstanding or conflict years later.

146

10

Maintenance

The mere mention of the word *maintenance* might stir emotions and start your stomach churning. If your spouse has filed for divorce and is seeking maintenance, you might see it as a double injustice—your marriage is ending and you feel like you have to pay your spouse so he or she can move forward to another life. If you are seeking maintenance, you may feel hurt and confused that your spouse is resistant to paying maintenance, even though you may have interrupted your career to care for your children.

Learning more about Wisconsin's maintenance laws, formerly known as alimony, may help you move forward from an emotional reaction to a recognition of the reality of maintenance under certain circumstances. Uncertainty about the precise amount of maintenance that may be awarded or the number of years maintenance will be paid also heightens the anxiety. Work closely with your lawyer to determine the appropriate amount and duration of maintenance given the specific facts and circumstances of your case. Be open to different options or possibilities. It never hurts to imagine reverse positions and to view the facts and circumstances through the eyes of your spouse.

10.1 Which gets calculated first, child support or maintenance?

According to Wisconsin's child-support guidelines, child support is calculated before determining the payor's maintenance obligation. In some circumstances there is insufficient

147

money for payment of child support and maintenance, so child support has top priority.

10.2 What is the difference between *alimony* and *maintenance*?

In Wisconsin, *alimony* and *maintenance* have the same meaning—spousal support.

10.3 How will I know if I am eligible to receive maintenance?

Talk with your attorney about whether you are a candidate for maintenance. A court may grant an order requiring maintenance payments to either party for a limited or definite length of time after considering the following factors:

- The length of your marriage
- The age and physical and emotional health of the parties
- The division of property
- The educational level of each party at the time of marriage and at the time the action is commenced
- The earning capacity of the party seeking maintenance
- The feasibility that the party seeking maintenance can become self-supporting at a standard of living reasonably comparable to that enjoyed during the marriage
- The tax consequences to each party
- Any mutual agreement made by the parties before or during the marriage
- The contribution by one party to the education, training, or increased earning power of the other
- Such other factors as the court may in each individual case determine to be relevant

Every case is unique. Providing your lawyer with clear and detailed information addressing the foregoing factors will allow your lawyer to weigh your rights or obligations relative to maintenance.

10.4 What information should I provide to my attorney if I want maintenance?

If your attorney advises you that you may be a candidate for maintenance, provide your attorney with the following facts:

- A history of the interruptions in your education or career for the benefit of your spouse, including transfers or moves due to your spouse's employment
- A history of the interruptions in your education or career for raising children, including periods during which you worked part-time
- Your complete educational background, including the dates of your schooling or training and degrees earned
- Your work history, including the names of your employers, the dates of your employment, your duties, your pay, and the reasons you left
- Any pensions or other benefits lost due to the interruption of your career for the benefit of the marriage
- Your health history, including any current diagnoses, treatments, limitations, and medications
- Your monthly living expenses, including anticipated future expenses such as health insurance and tax on maintenance
- A complete list of the debts owed by you and your spouse
- A marital history detailing the annual income earned by you and your spouse from all sources
- Tax returns for a period of five years, both personal and business
- Prenuptial agreement, if any

Also include any other facts that support your need for maintenance, such as other contributions you made to the marriage, upcoming medical treatment, or a lack of jobs in the field in which you were formerly employed.

No two maintenance cases are alike. The more information your lawyer has about your situation, the easier it will be for him or her to assess your case for maintenance.

10.5   My spouse told me that because I had an affair during the marriage, I have no chance to be awarded maintenance even though I quit my job when my first child was born and have cared for our children for many years. Is it true that I have no right to maintenance in that situation?

Wisconsin is a no-fault divorce state. Your right to maintenance will be based on many factors, but having an affair is not a factor in determining maintenance. The court may not consider marital misconduct as a relevant factor in granting maintenance payments.

10.6   How is the amount of maintenance calculated?

Unlike child support, there are no specific guidelines for determining the amount of maintenance. The court will weigh both the income and expenses of you and your spouse, after giving consideration to the payment and receipt of child support. The court will review your earning capacity, health, standard of living, and other factors to determine an award of maintenance. The court may begin its maintenance evaluation with the proposition that the financially dependent spouse may be entitled to 50 percent of the total earnings of both parties.

10.7   My spouse makes a lot more money than he reports on our tax return, but he hides it. How can I prove my spouse's real income to show he can afford to pay maintenance?

Alert your attorney to your concerns. Your lawyer can then take a number of actions to determine your spouse's income with greater accuracy, including the following:

- More thorough discovery
- An examination of check registers, bank deposits, and credit card statements
- Inquiries about travel
- Depositions of third parties who have knowledge of income or spending by your spouse
- Subpoena of records of places where your spouse has made large purchases or received income

- Comparison of income claimed with expenses paid
- Inquiries of purchases made in cash

Within legal perimeters and only after discussion with your attorney, consider the following sources for determining whether or not your spouse is hiding divorce assets and where those assets are located:

- Your spouse's computer history
- LinkedIn, Facebook, Twitter, Pinterest, and other social networks
- Your spouse's phone
- GPS on your spouse's phone or vehicles
- Bank statements and online accounts
- Your spouse's checking account and credit card information
- Google search of your spouse's name
- Your spouse's text messages
- PayPal account
- Income tax returns for the past years
- Websites your spouse routinely visits
- Public and paid online people search databases
- Photos and other downloads on your spouse's phone
- IT expert
- Your spouse's e-mails if the e-mail account is not password protected
- Your spouse's credit reports
- Loan applications your spouse may have submitted to any bank or credit card company
- Safe deposit box
- Ask—your spouse may be open and honest if the issue is pressed

All of the above ideas for locating hidden assets require prior review of legal restrictions on invading your spouse's right to privacy. There are also statutory limitations in effect so discuss with your lawyer before starting any investigations. Ask your attorney specifically what you can and cannot do. Much will depend on your legitimate access to computer passwords and usernames.

By partnering with your lawyer, you may be able to build a case to establish your spouse's actual income is greater than shown on tax returns. If you filed joint tax returns, discuss with your lawyer any other implications of incorrect information on those returns.

10.8   I want to be sure the records on the maintenance I pay are accurate, especially for tax purposes. What's the best way to ensure this?

Your maintenance payments should be made directly to the Wisconsin Support Collections Trust Fund (WI SCTF) in Milwaukee. Maintenance is generally withheld by wage assignment.

By avoiding direct payments to your former spouse, you and he or she will have accurate records. To avoid an audit by the Internal Revenue Service, you must deduct the same amount of maintenance that your spouse is reporting as income on your tax returns. Ask your attorney to consider inclusion of a provision in your judgment of divorce that provides that you and your spouse will agree to the amount of maintenance received and paid prior to submission of any income tax returns.

10.9   What effect does maintenance have on my taxes?

Generally, maintenance is deductible to the payor and income to the payee.

10.10 What types of payments are considered maintenance?

Maintenance payments do not just include monthly monetary payments. Payments to a third party on behalf of your spouse, according to the terms of the judgment of divorce, may also be treated as maintenance.

These third-party payments may include court-ordered payments for your spouse's medical expenses, mortgage payments, housing costs, taxes, and/or tuition. These payments may be treated as if they were received by your spouse as maintenance then paid to the third party, but the issue must be specifically addressed and identified in writing in your marital settlement agreement.

Additionally, if you pay the premiums on a life insurance policy that is owned by your spouse, those payments may be considered maintenance. This is a very fine-line determination and again must be specifically addressed and identified in the judgment of divorce. This is an issue that must be determined prior to the actual divorce—not after. You and your spouse must agree on the definition of maintenance or an audit by the IRS may not be too far in the future.

10.11 What is the reason for allocation of maintenance? Does maintenance differ from property division?

Maintenance and property division serve two distinct purposes, even though many of the factors for determining them are the same. The purpose of maintenance is to provide support. In contrast, the purpose of a property division is to distribute the marital assets fairly between you and your spouse.

10.12 My spouse makes a lot more money than I do. Will I be awarded maintenance to address the difference in our income?

Generally, the answer to your question is yes, but there are a number of factors that go into any maintenance award. The length of the marriage is one significant criteria. If you have been married for only a short time, the court may not address the difference in your incomes because of the short length of your marriage. If you have a long marriage, it is likely that the court may begin its maintenance evaluation with the presumption that you may be entitled to 50 percent of the total earnings of both you and your spouse. Discuss this issue at length with your attorney. Your attorney will be able to advise you relative to his or her analysis of the range of the amount and duration of maintenance the court is likely to award.

10.13 What is a *buyout of maintenance*?

You and your spouse may agree to a *buyout of maintenance,* which is the payment of maintenance in one lump sum. A maintenance buyout will provide each party with certainty as to the amount of maintenance each will pay or receive. This is a very complicated issue that must be discussed with your attorney, taking into consideration tax issues. You should also consult your financial planner or accountant before agreeing to a buyout of maintenance.

10.14 How long may I expect to receive maintenance?

Like your right to receive maintenance, how long you will receive maintenance will depend on the facts of your case, Wisconsin case law, and the court's use of discretion in determining the amount and duration of maintenance. In general, the longer your marriage, the longer you may expect to receive maintenance, but this is a general rule subject to modification based on the individual facts and circumstances of your case.

Unless you and your spouse agree otherwise (which would be highly unusual), maintenance terminates on the remarriage of the recipient or the death of either party.

10.15 Does remarriage affect my maintenance?

Yes. Under Wisconsin law, unless your judgment of divorce provides otherwise, maintenance ends on the remarriage of the recipient.

10.16 Does my spouse's cohabitation allow me to discontinue maintenance?

It is not allowable in Wisconsin to discontinue maintenance payments to a former spouse solely on the grounds of cohabitation with another person. Cohabitation is a factor to be considered by the court, but is not the only factor that the court will consider in determining whether maintenance should be terminated, modified, or reduced under those circumstances.

10.17 Does the death of my former spouse affect my maintenance?

Yes. Under Wisconsin law, unless your judgment of divorce provides otherwise, maintenance ends on the death of either party.

10.18 May I continue to collect maintenance if I move to a different state?

Yes. The duty of your former spouse to follow a court order to pay maintenance does not end simply because you move to another state, unless this is a specific provision in your judgment otherwise.

10.19 What should I do if my spouse stops paying maintenance?

If your spouse stops paying maintenance, talk to your attorney about your enforcement options. If you are not already being paid by wage assignment, that should be your first option. Contact the child-support agency in your county or your attorney to assist you in implementing a wage assignment. You may also file the appropriate contempt motion to ask the court's assistance in enforcing the maintenance order.

10.20 May I return to court to modify maintenance?

It depends. If your judgment of divorce provides that your maintenance order is "non-modifiable," then it may not be modified. Your judgment of divorce may not be modified to award maintenance if maintenance was already terminated at the final divorce. A request to modify maintenance for the purposes of seeking additional maintenance may not be filed if you were awarded limited-term maintenance and the limited term has passed.

If there has been a substantial change in circumstances that impacts your need for maintenance or your spouse's ability to pay maintenance, a motion for modification of maintenance may be filed. Examples of a substantial change in circumstances may include serious illness, job loss, substantial increase or decrease in your ex-spouse's income, and more.

If you think you have a basis to modify your maintenance, contact your attorney at once to be sure a timely modification request is filed with the court.

11

Division of Property

You never imagined that you would face losing the
house you and your spouse so happily purchased—
the house where you celebrated family traditions and spent
countless hours making it "home." Your spouse wants it and
your lawyer says it might be sold.

During a divorce, you will decide whether you or your
spouse will take ownership of everything from bathroom towels to your stock portfolio. Suddenly you find yourself having a
strong attachment to that lamp in the family room or the paint-
ing in the hallway. Why does the collection of coins suddenly
take on new meaning?

It is important that you and your spouse do your best to
jointly divide personal property. Fighting over personal property can be very costly, so personal property such as dishes,
towels, tools, and furniture is generally divided by negotiation
between the parties—not by litigation by attorneys. However,
some assets do require formal valuation. Enlist the support of
your attorney in deciding which assets should be valued by
an expert, such as the family business or real estate. From tax
consequences to replacement value, there are many factors to
consider in deciding whether to fight to keep an asset, award
it to your spouse, or ask that the item be sold.

Like all aspects of your divorce, take one step at a time.
By starting with the items most easily divided, you and your
spouse may avoid paying lawyers to litigate the value of personal property.

Division of Property

11.1   What system does Wisconsin use for dividing property?

No matter how title is held, the court may use its discretion in determining a division of the marital assets and marital debts. The court must presume that all property, except inherited or gifted property (from a person other than the other party), shall be divided equally between the parties. The factors the court considers in reaching a property division award include the following:

- The length of the marriage
- The property brought to the marriage by each party
- Whether one of the parties has substantial assets not subject to division by the court
- The contribution of each party to the marriage, giving appropriate economic value to each party's contribution in homemaking and child-care services
- The age and physical and emotional health of the parties
- The contribution by one party to the education, training, or increased earning power of the other
- The earning capacity of each party
- The desirability of awarding the family home to the party having physical placement for the greater period of time
- The amount and duration of any order granting maintenance or family support payments to either party and whether the property division is in lieu of such payments
- Other economic circumstances of each party, including pension benefits, vested or unvested, and further interests
- The tax consequences to each party
- Any written agreement made by the parties before or during the marriage
- Such other factors as the court may in each individual case determine to be relevant

11.2   How is it determined who gets the house?

The award of the marital residence is a significant consideration in any divorce. The court looks at a number of factors including the desire of the parties relative to that issue. The court also addresses the desirability of awarding the family home or the right to live therein for a reasonable period to the party having physical placement for the greater period of time. The decision as to which party will reside in the home on a temporary basis, until the divorce is final, is also a significant consideration.

Other factors the court considers relative to the disposition of the marital residence include the following:

- Which party, if either, can afford the mortgage and expenses associated with the home
- Which party, if either, will be able to refinance the parties' residence
- Whether either party owned or purchased the residence prior to the marriage
- Whether the residence was purchased with inherited or gifted funds from either party
- Whether there are other assets in the marital estate to offset the value of the home

Talk with your lawyer about your options. If you and your spouse are unable to reach an agreement regarding the house, the court will decide which party will be awarded the residence or whether the residence will be placed on the market for sale.

11.3   Should I sell the house during the divorce proceedings?

Selling your home is a big decision. To help you decide what is right for you, ask yourself these questions:

- How will the sale of the marital home affect my children?
- Can I afford to pay the mortgage, real estate taxes, utilities, and maintenance?
- After the divorce, will I be willing to give the house and yard the time, money, and physical energy required for its maintenance?

- Are there other assets available to buy out my spouse's financial interest in the residence?
- Would my life be easier if I were in a smaller or simpler home?
- Would I prefer to move closer to friends and family?
- What is the state of the housing market in my community?
- What are the benefits of remaining in this house?
- Will I have a higher or lower interest rate if I sell the house and buy a new one?
- Will I have the means to acquire another home?
- If I don't retain the home and my spouse asks for it, what effect will this have on my custody case?
- Will my spouse agree to the sale of the house?
- What is the real estate commission if the residence is sold?
- What will be the costs of preparing the house for sale?
- Financially, would I be better served by retaining retirement benefits rather than the residence?

Selling a home is more than just a legal or financial decision. Consider what is important to you in creating your life after divorce.

11.4   How do I determine how much our house is worth?

In a divorce, the value of your home may be determined in a number of ways. You and your spouse may agree to the value of your home. You may seek advice from a local real estate agent on the approximate value of your home through a market analysis. Or, for a more authoritative valuation, you may hire a professional real estate appraiser to determine the value of your home. You may also use the fair market value or assessed value of your residence, as determined by your most recent real estate tax bill. Talk to your attorney to determine the best method to value your home in your divorce.

11.5 My house is worth less than what is owed. What are my options?

Talk with your lawyer and consider consulting a mortgage specialist. It is important to get an accurate assessment of the value of your house. If your house is "under water," meaning you owe more on the mortgage than your house is worth, you may decide to list your house for sale while continuing to make your mortgage payments in order to maintain your good credit rating. Another option to consider is a short sale, where the lender accepts less money for your house than is actually owed. A deed in lieu of foreclosure is also an option if all parties and the mortgage holder(s) cooperate. Seek advice from your lawyer and other financial experts to determine which option is best for you. There is no one easy answer.

11.6 What is meant by *equity* in my home?

Equity is the difference between the value of the home and the amount owed in mortgages or other liens against the property. For example, if the first mortgage is $50,000 and the second mortgage from a home equity loan is $10,000, the total debt owed against the house is $60,000. If your home is valued at $100,000, the equity in your home is $40,000. (The $100,000 value less the $60,000 in mortgages equals $40,000 in equity.)

No matter which party is awarded the marital residence, the court will consider whether the spouse not awarded the home should be compensated for the equity in the house. In Wisconsin, it is presumed that there will be a 50/50 split of equity in the residence. If one of the parties remains in the home that party will have to buy out the other party's 50 percent share of equity in the residence, which would be $20,000 using the above example.

11.7 How will the equity in our house be divided?

If your home is sold, the equity in the home will be divided at the time of closing, after the costs of the sale have been paid.

If either you or your spouse is awarded the residence as part of the divorce property division, the other party must be compensated for his or her share of the equity in the residence.

There are different options for payment of this equity, including the following:

- Allocation of other assets of equal value, such as cash, retirement accounts, or personal property
- The spouse who remains in the home must refinance the residence to remove the other party's name from any existing mortgages or liens and to obtain the amount of any equalization payment to the other party.
- The parties may agree that payment will be made at the time of the sale of the residence at some future date.

11.8   If my spouse signs a *quitclaim deed,* does that remove his or her obligation to repay the mortgage?

No. A *quitclaim deed* is a legal document that transfers one person's interest in real property to another person. However, removing your spouse's name from the title of the real estate does not remove that spouse's obligation on the mortgage, home equity loan, or other liens. Both you and your spouse signed a contract with the lender to repay debt borrowed to purchase your home. Removing your spouse's name from the title of the real estate does not remove that spouse's obligation to repay the underlying debt. To remove your spouse from the mortgage or home equity line of credit, the retaining spouse must refinance the mortgage and other liens. Refinancing involves obtaining a new mortgage loan to pay off all existing debt in the name of both parties.

11.9   Who keeps all the household goods until the judgment is signed?

At a temporary hearing, the family court commissioner will decide who gets what personal property and household goods on a temporary basis if the parties cannot agree on that division. Most couples attempt to resolve the division of personal property on their own rather than incur legal fees for such division, because fees may far exceed the value of the personal property in question.

11.10 How can I reduce the risk that assets will be hidden, transferred, or destroyed by my spouse?

Consider the following actions to reduce the risk that assets will disappear or be difficult to locate before and during the divorce process:

- Place your family heirlooms or other valuables in a safe location.
- Consider the transfer of some financial accounts to your individual name prior to filing for divorce. This does not mean spending the asset. It is simply a question of title. Discuss this type of action with your attorney in advance of any such transfer and generally limit any such action to 50 percent of the value of the asset.
- Prepare an inventory of the personal property.
- Take photographs or video of the property.
- Obtain copies of important records or statements.
- Make copies of your income tax returns for the last five years.
- Record account numbers and passwords to all assets.
- Obtain copies of pension plan, 401(k), IRA, and other documents and statements.
- Obtain real estate information, including copies of deeds, mortgage statements, escrow account information, and tax bills.
- Obtain copies of any debts or liabilities, including credit card statements.
- Prepare a list of any premarital assets, including gifts or inheritances.

Speak candidly with your lawyer about your concerns so that a plan can be developed that provides a level of protection that is appropriate to your circumstances.

11.11 How are assets such as cars, boats, and furniture divided, and when does this happen?

In most cases, spouses are able to reach their own agreement relative to the division of personal property. If you and your spouse disagree about the value and allocation of certain items, prioritize those items that are the most significant to you, emotionally, financially, or otherwise. Remember, some items can be replaced at a reasonable cost that is well below the cost of fighting with your spouse over the item.

Always determine whether it is a good use of your attorney fees to argue over an item of personal property. If a negotiated settlement cannot be reached, the issue of property division will be determined by the court.

11.12 How do I value our used personal property?

In a divorce, your personal property will be valued at its fair market value. The fair market value is the price a buyer would be willing to pay for the item at a garage sale or on an online auction website. For example, if you bought a sofa for $3,000 five years ago, the fair market value is not how much the sofa cost when you purchased it or how much it will cost to replace it. Instead, the value of the sofa or other personal property is what you could reasonably expect to pay if the sofa was for sale at a garage sale.

11.13 My wife and I own a coin collection. How will our collection be valued and divided in our divorce?

If you own a unique collection, such as a gun, art, or coin collection, talk with your attorney about how to value the collection in your divorce. You will probably be compelled to have the collection appraised by an expert with specialized knowledge and training in that area. If you and your spouse cannot agree on who will keep the collection, the court may order the collection to be sold. The court may also divide the collection between you and your spouse. The bottom line is that the court will make the decision if you and your spouse cannot agree to the value of the collection and its allocation.

11.14 What is meant by a *property inventory* and how detailed should mine be?

A *property inventory* is a listing of the property you own. It may also include a brief description of the property. Discuss with your attorney the level of inventory detail needed to benefit your case.

Factors to consider when creating your inventory may include:

- Whether you anticipate a dispute regarding the value of the property
- Whether you will have continued access to the property if a later inventory is needed
- Whether you or your spouse are likely to disagree about which items are premarital, inherited, or gifts from someone other than your spouse

In addition to creating an inventory, your attorney may request that you prepare a list of the property that you and your spouse have already divided or a list of the items you want but your spouse has not agreed to allocate to you. Make sure your list is comprehensive. Do not forget frequently overlooked things such as tickets for social events, frequent flyer miles, club memberships, and more.

If you do not have continued access to your property, talk to your attorney about taking photographs or obtaining access to the property to complete your inventory. Your best option is to take photographs of your personal property. A video is another option.

11.15 What happens to our individual checking and savings accounts during and after the divorce?

No matter whose name is listed on the account, bank accounts are generally considered marital assets and may be divided by the court unless the funds are gifted or inherited. Your attorney may want to obtain a temporary order addressing the disposition of any financial marital assets. Make sure you have a list of all accounts as well as password access. Discuss with your attorney whether these accounts may be used during the pendency of the divorce action. Each case is different, so allocation of bank accounts must be individually considered by you and your attorney.

11.16 How and when are liquid assets like bank accounts and stocks divided?

In some cases couples will agree to divide bank accounts equally at the outset of the case. However, this may not be advisable in your case. Discuss with your attorney whether you should keep an accounting of how money is spent while your divorce is in progress.

Stocks are ordinarily a part of final property division and are valued as of the date of divorce. If you and your spouse cannot agree on how your investments should be divided, the court will make the decision at trial.

11.17   How is pet custody determined?

There is currently no such thing as pet custody in Wisconsin. Even though many people treat their animals as important members of their family, when it comes to divorce, Wisconsin pets are generally considered property and are not treated as "children." The court does not award "placement." But the issue of pet allocation in divorce is changing from a traditional property approach to a more caring recognition that a pet is far more than property. You cannot use the same analysis for a pet as you would use for a sofa or a car.

The Wisconsin Supreme Court in *Rabideau v. City of Racine* addressed the pet issue as follows: "[W]e are uncomfortable with the law's cold characterization of a dog...as mere 'property.' Labeling a dog 'property' fails to describe the value human beings place upon the companionship that they enjoy with a dog...."

Although not to be given the same consideration of best interest as in a child custody or placement determination, courts are beginning to look at not only who may have purchased the pet but where the pet prefers to spend time, who takes the pet to the vet, who feeds the pet, and who gets the most companionship from the pet. Courts are taking a middle-of-the-road position, weighing all relevant factors, determination of which is left to the court's reasoned analysis.

11.18   How will our property in another state be divided?

For the purposes of dividing your assets, out-of-state property is treated the same as property in Wisconsin.

11.19 Are all of the assets—such as property, bank accounts, and inheritances—that I owned prior to my marriage going to be awarded to me in the divorce?

Not necessarily. The only property that is nonmarital in Wisconsin is gifted and inherited property. The decision is ultimately left to the court, which has discretion to divide the property if the parties cannot come to their own resolution.

In some cases the court will allow a party to retain an asset brought into the marriage, but the following are questions the court will consider in making its determination:

- Can the premarital asset be clearly traced? For example, if you continue to own a vehicle that you brought into the marriage, it is likely that it will be awarded to you as your separate property. However, if you brought a vehicle into the marriage, sold it during the marriage, and spent the proceeds, it is less likely that the court will consider awarding you its value.
- Did you keep the property separate and titled in your name, or did you commingle it with marital assets?
- Did the other spouse contribute to the increase in the value of the premarital asset, and can the value of that increase be proven? For example, suppose a woman owned a home prior to her marriage. After the marriage, the parties lived in the home, continuing to make mortgage payments and improvements to the home.

The award of premarital assets in a divorce is a difficult subject. If you have premarital assets, a prenuptial agreement will generally address the issue of how those assets can be individually maintained during the marriage. Otherwise, Wisconsin operates under the premise that property brought into the marriage that is not gifted or inherited is marital property. While the court retains the discretion to divide property, there is certainly no guarantee that you will be allocated assets that you brought into the marriage. Talk to your attorney about this issue at the onset of your divorce so that discovery and sufficient verification can be completed to substantiate reasons why this premarital property should be allocated to you in the divorce.

11.20 Will I get to keep my engagement ring?

Not necessarily. It is something you must negotiate as part of the divorce process because an engagement ring is generally considered to be marital property. In Wisconsin an engagement ring is considered to be a gift from one spouse to the other. Although gifts are in most instances individual property, there is an exception to that rule. The gift must be from a person other than the other party. Gifts between husband and wife are marital property. The engagement ring is part of the marital estate subject to division and negotiation between the parties.

11.21 What does it mean to *commingle* property?

Commingling occurs when one spouse's individual property is mixed or combined with the parties' marital property, such that the individual property can no longer be distinguished from the marital property.

11.22 May I keep gifts and inheritances I received during the marriage?

Gifts that you and your spouse gave to each other are treated as any other marital asset. Gifts received from third parties are individual property if the gift was awarded to one party and not to the parties jointly as husband and wife. Inherited property is generally individual property unless the assets have been commingled with joint assets. Inherited property should be separately maintained under the recipient's sole name. Once inherited property is titled jointly, there is a good probability that the asset may be considered joint.

The following factors increase the probability that inherited property will remain individual property:

- The inheritance has been kept in a separate account under the recipient's individual name.
- The inheritance is clearly identifiable.
- It has not been commingled with marital assets.
- Your spouse has not contributed to its care, operation, or improvement.

It is less likely that you will be awarded your full inheritance if:

- It was commingled with marital assets.

- Its origin cannot be traced.
- You have placed your spouse's name on the title.
- Your spouse has contributed to the increase in the value of the inheritance.

If keeping your inheritance is important to you, talk to your attorney about the information needed to build your case.

11.23 If my spouse and I can't decide who gets what, who decides?

If you and your spouse cannot agree on the division of your property, the court will make the determination after considering the evidence at your divorce trial.

11.24 How are the values of property determined?

The value of some assets, like bank accounts, is usually not disputed. The value of other assets, such as homes or personal property, is more likely to be disputed.

If your case proceeds to trial, you may give your opinion of the value of property you own. You or your spouse may also have certain property appraised by an expert. In such cases it may be necessary to have the appraiser appear at trial to give testimony regarding the appraisal and the value of the asset.

If you own substantial assets for which the value is likely to be disputed, talk to your attorney early in your case about the benefits and costs of expert witnesses and appraisals.

11.25 What does *date of valuation* mean?

Because the value of assets may go up or down while a divorce is pending, it can be necessary to determine a set date for valuing the marital assets. This is referred to as the *date of valuation.* You and your spouse may agree on the date the assets should be valued, but generally assets are valued as of the date of divorce.

11.26 Who gets the interest from certificates of deposit or dividends from stock holdings during the divorce proceedings?

Whether you or your spouse receive interest from these assets is decided as a part of the overall division of your property and debts. Generally, because assets are divided as of the date of divorce, the interest is considered marital and split on a 50/50 basis except if the asset is gifted or inherited.

11.27 Do each one of our financial accounts have to be divided in half if we agree to an equal division of our assets?

No. Rather than incurring the administrative expense of dividing each asset in half, you and your spouse may decide that one of you will take certain assets equal to the value of assets taken by the other spouse. If necessary, one of you may agree to make a cash payment to the other to make an equitable division. Talk to your attorney about the specifics of property division.

11.28 Is my *health savings account* an asset that can be divided in the divorce?

Yes. A *health savings account (HSA)* is a tax-advantaged medical savings account to which contributions may be made by employees, employers, or both. Your HSA is an asset to be included in the property division and may be divided according to your judgment of divorce and transferred to another HSA. A division according to a judgment of divorce does not constitute a distribution and is thus a tax-free transfer.

11.29 I worked very hard for years to support my family while my spouse completed an advanced degree. Do I have a right to any of my spouse's future earnings?

Your contributions during the marriage are a factor to be considered in both the division of the property and debts, as well as any award of maintenance. Generally, in Wisconsin, however, the contributions will be considered in the award of maintenance rather than property division. Be sure to give your attorney a complete history of your contributions to the marriage and ask about their impact on the outcome of your case.

11.30 What factors determine whether I can get a share of my spouse's business?

Many factors determine whether you will get a share of your spouse's business and in what form you will receive it. Among the factors the court will consider are the following:

- Whether your spouse owned the business prior to your marriage
- Your role, if any, in operating the business or increasing its value
- The overall division of the property and debts

If you or your spouse own a business, it is important that you work with your attorney early in your case to develop a strategy for valuing the business and making your case about how it should be treated in the division of property and debts. Remember, there is presumed a 50/50 split of property in a divorce. That does not mean that you get one-half of every asset. For example, your spouse may be awarded the business, while you are awarded the marital residence. It is very important to have a business valuation done by a competent evaluator in order to fully determine the value of the business so that it may be appropriately divided at divorce.

11.31 My spouse and I have owned and run our own business together for many years. Can I be forced out of it?

Deciding what should happen with a family business when divorce occurs can be a challenge. Because of the risk for future conflict between you and your spouse, the value of the business is likely to be substantially decreased if you both remain owners.

In discussing your options with your lawyer, consider the following questions:

- If one spouse retains ownership of the business, are there other assets subject to division that will provide the other spouse with his or her fair share of property division?
- Which spouse has the skills and experience to continue running the business?
- Does either spouse have other vocation options?
- What is the value of the business?

- What is the market for the business if it were to be sold?
- Are the parties able to work together as co-owners of the business?

You and your spouse know your business best. With the help of your lawyers, you may be able to create a settlement that can satisfy you both. If not, the judge will make the decision for you at trial. This is a very difficult determination that impacts the financial and emotional well-being of all parties. Bring this issue to the attention of your attorney at the onset of your divorce.

11.32 I suspect my spouse is hiding assets, but I can't prove it. How can I protect myself if I discover later that I was right?

Ask your lawyer to include language in your judgment of divorce to address your concern. Insist that it include an acknowledgment by your spouse that the agreement was based on a full and complete disclosure of your spouse's financial condition. Discuss with your lawyer a provision that allows for setting aside the agreement if it is later discovered that assets were hidden.

11.33 My spouse and I own and operate an agricultural operation. What do I need to know about dividing our assets?

Agricultural operations may be complex because income and debts can be derived from many sources. Retain an attorney experienced in agricultural divorces who is familiar with all aspects of federal programs including the *Federal Farm Bill* on federal funding for farmers. These are some of the actions that might be needed in your case:

- Sending copies of your temporary order regarding property to financial institutions, major customers, or agencies that might be involved with the transfer of the farm assets
- Conducting in-depth discovery in order to gather information such as the timing of payments, contracts, agreements to withhold payment, prepurchased feed

or fertilizer, and grain delivered but not receipted, and the value and location of all assets held

- Obtaining information under the *Freedom of Information Act (FOIA)* from federal agencies such as the Department of Agriculture or the Farm Credit Administration

- Using a forensic accountant to help value the farming business, including evaluation of balance sheets and tracing cash flow

Work closely with your lawyer to be sure that you have a complete and accurate picture of your financial situation before entering settlement negotiations or proceeding to trial.

11.34 My spouse says I'm not entitled to a share of his stock options because he gets to keep them only if he stays employed with his company. What are my rights?

Stock options are sometimes a very valuable marital asset. You are entitled to a share of your spouse's stock options, but proper valuation is critical. In making a determination of the value of stock options, consider the following factors:

- Each company has its own rules about awarding and exercising stock options.

- Obtain a complete copy of the regulations relative to exercise of the stock options.

- Know and review with your attorney the different methods for calculating the value of stock options.

- The reasons the options were given may impact the valuation and division. For example, some are awarded for future performance and may be considered individual property subsequent to the final divorce but may potentially be income for support purposes as well. Read all the documents relative to the stock options in question.

- Recognize that there are cost and tax considerations when options are exercised.

Rather than being awarded a portion of the stock options, you may be awarded a share of the proceeds when the stock options are exercised. Make sure notice requirements are included in your judgment of divorce.

If either you or your spouse owns stock options, begin discussing this asset with your attorney early in your case to allow sufficient time to address the issue.

11.35 What is a *prenuptial agreement* and how might it affect the property settlement phase of the divorce?

A *prenuptial agreement,* sometimes referred to as a *premarital* or *antenuptial agreement,* is a contract made by a couple before they marry, which may include provisions for how assets and debts will be divided in the event the marriage is terminated, as well as provisions regarding maintenance.

Your divorce property settlement is likely to be impacted by the terms of your prenuptial agreement. The court must presume that any written agreement made by the parties before or during the marriage is equitable to both parties. The court may invalidate the agreement only if its terms are found to be inequitable.

11.36 Can a prenuptial agreement be contested during the divorce?

Yes. The court may consider many factors in determining whether to uphold your prenuptial agreement. Those factors include:

- Whether your agreement was entered into voluntarily
- Whether your agreement was fair and reasonable at the time it was signed
- Whether you and your spouse gave a complete disclosure of your assets and debts
- Whether you and your spouse each had your own lawyer
- Whether you and your spouse each had enough time to consider the agreement
- Whether the prenuptial agreement is fair now

If you have a prenuptial agreement, bring a copy of it to the initial consultation with your attorney. Be sure to provide your lawyer with a detailed history of the facts and circumstances surrounding reaching and signing the agreement. Generally, the court will divide into two parts the actual divorce trial from a determination of the validity of a prenuptial agreement.

The validity of the prenuptial agreement has such a substantial impact on the final divorce determination that the issue of the validity of the prenuptial agreement will be considered first.

11.37 I'm Jewish and want my spouse to cooperate with obtaining a *get,* which is a divorce document under our religion. Can I get a court order for this?

Talk to your lawyer about obtaining a *get* cooperation clause in your judgment of divorce, including a provision regarding who should pay for it. In Wisconsin, the court cannot order a party to cooperate in obtaining a get or in obtaining an annulment through the Catholic Church. If the parties agree to such cooperation, it may be included in the judgment of divorce.

11.38 Who will get the frozen embryo of my egg and my spouse's sperm that is stored at the health clinic?

The terms of your contract with the clinic may impact the rights you and your spouse may have to the embryo, so provide a copy to your attorney for review. If permissible under your contract, you and your spouse may want to consider donating the embryo to another couple or dividing the embryos equally.

According to *A Look at Embryos in Divorce,* by Charles P. Kindregan Jr., professor of law, and Maureen McBrien, adjunct professor, family lawyer, the current law as interpreted by divorce courts has recognized four options regarding the enforcement of contracts providing for disposition of embryos. These options are: (1) enforcing a dispositional agreement and, in the absence of a contract, giving preference to the party wishing to avoid parenthood; (2) refusing on public policy grounds to enforce a preexisting agreement and enforcing the right of one of the divorcing parties to refuse parenthood; (3) recognizing agreements to dispose of embryos made prior to divorce, but permitting a party to change his or her mind up to the point of use or destruction of the embryos; and (4) enforcing an agreement to dispose of the embryos for nonreproductive use. This is a difficult issue that should be addressed in the original in vitro fertilization contract.

11.39 Will debts be considered when determining the division of the property?

Yes. The court will consider any debts incurred during the course of the marriage as part of property division. For example, if you are awarded a car valued at $12,000, but you owe a $10,000 debt on the same vehicle, the court will take that debt into consideration in the overall division of the assets. Similarly, if one spouse agrees to pay substantial marital credit card debt, this obligation may also be considered in the final determination of the division of property and debts.

If your spouse incurred debts that you believe should be his or her sole responsibility, advise your attorney of the fact. Some debts may be considered nonmarital and treated separately from other debts incurred during the marriage. For example, if your spouse spent large sums of money on gambling or illegal drugs without your knowledge, you may be able to argue that those debts should be the sole responsibility of your spouse.

11.40 What happens to the property distribution if one of us dies before the divorce proceedings are completed?

If your spouse dies prior to your judgment of divorce being entered, you will be considered married and your divorce will be dismissed.

11.41 After our divorce is final, can the marital settlement agreement provision regarding property division be modified?

Generally, provisions in your marital settlement agreement dealing with the distribution of your assets and debts are not modifiable after the final divorce. Absent an uncommon instance of fraud, duress, or newly discovered evidence, the judgment of divorce relative to property division cannot be modified.

12

Benefits: Insurance, Retirement, and Pensions

During your marriage, you may have taken certain employment benefits for granted. You may not have given much thought each month to having health insurance through your spouse's employer. When you find yourself in a divorce, suddenly these benefits come to the forefront of your mind.

You may also have believed that your employment retirement benefits belonged exclusively to you and not to your spouse. You may have referred to "my 401(k)" or "my pension." After all, you are the one who worked every day to earn these benefits.

When you divorce, some benefits arising from your spouse's employment will end, some may continue for a period of time, and others may be divided between you. Retirement funds, in particular, are often one of the most valuable marital assets subject to division at divorce.

Whether benefits derive from your employment or from your spouse's employment, with your attorney's help you will develop a better understanding of which benefits the law considers to be "yours" "mine," or "ours" for divorce purposes.

12.1 Will my children continue to have health insurance coverage through my spouse's work even though we're divorcing?

If either you or your spouse currently provides health insurance for your children, it is very likely that the court will order the insurance to remain in place until your child reaches the age of majority, or for as long as employer-provided health insurance remains available at a reasonable cost to cover your minor children. Although the court cannot order it, you may also voluntarily address health insurance coverage for your adult children. *The Affordable Care Act* allows young adults to stay on a parent's health care plan until age twenty-six.

The cost of insurance for your children may be one factor taken into consideration in determining the amount of child support to be paid.

12.2 Will I continue to have health insurance through my spouse's work after the divorce?

It depends. If your spouse currently provides health insurance for you, you may be treated as a spouse for health insurance until the end of the month following your divorce. However, some insurance companies refuse to treat a person as a spouse after the entry of the judgment of divorce. It is important that you read the terms of the contract to specifically address the coverage, if any, you will receive subsequent to the date of the default divorce.

Investigate the cost of continuing on your spouse's employer-provided plan under a federal law known as *COBRA* after the expiration of your previous coverage. This coverage may be maintained for three years. However, the cost may be very high, so you will want to determine whether it's a realistic option. Also explore the possibility of coverage under the *Affordable Care Act.*

The cost of health care is an important factor when determining maintenance and planning your postdivorce budget, so start early to determine your health insurance options postdivorce.

12.3 What is a *QMSO*?

A *QMSO (qualified medical support order)* is a court order providing continued group health insurance coverage for a minor child. A QMSO may also enable a parent to obtain other information about the plan, without having to go through the parent who has the coverage. Rather than allowing only the parent with the insurance to be reimbursed for a claim, under a

QMSO, a health insurance plan is required to reimburse directly whichever parent actually paid the child's medical expense.

12.4 What is a *qualified domestic relations order*?

A *qualified domestic relations order (QDRO)* is a court order that requires a retirement or pension plan administrator to pay the receiving spouse his or her share of the former spouse's retirement that was awarded to the other party in the judgment of divorce. In the case of federal retirement plans, this order is called a *court order acceptable for processing (COAP)*. These orders help ensure that a nonemployee spouse receives his or her share of the retirement or pension plan directly from the employee spouse's plan.

Obtaining a QDRO or COAP is a critical step in the divorce process. These are complex documents, and a number of steps are required to reduce future concerns about enforcement and to fully protect your rights. These court orders must comply with numerous technical rules and be approved by the plan administrator, which is often located outside Wisconsin. More often than not an expert is hired by the parties to draft a QDRO. Each party's attorney will then review the documents and approve them for submission to the court for approval.

12.5 How many years must I be married before I'm eligible to receive a part of my spouse's retirement fund or pension?

There is a presumption of a 50/50 split of marital property in Wisconsin. So no matter how long you are married you may be entitled to a share of your spouse's retirement or pension fund. Discuss this issue with your attorney.

12.6 I contributed to my pension plan for ten years before I got married. Will my spouse get half of my entire pension?

When you marry in Wisconsin, it is presumed that your property is marital property with the exception of gifted or inherited property. That being said, it is discretionary with the court whether or not you will receive any credit for the ten years of pension accumulation before marriage. It is important to provide the court with information regarding the actual premarital value of your pension so that a reasonable assessment of premarital and postmarital value may be ascertainable.

If either you or your spouse made premarital contributions to a pension or retirement plan, be sure to let your attorney know. This information is essential to determine whether an argument should be made that a portion of the pension or retirement plan was accrued premarital and therefore should be excluded from division in the divorce action. Again, this is totally discretionary by the court. Absent a valid prenuptial agreement, you have no absolute right to your premarital portion of your pension or retirement plan earned prior to marriage.

12.7 I plan to keep my same job after my divorce. Will my former spouse get half of the money I contribute to my retirement plan after my divorce?

Your spouse is not entitled to your postdivorce retirement benefits. Talk with your attorney so that the language of the court order ensures protection of your postdivorce retirement contributions.

12.8 Am I still entitled to a share of my spouse's retirement even though I never contributed to my own retirement account during our twenty-five-year marriage?

Yes. Retirements are often the most valuable asset accumulated during a marriage. Consequently, the court will consider the retirement along with all other marital assets and debts when determining a fair division of the marital assets. In Wisconsin, you may expect to receive 50 percent of your spouse's retirement or an equal value to that 50 percent from some other marital asset.

12.9 My lawyer says I'm entitled to a share of my spouse's retirement. How can I find out how much I get?

Multiple factors will determine your rights to collect from your spouse's retirement. One factor will be the terms of the court order dividing the retirement. The court order will determine whether you are entitled to receive a specific dollar amount or a percentage of the retirement account as well as the exact amount of your benefit. In order to calculate this amount, it is ordinarily necessary to value the benefit to determine each party's applicable share.

12.10 If I am eligible to receive my spouse's retirement benefits, when am I eligible to begin collecting it? Do I have to be sixty-five to collect it?

It depends on the terms of your spouse's retirement plan. In some cases it is possible to begin receiving your share at the earliest date your spouse is eligible to retire regardless of whether or not he or she actually retires. Check the terms of your spouse's plan to learn your options.

12.11 What happens if my former spouse is old enough to receive benefits but I'm not?

Ordinarily you will be eligible to begin receiving your share of the benefits when your former spouse begins receiving benefits. It is imperative that you review the plan's terms in order to address these concerns specifically.

12.12 Am I entitled to *cost-of-living* increases on my share of my spouse's retirement?

If your spouse has a retirement plan that includes a provision for a *cost-of-living allowance (COLA),* talk to your lawyer about whether you will be able to include this provision in the court order dividing the retirement.

12.13 What circumstances might prevent me from receiving part of my spouse's retirement benefits?

Some government pension plans, if they are in lieu of a Social Security benefit, are not subject to division. If you or your spouse is employed by a government agency, talk with your lawyer about whether you are entitled to any other retirement benefits and how this may affect the property settlement in your case. If a plan is not subject to division but is part of the marital estate, you will receive your equalization from another marital asset.

12.14 How do I determine what my spouse's pension plan is worth?

There are a number of ways to determine how much your spouse's pension plan or retirement account is worth. The company itself may issue a quarterly report that states the value of the asset. You may also contact the company directly for the value of the pension or retirement account. There are also experts who are able to make the determination of the value of the pension or retirement account.

12.15 What is a *defined benefit plan*?

A *defined benefit plan* is a plan to which the employer contributes to guarantee that the employee receives a certain amount at a guaranteed retirement date.

12.16 Does the death of my spouse affect the payout of retirement benefits to me or to our children?

It depends on both the nature of your spouse's retirement plan and the terms of the court order dividing the retirement. If you want to be eligible for survivorship benefits from your spouse's pension, discuss the issue with your attorney before your final divorce. Your attorney can advise you. Survivorship benefits should always be addressed in the qualified domestic relations order.

12.17 May I still collect on my former spouse's Social Security benefits if he or she dies before I do?

You may be eligible to receive benefits if:

- You were married to your spouse for ten or more years.
- You have not remarried.
- You are at least sixty-two years old.
- The benefit you would receive based on your own earning record is less than the benefit you would receive from your former spouse.

If your ex-spouse gets remarried after you were previously married to your spouse for ten years, you will still be entitled to half of your former spouse's Social Security benefit. This will not reduce your former spouse's Social Security.

181

If you remarry and you are married to your second husband for ten years or longer and then get divorced, you will be able to receive half of your new husband's Social Security on retirement or half of your first husband's Social Security on retirement, whichever is higher. If your ex-husband dies before he turns sixty-five and if you have not remarried by age sixty, you will receive your ex-husband's full Social Security benefits.

For more information, contact your local Social Security Administration office or visit the SSA website at www.ssa.gov.

12.18 What orders might the court enter regarding life insurance?

Generally, you cannot remove your spouse from insurance policies during the divorce. You must wait until the divorce is final. The court routinely enters an order that all insurance policies and beneficiaries shall remain in full force and effect, without modification, during the pendency of the divorce.

If you are the family's primary breadwinner, you may also be ordered to maintain your life insurance policy after the divorce is final, naming your spouse and children as sole and exclusive beneficiaries in order to secure future support payments. This is a significant issue to be addressed in your marital settlement agreement. You should identify whether you, your spouse, or both of you must maintain life insurance for the benefit of the other or the minor children; who is responsible for payment of premiums; and the duration of the coverage, which is often dependent on the length of your maintenance and/or child-support obligation.

In most cases you will be required to pay your own life insurance premiums after your divorce. You should include this as an expense in your monthly budget. Determine how much coverage you will need and whether any trust documents should be created for life insurance proceeds. You may want to contact your financial planner or an estate planning attorney to help you address these issues.

12.19 Because we share children, should I consider my spouse as a beneficiary on my life insurance?

If it is your intention to give the proceeds to your former spouse, name him or her as beneficiary of your life insurance death benefit. However, if you intend the life insurance proceeds to be used for the benefit of your children, talk with your attorney about your options. You may want to name a trustee to manage the life insurance proceeds on behalf of your minor children. There may or may not be reasons to choose someone other than your former spouse to act as trustee. This is a personal decision that requires significant thought and financial planning.

12.20 Will the court order that I be named the beneficiary of my spouse's insurance policy so long as the children are minors or as long as I am receiving maintenance?

When a court order is entered for life insurance, it is ordinarily for the purposes of ensuring payment of future support and will terminate when the support obligation has ended or the children reach majority. Naming you as the beneficiary on your spouse's insurance policy for purposes of ensuring payment of future support is one option. The court may also name the children as beneficiaries or require that a trust be established to receive the life insurance proceeds on behalf of your children. This type of provision is discretionary with the court. You should make every effort to address and resolve this issue in negotiations.

12.21 My spouse is in the military. What are my rights to benefits after the divorce?

As the former spouse of a military member, the types of benefits to which you may be entitled are typically determined by the number of years you were married, the number of years your spouse was in the military while you were married, and whether or not you have remarried. Be sure you obtain accurate information about these dates.

The benefits for which you may be eligible include the following:

- A portion of your spouse's military retirement pay
- A survivor benefit in the event of your spouse's death
- Health care or participation in a temporary, transitional health care program

- Ability to keep your military identification card
- Use of certain military facilities, such as the commissary

While your divorce is pending, educate yourself about your rights to future military benefits so that you may plan for your future with clarity. Contact your base's legal office, or for more information, visit the website for the branch of the military of which your spouse was a member (www.benefits.va.gov/benefits/) or (http://militarypay.defense.gov/benefits/).

13

Division of Debts

Throughout a marriage, most couples will have some disagreements about money. You may think extra money should be spent on a family vacation, but your spouse may insist it be saved for retirement. You may think it's time to finally buy a new car, but your spouse may think driving your ten-year-old van for another two years is a better idea.

If you and your spouse had different philosophies about saving and spending during your marriage, chances are you will have differing opinions when dividing your debts in divorce. Similar to the division of marital assets, there is a presumption of a 50/50 split of marital debt in Wisconsin.

There are steps you should take to address the division of marital debt. Make sure you provide accurate and complete debt information to your lawyer. Ask your lawyer to include provisions in your divorce judgment to provide future protection if your spouse does not pay his or her share of the marital debt. Remember, however, that your marital settlement agreement is between you and your spouse and not between you, your spouse, and your creditors. That is why it is important to provide indemnification and hold-harmless provisions in your judgment of divorce in the event your spouse does not pay his or her share of the debt.

13.1 Who is responsible for paying credit card bills and making house payments during the divorce proceedings?

Work with your attorney and your spouse to reach a temporary agreement. Discuss the importance of making timely, not less than minimum, payments on your debt in order to avoid finance charges and late fees.

Generally, in Wisconsin it is important to reach a temporary stipulation relative to the payment of debt including credit card debt, home mortgages, taxes, and car payments. If you cannot reach a stipulation, you should file an *order to show cause for temporary order* or a *motion for temporary order* addressing debt payment as well as other areas of disagreement. If there is any possibility that you and your spouse will not be able to reach an agreement on debt payment, schedule the temporary hearing as soon as possible so you are not already behind in payments before debt allocation is addressed.

13.2 When should the credit card companies be advised of the pending divorce?

Don't simply advise the credit card companies that you are going through a divorce. Rather, obtain separate credit prior to the filing of the divorce action if it is at all possible. Try to get a credit card in your own name; this will allow you to move forward financially during and after the divorce.

Begin by obtaining a copy of your credit report from at least two of the three nationwide consumer reporting companies: Experian, Equifax, and TransUnion. *The Fair Credit Reporting Act* entitles you to a free copy of your credit report from each of these three companies every twelve months. To order your free annual report online, visit www.annualcreditreport.com or call toll-free (877) 322-8228 or complete an Annual Credit Report Request Form and mail it to: Annual Credit Report Request Service, P.O. Box 105283, Atlanta, Georgia 30348-5283. You can print the form from the Federal Trade Commission website at www.ftc.gov/credit. Once you receive a copy of your credit report you will have a better understanding of your credit score, total debt, and related information that will be necessary in your divorce and will guide you in your future credit efforts.

Your spouse may have incurred debt using your name. This information is important to relay to your attorney. If you and your spouse have joint credit card accounts, talk to your attorney about contacting the credit card company to close the accounts. Do the same if your spouse is an authorized user on any of your personal accounts.

If you want to maintain credit with a company, ask to have a new account opened in your individual name. Be sure to let your spouse know if you close an account he or she has been using.

13.3   How is credit card debt divided?

Credit card debt will be divided as part of the overall division of the marital assets and debts. Just as in the division of property, the court considers what is equitable, or fair, in your case and starts with the presumption that a 50/50 division of the marital debt is reasonable.

If your spouse has exclusively used a credit card for purposes that did not benefit the family, such as gambling or infidelity, discuss this issue with your attorney to determine whether it is in your best interest to challenge your spouse's spending. This type of challenge involves significant time and costly discovery, so it is necessary to balance the benefits with the cost before proceeding with this type of challenge.

13.4   Am I responsible for repayment of my spouse's student loans?

If your spouse incurred student loans prior to the marriage, it is most likely that he or she will be ordered to pay that debt. If the debt was incurred during the marriage, how the funds were used may have an impact on who is ordered to pay the student loans, but start with the presumption that the debt is marital. If your spouse borrowed money during the marriage for tuition, and your spouse increased his earning potential as a result of his or her education, the student loan may be allocated to the student spouse. If the loan was used for family living expenses while your spouse was in school, the loan will almost certainly be considered marital. If the student loan was used solely for educational expenses and you are divorced before your spouse joined the job market, some Wisconsin courts may consider the obligation to be your student spouse's responsibility. This is an expanding issue in Wisconsin, subject to the facts and circumstances of each individual case.

13.5 During the divorce proceedings, am I still responsible for debt my spouse continues to accrue?

In most cases, the court will order each of the parties to be responsible for his or her own post-separation debts. In some cases, the date for dividing debt is determined as of a specific date, for example, the date of divorce or the date of divorce filing. This is an issue that should be specifically addressed in the judgment of divorce so there is no uncertainty relative to the allocation of debt.

13.6 During the marriage my spouse applied for and received several credit cards without my knowledge. Am I responsible for them?

The court will consider the overall fairness of the property and debt division when deciding who should pay this debt. If your spouse bought items with the cards and intends to keep those items, it is likely that she or he will be ordered to pay the debt incurred for the purchases. For example, if your spouse purchased a large-screen TV on his or her credit card and he or she is allocated the large-screen TV as part of the divorce, your spouse will most likely be allocated that credit card debt. If the credit card was used for marital purposes, such as groceries, children's clothes, or a family vacation, the debt is likely to be allocated on a 50/50 basis.

13.7 During our marriage, we paid thousands of dollars of debt incurred by my spouse before we were married. Will the court take this into consideration when dividing our property and debt?

Just as premarital assets may have an impact on the overall division of property and debts, premarital debt is no different. Depending on the length of the marriage, the evidence of the debt, and the amount paid, payment of one party's premarital debt may be a factor for the court to consider. However, this issue is totally discretionary with the court.

13.8 Relative to debt allocation, what is a *hold-harmless provision,* and why should it be in the judgment of divorce?

A *hold-harmless provision* is intended to protect you in the event your spouse fails to follow a court order to pay a debt after the divorce is granted. The language typically provides that your spouse shall "indemnify and hold [you] harmless from liability" on the debt.

If you and your spouse have a joint debt and your spouse fails to pay, the creditor may nevertheless attempt to collect from you. This is because the court is without power to change the creditor's rights and can make orders affecting only you and your spouse.

In the event your spouse fails to pay a court-ordered debt and the creditor attempts collection from you, the "hold-harmless" provision in your judgment of divorce may be used in an effort to insist that payment is made by your former spouse. Generally, a hold-harmless provision will include indemnification as well as a provision for payment of any attorney's fees, interests, costs, and related expenses.

13.9 My spouse and I have agreed that I will keep our home. Why must I refinance the mortgage?

There may be a number of reasons why your spouse is asking you to refinance the mortgage. First, the mortgage company cannot be forced to take your spouse's name off the mortgage note. If you for some reason do not make the house payment, the mortgage lender will seek payment from your spouse. It also makes no sense for your spouse to give up his or her interest in the residence while remaining on the mortgage.

Second, your spouse may want to receive his or her share of the home equity. It may be possible for you to borrow additional money at the time of refinancing to pay your spouse his or her share of the equity in the home.

Third, the mortgage on your family home may prevent your spouse from buying a home in the future. Because there remains a risk that your spouse could be pursued for the debt to the mortgage company, it is unlikely that a second lender will want to take the risk of extending further credit to your spouse.

13.10 May I file for bankruptcy while my divorce is pending?

Yes, but consult with your attorney if you are considering filing for bankruptcy while your divorce is pending. There are two types of bankruptcy, Chapter 7 and Chapter 13 bankruptcy.

In a *Chapter 7 bankruptcy,* debts are generally discharged. A bankruptcy discharge releases the debtor from personal liability for certain specified types of debts. In other words, the debtor is no longer legally required to pay any debts that are discharged.

Chapter 13 bankruptcy is a repayment bankruptcy. The debtor is provided with a plan for paying back a portion of the debt over three to five years. These repayment plans range anywhere from 0 to 100 percent payment of debt depending on the debtor's net income after payment of basic expenses. Consider consulting with a bankruptcy attorney, not just your divorce attorney because you need knowledge and expertise in the bankruptcy area if you are making the decision to file for bankruptcy. A number of issues must be addressed, including the following:

- Should I file for bankruptcy individually or jointly with my spouse?
- How will filing for bankruptcy affect my ability to purchase a home in the future?
- Which debts can be discharged in bankruptcy, and which cannot?
- How will a bankruptcy affect the division of property and debts in the divorce?
- How might a delay in the divorce proceeding due to a bankruptcy impact my case?
- What form of bankruptcy is best for my situation?

Bankruptcy is an important decision. Your divorce will be stayed during the bankruptcy process unless the appropriate order is filed to lift the stay. Consult with your spouse, financial planner, bankruptcy attorney, divorce attorney, and family before making the decision to file for bankruptcy.

Division of Debts

13.11 If I am awarded child support or maintenance in my judgment of divorce, can these obligations be discharged if my former spouse files for bankruptcy after our divorce?

No, support obligations such as child support and maintenance are not dischargeable in bankruptcy, meaning these support obligations cannot be eliminated in a bankruptcy proceeding. Arrearages for past-due child support or maintenance are not discharged in bankruptcy.

13.12 What happens if my former spouse does not pay his or her obligations as listed in the judgment of divorce?

If your former spouse does not pay the debts assigned to him or her in the judgment of divorce, you may be able to pursue an action for contempt of court against your former spouse. A party is in contempt if he or she willfully disobeys or disregards a court order. Talk with your attorney to determine whether a contempt action is the right option in your case.

14

Taxes

Nobody likes a surprise letter from the Internal Revenue Service. During and after your divorce, you don't want to learn that you owe taxes that you were not expecting to pay.

A number of tax issues may arise in your divorce. Your attorney may not be able to answer all your tax questions, so do not be afraid to consult with an accountant or other tax advisor for additional accounting and tax advice.

Taxes are important considerations in both settlement negotiations and trial preparation. They should not be overlooked. Taxes may impact many of your decisions, including those regarding maintenance, division of property, and the receipt of benefits.

Be sure to be absolutely aware of the tax implications of your divorce so you don't get that letter in the mail that begins, "Dear Taxpayer:..."

14.1 Will either my spouse or I have to pay income tax when we transfer property or pay a property settlement to each other according to our judgment of divorce?

No, property division is generally a tax-free occurrence. However, it is imperative that you be knowledgeable about the future tax consequences of a subsequent withdrawal, sale, or transfer of certain assets you receive in your divorce.

It is important to ask your attorney to take tax consequences into consideration when looking at the division of your assets.

14.2   Is the amount of child support I pay tax deductible?

Child support is not deductible to the payor.

14.3   Do I have to pay income tax on any child support I receive?

Child support is not income to the payee.

14.4   Is maintenance taxable?

Maintenance paid according to the judgment of divorce or legal separation is income to the payee and deductible to the payor. You may deduct maintenance payments if you answer yes to all the following questions:

- Are your maintenance payments made according to a written agreement or judgment of divorce?
- Are you and your spouse members of different households?
- Are payments not child support?
- Do payments cease on your ex-spouse's death?

Maintenance is generally labeled as such, so the determination of whether a payment is actually maintenance is usually determinable. If you are receiving maintenance, in some situations you will be compelled to make estimated tax payments to avoid penalties when you file income tax returns. Your judgment of divorce should specifically delineate that maintenance is deductible to the payor and taxable to the recipient.

14.5   Are other forms of support I pay my spouse tax deductible?

Maintenance paid according to a court order is deductible. This may also include other forms of support provided to your former spouse (but not child support) such as mortgage payments, if the residence is in your spouse's name, health insurance payments, and more. You and your attorney must be very careful to make sure that the tax consequences of any payment is specifically addressed in the judgment of divorce.

14.6 Is there anything else I should know about maintenance and taxes?

If your maintenance payments to your spouse decrease or end during the first three calendar years after your divorce, you may be subject to the *recapture rule*. You are subject to the recapture rule if the maintenance you pay in the third year decreases by more than $15,000 from the maintenance paid in the second year, or if the maintenance paid in the second and third year decreases significantly from the first year.

If you are subject to the recapture rule, you must claim a portion of the maintenance payments you've previously deducted as income in the third year, and your spouse may deduct part of the maintenance payments received as income in the third year. This is a very complicated IRS delegation of income. In addition to your attorney, it would be wise to also discuss this issue with your accountant or financial advisor.

One more thing, if maintenance is scheduled to end within six months of a child's eighteenth birthday, the IRS may consider the maintenance to be disguised child support. This is another issue that should be addressed by your lawyer, accountant, or financial advisor.

You should also be aware that if both maintenance and child support are awarded in the judgment of divorce, and there is an underpayment, the payments will first be applied to child support and then to maintenance. For example, if your spouse is ordered to pay $1,000 in maintenance and $1,200 in child support, but only pays $1,500, the first $1,200 will be allocated to child support, with the balance of $300 qualifying as maintenance. So only $300 of the total $1,500 payment would be deductible to the payor and income to the recipient.

14.7 Is family support taxable?

If you are receiving family support, which is considered to be a mixture of both maintenance and child support, family support is fully taxable to the recipient and fully deductible to the payor, just like maintenance.

14.8 During the divorce proceedings, is our tax filing status affected?

It can be. You are considered unmarried if your judgment of divorce is final by December 31 of the tax year.

If you are considered unmarried, your filing status is either "single" or, under certain circumstances, "head of household." If your judgment of divorce is not final as of December 31, your filing status is either "married filing a joint return" or "married filing a separate return," unless you live apart from your spouse and meet the exception for "head of household." You may file as "head of household" if the following conditions are met:

- You maintain a household for your dependent child.
- The household is the taxpayer's home and the main home of the dependent child for more than half the year.
- The taxpayer provides more than 50 percent of the cost of maintaining the household.
- The taxpayer's spouse was not a member of the household during the last six months of the year.
- The taxpayer is entitled to claim the child as a dependent.

It is possible for each spouse to file as "head of household" if there are at least two children.

While your divorce is in progress, talk to both your tax advisor and your attorney about your filing status. It may be beneficial to figure your tax on both a joint return and a separate return to see which gives you the lower tax. IRS Publication 504, Divorced or Separated Individuals (www.irs.gov/pub/irs-pdf/p504.pdf), provides more details on tax issues while you are going through a divorce.

14.9 Should I file a joint income tax return with my spouse while our divorce is pending?

Consult your tax advisor and attorney to determine the risks and benefits of filing a joint return with your spouse. Compare this with the consequences of filing your tax return separately. Often the overall tax liability will be less filing a joint return, but other factors are important to consider.

When deciding whether to file a joint return with your spouse, consider any concerns you have about the accuracy and truthfulness of the information on the tax return. If you have any doubts, consult both your attorney and your tax advisor before agreeing to sign a joint tax return with your spouse. Prior to filing a return with your spouse, try to reach a written agreement about how any tax liability or refund will be shared.

14.10 My spouse will not cooperate in providing the necessary documents to prepare or file our taxes jointly. What options do I have?

Talk with your attorney about requesting your spouse to cooperate in the preparation and filing of your joint return. Although the court cannot order your spouse to sign a joint return, it can penalize your spouse for his or her unreasonable refusal to do so. The court may also order both you and your spouse to file your taxes cooperatively.

14.11 For tax purposes, is one time of year better to divorce than another?

It depends on your tax situation. If you and your spouse agree that it would be beneficial to file joint tax returns for the year in which you are divorcing, you may wish to finalize your divorce after January 1 of the following year.

Your marital status for filing income taxes is determined by your status on December 31. Consequently, if you both want to preserve your right to file a joint return, your judgment of divorce should not be entered before December 31 of that year.

14.12 What tax consequences should I consider regarding the sale of our home?

When your home is sold, whether during your divorce or after, the sale may be subject to capital gains tax. If your home was your primary residence and you lived in the home for two of the preceding five years, you may be eligible to exclude up to $250,000 of the gain on the sale of your home. If both you and your spouse meet the ownership and residence tests, you may be eligible to exclude up to $500,000 of the gain.

If you anticipate the gain on the sale of your residence to be over $250,000, talk with your attorney early in the divorce process about a plan to minimize the tax liability. For more information, see IRS Publication 523, Selling Your Home, or visit the IRS website at www.irs.gov and talk with your tax advisor.

14.13 How might capital gains tax be a problem for me years after the divorce?

Future capital gains tax on the sale of property should be discussed with your attorney during the negotiation and trial preparation stages of your case. This is especially important if the sale of the property is imminent. Failure to do so may result in an unfair outcome.

For example, suppose you agree that your spouse will be awarded the proceeds from the sale of your home valued at $200,000, after the real estate commission, and you will take the stock portfolio also valued at $200,000. Suppose that after the divorce, you decide to sell the stock. It is still valued at $200,000, but you learn that its original price was $120,000 and that you must pay capital gains tax of 15 percent on $80,000 gain. You pay tax of $12,000, leaving you with $188,000. Meanwhile, your former spouse sells the marital home but pays no capital gains tax because he qualifies for the $250,000 exemption. He is left with the full $200,000.

Tax implications of your property division should always be discussed with your attorney, with support from your tax advisor as needed.

14.14 During and after the divorce, who gets to claim the children as dependents?

This issue should be addressed in settlement negotiations or at trial if settlement is not reached. This issue should be specifically addressed in the judgment of divorce. Unless your divorce judgment says otherwise, the right to claim a child as a dependent belongs solely to the custodial parent. The custodial parent, according to the IRS, is the parent who has the child more than one-half of the year. If both parents have placement on a 50/50 basis, then it is the parent who pays support who claims the dependency exemption. If neither party pays child support, then the person with the higher adjusted gross income is allocated the exemption.

The court has discretion to determine which parent will be entitled to claim the children as exemptions for income tax purposes. Many judges order that the exemptions be shared or alternated. However, most judges will order that the payor of child support be current on his or her child-support obligation to be eligible to claim the income tax dependency exemption. Additionally, if one party has income so low or so high that he or she will not benefit from the dependency exemption, the court may award the exemption to the other parent.

Before you start preparing your income tax return, visit the IRS website (www.irs.gov/pub/irs-pdf/p504.pdf) to assess the Tax Information for Divorced and Separated Individuals booklet.

14.15 My judgment of divorce says I have to sign IRS Form 8332 (Release/Revocation of Release of Claim to Exemption for Child by Custodial Parent) so my former spouse may claim our child as an exemption. Should I sign it once for all future years?

No, child custody and child support may be modified in the future. If there is a future modification of custody or support, which parent is entitled to claim your child as an exemption could change. The best practice is to provide your former spouse with a timely copy of Form 8332 signed by you for the appropriate tax year only. Form 8332 allows your spouse to claim the tax exemption for children who spend less than six months of the year with that spouse.

However, if a parent has incorrectly signed a future Form 8332, that parent may revoke, or withdraw, Form 8332 by providing written notice of the revocation to the other parent. The parent revoking Form 8332 must make reasonable efforts to provide actual notice to the other parent. The revocation may be effective no earlier than the next taxable year.

Form 8332 must be attached to the noncustodial parent's return when it is filed. If Form 8332 is not attached to the return, then the noncustodial parent may not claim the exemption.

14.16 May my spouse and I split the child-care tax credit?

If you are the custodial parent and you incur work-related child care for children under the age of thirteen, you may be able to claim a child-care credit for a portion of the child-care costs. For more information visit www.irs.gov/Help-&-Resources/Tools-&-FAQs/FAQs-for-Individuals/Frequently-Asked-Tax-Questions-&-Answers/Child-Care-Credit,-Other-Credits. The child-care credit is available only to the custodial parent. However, if you and your spouse have shared placement and variable expenses are ordered shared, the value of the federal child-care tax credit may sometimes be subtracted from the actual costs of child care to arrive at a figure for net child-care expenses owed by the spouse paying support.

If you are a noncustodial parent and paying child support, talk to your lawyer about how to address this issue in your judgment of divorce.

14.17 Are there any other tax credits available to parents other than the child-care tax credits?

The education tax credit follows the dependent exemption and is a tax credit for post-high-school-education expenses. More information is available at www.irs.gov/Individuals/Education-Credits.

The earned-income tax credit is available to custodial parents with earned income below a certain amount. For more earned-income credit information visit: www.irs.gov/Individuals/EITC,-Earned-Income-Tax-Credit,-Questions-and-Answers.

Check with your accountant for additional tax credits that may be available to you.

14.18 Do I have to pay taxes on the portion of my spouse's 401(k) that was awarded to me in the divorce?

If you have been awarded a portion of your former spouse's 401(k) or 403(b) retirement plan, the mere division of the 401(k) or 403(b) is not taxable. However, any actual distribution of these funds to you will be subject to regular income tax. It will generally be possible for you to elect to receive all or a portion of these assets without incurring the 10 percent early-withdrawal penalty (applicable if you are under age 59 ½) if you decide to take the money rather than keeping an account in your name or rolling over the assets to an IRA or other permitted retirement account. Talk with your attorney and your tax advisor to determine your options.

14.19 Is the cost of getting a divorce, including my attorney fees, tax deductible under any circumstances?

Your legal fees are generally not tax deductible. However, there are exceptions to that rule, including the following:

- Fees paid to obtain taxable income, such as maintenance or family support
- Fees to prepare a new title for rental property
- Fees paid for tax advice and planning
- Fees paid for securing an interest in a qualified retirement plan

Attorney fees are "miscellaneous" deductions for individuals and are consequently limited to 2 percent of your adjusted gross income. More details can be found in IRS Publication 529, Miscellaneous Deductions (www.irs.gov/pub/irs-pdf/ p529.pdf).

Talk to your attorney and tax advisor about whether any portion of your attorney fees or other expenses from your divorce are deductible.

14.20 Do I have to complete a new Form W-4 for my employer because of my divorce?

Completing a new Form W-4, Employee's Withholding Certificate, will help you claim the proper withholding allowances based on your marital status and exemptions. Also, if you are receiving maintenance, you may need to make quarterly estimated tax payments. Consult with your tax advisor to ensure you are making the most preferable tax-planning decision.

14.21 What is *innocent spouse relief* and how may it help me?

Innocent spouse relief refers to a method of obtaining relief from the Internal Revenue Service for taxes owed as a result of a joint income tax return filed during your marriage. Numerous factors affect your eligibility for innocent spouse tax relief, such as:

- You would suffer a financial hardship if you were required to pay the tax.
- You did not significantly benefit from the unpaid taxes.
- You suffered abuse during your marriage.
- You thought your spouse would pay the taxes on the original return.

Talk with your attorney or your tax advisor if you are concerned about liability for taxes arising from joint tax returns filed during the marriage. You may benefit from a referral to an attorney who specializes in tax law.

See also www.irs.gov/Individuals/Tax-Information-for-Innocent-Spouses.

14.22 How do I obtain a copy of past income tax returns?

You may obtain a copy of your own income tax returns by contacting the IRS. If you file a joint return, either spouse will be entitled to the return information. See www.irs.gov/uac/How-to-Get-Your-Prior-Year-Tax-Information-from-the-IRS.

15

Going to Court

For many of us, our images of going to court are created by movie scenes and our favorite television shows. We picture the witness breaking down in tears after a grueling cross-examination. We see lawyers strutting around the courtroom, waving their arms as they plead their case to the jury.

Hollywood drama, however, is a far cry from reality. Going to court for your divorce can mean many things, ranging from sitting in a hallway while waiting for the lawyers and judge to conclude a conference, to sitting in the witness chair giving mundane answers to questions about your monthly living expenses, to contentious arguments between lawyers and more.

No matter what the nature of your court proceeding is, attendance at court often results in anxiety. Your divorce may be the first time in your life that you have been in a courtroom. Feelings of nervousness and uncertainty are normal and to be expected.

Understanding what will occur in court and being well prepared for any court appearances will help alleviate your stress. Knowing the order of events, the role of the people in the courtroom, etiquette in the courtroom, and what is expected of you will make the entire experience easier.

Your lawyer will be present whenever you make a court appearance. Remember, every court appearance moves you one step closer to completion of your divorce and your first steps into the future.

15.1 What do I need to know about appearing in court and court dates in general?

Court dates are important. As soon as you receive a notice about a court date in your case, confirm whether your attendance will be required and put the date in your calendar.

Ask your attorney about the reason for the hearing, including whether the judge will be listening to the testimony of witnesses, hearing oral arguments by the attorneys, or handling routine matters such as scheduling or pretrial conferences.

Ask whether it is necessary for you to meet with your attorney or take any other action to prepare for the hearing, such as providing additional information or documents. Find out how long the hearing is expected to last. It may be as short as a few minutes or as long as a day or more.

If you plan to attend the hearing, determine where and when to meet your attorney in advance of the hearing. Depending on the type of hearing, your lawyer may want you to meet at his or her office one or two days before the hearing in order to prepare for your court appearance.

Make sure you know the location of the courthouse, where to park, and the floor and room number of the courtroom. Planning in advance can eliminate unnecessary stress.

15.2 How often will I need to go to court?

How often your case will require a court hearing depends on the number of disputed issues in your case and the overall cooperation between you and your spouse, and between your attorney and your spouse's attorney. Depending on these issues, you may have only one, two, or numerous court hearings throughout the course of your divorce.

Some hearings, usually those on procedural matters, may be attended only by the attorneys. This type of hearing generally includes scheduling conferences. These hearings are brief. Other hearings, such as temporary hearings for custody or support, are typically attended by both parties and their attorneys.

Every divorce in Wisconsin requires at least one court appearance at the default divorce hearing where you and your spouse testify to basic identification information, the accuracy and completeness of your financial disclosure, the irretrievable breakdown of your marriage, and your understanding and agreement with the marital settlement agreement.

15.3 How much notice will I receive of upcoming court hearings?

The amount of notice you will receive for any court hearing may vary from a few days to several weeks. Ask your attorney whether and when it will be necessary for you to appear in court on your case.

15.4 I am afraid to be alone in the same room with my spouse. What should I do?

Talk to your lawyer. Prior to any court hearing, you and your spouse may be asked to wait while your attorneys meet with the judge in chambers to discuss preliminary matters. If you are in the courtroom outside the presence of your attorney and have safety concerns, advise your attorney and the judge's clerk who will request a bailiff to sit in attendance while the attorneys are in chambers.

15.5 Do I have to be present every time there is a court hearing on any motion?

Not necessarily. Some matters will be decided by the judge after listening to the arguments of the lawyers. Sometimes court hearings are held by phone. This is an issue to be discussed with your attorney. Your attorney will know whether your presence is mandatory, and/or whether you can appear by telephone.

15.6 My spouse's lawyer keeps asking for adjournments of court dates. Is there anything I can do to stop these adjournments?

Adjournments, or postponements, of court dates are not unusual in divorces. A court date might be rescheduled for many reasons, including a conflict on the calendar of one of the attorneys or the court, the lack of availability of one of the parties or an important witness, or the need for more time to prepare.

Discuss with your attorney your desire to move your case forward without further delay so that repeated requests for continuances can be resisted.

15.7 If I have to go to court, will I be put on the stand? Will there be a jury?

In Wisconsin, divorce matters are heard before a judge or family court commissioner. Juries do not hear divorces. Whether or not you will be called to testify depends on the nature of the hearing and the issues in dispute.

15.8 My lawyer said I need to be in court for our temporary hearing next week. What's going to happen?

At a temporary hearing terms are determined for the time period between the commencement of the divorce and the final divorce. These terms include a determination of who remains in the house while your divorce is pending, temporary custody and placement, temporary child support and maintenance, debt allocation, and division of personal property and automobiles. The procedure for your temporary hearing may vary depending on the county in which your case is filed, the judge or family court commissioner to which the case is assigned, and whether temporary custody and placement is disputed.

Talk to your lawyer about the procedure you should expect for the temporary hearing in your case. Generally, a temporary hearing is based on arguments by each attorney, but there are exceptions to this rule where individual testimony of the parties is given.

15.9 Are there any rules about courtroom etiquette that I should know?

Yes. The following recommendations will go a long way toward making any court appearance a little easier and less stressful:

- Dress appropriately. Avoid overly casual dress, lots of jewelry, sunglasses, revealing clothing, and extreme hairstyles.
- Don't bring beverages into the courtroom. Most courts have rules that do not allow food and drink in courtrooms. If you need a drink of water, ask your lawyer.
- Dispose of chewing gum before entering the courtroom.

- Don't talk loudly in the courtroom unless you're on the witness stand or being questioned by the judge.
- Do not even think of trying to enter the judge's chambers.
- Stand up whenever the judge is entering or leaving the courtroom.
- Be sure to turn off your electronic devices, including cell phones.
- Be aware that the judge may be observing you at all times.

Although you may feel anxious initially, you'll likely feel more relaxed about the courtroom setting once your hearing gets underway.

15.10 What is the role of the *bailiff*?

The *bailiff* provides support for the judge and lawyers in the management of the court calendar and courtroom security. He or she assists the judge in maintaining the decorum and order of the courtroom.

15.11 What is the role of the *clerk*?

The *clerk,* or *judicial assistant,* assists with administrative and legal tasks, leaving the judge more time for judicial duties. Although the specific duties of a clerk vary from judge to judge, the clerk assembles files and documents, schedules trials and hearings, swears in witnesses, and marks exhibits. The clerk manages the chambers, organizes the judge's calendar, makes travel arrangements, coordinates judicial committee activities, maintains office records and files, and performs numerous other tasks that keep the chambers running smoothly. The clerk may also deal with lawyers and members of the public on behalf of the judge. Many lawyers consider the work of clerks invaluable, and respect for the clerk and his or her responsibilities is mandatory.

15.12 Will there be a *court reporter,* and what will he or she do?

A *court reporter* is a professional trained to make an accurate record of the words spoken and documents offered into evidence during court proceedings. Some counties use tape-recording devices rather than court reporters.

A written transcript of a court proceeding may be purchased from the clerk of court's office. If your case is appealed, the transcript prepared by the court reporter will be used by the appeals court to review the facts of your case.

Some hearings are held "off the record," which means that the court reporter is not making a record of what is being said. Ordinarily these are matters for which no appeal is expected to be taken.

15.13 Do I have to appear in court if all of the issues in my case are settled?

Yes. Your case will be scheduled for a default divorce hearing and you will be compelled to testify. A *default hearing* is a brief hearing in which your attorney will ask you questions relating to the agreements you and your spouse reached. At this hearing, the judge will review and approve your marital settlement agreement and may ask you a few questions as well.

15.14 What documents must be provided to the court at the final divorce hearing?

The following documents are required at your final default divorce hearing:

- Financial disclosure statement
- Marital settlement agreement addressing all issues
- *Interim Financial Summary* to the child-support agency that provides for payment of child support, family support, or maintenance
- Vital statistics form completed in black ink only
- Report verifying the completion of parenting education requirements
- *Order for Appearance* if applicable
- Family medical history questionnaire prepared by the noncustodial parent if the court awards sole custody

15.15 What questions will my attorney ask during the default divorce hearing?

Your attorney will ask the following questions, as applicable to your case, in a default divorce hearing. These questions will not always be asked in a "yes" or "no" format so be sure you are able to answer the questions accurately and correctly.

- State your name.
- State your address.
- State your birth date.
- State the last four digits of your Social Security number.
- What is your occupation?
- What is the date of your marriage?
- Did you reside in _____ County for thirty days and in the state of Wisconsin for six months prior to the commencement of this action?
- How many children were born to you during the marriage?
- What are their dates of birth and ages if they are minors?
- Were any other children born or adopted by you during the marriage?
- Are you pregnant?
- Do you believe this marriage is irretrievably broken and that there is no hope for reconciliation?
- Have either you or your spouse commenced any other actions for divorce, annulment, or legal separation at any time? Are there currently any such actions pending in any other court?
- Were you previously married? How many times? Why did these marriages end? When did these marriages end?
- Have you filed a financial disclosure statement with the court today? (The commissioner/judge hands you the document.) Is that your signature on the final page of that document?
- Does this financial disclosure statement contain a complete disclosure of all of your income, assets, expenses, and debts?

- Have you had an opportunity to review your spouse's financial disclosure statement?
- Do you believe your spouse has made a complete disclosure of all his or her income, assets, liabilities, and expenses?
- Have you filed with the court today a marital settlement agreement?
- Does your signature appear on the final page of that agreement?
- Have you had an opportunity to review this agreement with your attorney?
- Did anybody force you or coerce you to sign this agreement?
- Do you believe you understand all of the terms of this agreement?
- Do you believe the custody and placement provisions of this agreement are in your children's best interest?
- Do you believe the property division is fair and equitable considering all of the facts and circumstances in your case?
- Did both you and your spouse make compromises to arrive at this agreement?
- Do you understand that you have a right to have a trial of all issues in this divorce action and that you are giving up that right by entering into this agreement?
- Do you understand that your waiver of maintenance (if applicable) is irrevocable and that you can never ask this court, or any other court, to award you maintenance?
- Do you understand that the terms of the final agreement as to maintenance (assuming there is no waiver), child support, and family support may be modified by the court on a showing of a substantial change in the financial circumstances of the parties?
- Are there any arrearages owing under any temporary order or agreement in existence during the pendency of this action?

- Have you received any public funds or any form of public assistance during the pendency of this action?
- Are you in good health?
- Are you currently in the active service of the Armed Forces of the United States?
- Has anyone promised you anything to get you to sign the marital settlement agreement?
- Are you asking that the court approve this agreement and incorporate it into the judgment of divorce in your case?

Your spouse will testify to the same questions.

15.16 Will I be able to talk to my attorney while we are in court?

During court proceedings it is important that your attorney give his or her attention to anything being said by the judge, witnesses, or your spouse's lawyer. For this reason, your attorney will avoid talking with you when anyone else in the courtroom is speaking.

It is critical that your attorney hear each question asked by the other lawyer and all answers given by each witness. If not, opportunities for making objections to inappropriate evidence may be lost. You can support your attorney in doing an effective job by avoiding talking to him or her while a court hearing is in progress.

Plan to have pen and paper with you when you go to court. If your court proceeding is underway and your lawyer is listening to what is being said by others in the courtroom, write him or her a note with your questions or comments.

If your court hearing is lengthy, breaks will be taken. You can generally use this time to discuss with your attorney any questions or observations you have about the proceeding.

15.17 What is a *pretrial conference*?

A *pretrial conference* is a hearing with the lawyers, parties, and the judge to review the status of the case prior to trial. Sometimes there is more than one pretrial conference if the divorce issues are complex and progress is slow.

Often the trial date is set at the pretrial conference. If a pretrial conference is held in your case, ask your attorney whether or not you are required to attend. Generally, your attendance is required.

15.18 My lawyer said that the judge has issued a pretrial order. What is a *pretrial order*?

A *pretrial order* is generally issued after the pretrial conference in anticipation of a divorce trial and to make sure that each party is actually ready for trial. Your attorney will provide you with a copy of the pretrial order. The pretrial order generally contains mandates for the completion of discovery and the exchange of information. A pretrial order will usually mandate that actions occur by a certain date. These actions usually include the following:

- Identification of the issues that have been settled between the parties (Generally, these issues are put in the form of a *stipulation* or partial marital settlement agreement signed by both parties so that there is no need to further address these issues in trial.)
- The status of mediation, settlement negotiations, or other alternative dispute resolution
- Identification of remaining disputed issues
- Identification of witnesses and a brief synopsis of each witness's anticipated testimony
- List of exhibits
- Proposed findings of fact and conclusions of law
- Deadlines for completion of discovery, naming of experts, exchange of information, and submission of financial disclosure statements

15.19 In addition to meeting with my lawyer, is there anything else I should do to prepare for trial if my divorce can't be settled by agreement?

Yes. Be sure to review your deposition and any information you provided in your discovery, such as answers to interrogatories. Review any information or affidavits previously submitted to the court, such as your financial disclosure statement or the supporting affidavit prepared for your temporary hearing. At trial, it is possible that you will be asked some of the same questions that you were asked in prior discovery. If you think you might give different answers at trial, discuss how to handle that situation with your lawyer. It is important that your attorney know in advance of trial whether any information you provided during the discovery process has changed.

15.20 I'm meeting with my lawyer to prepare for trial. How do I make the most of these meetings?

Meeting with your lawyer to prepare for your trial is important to achieving a good outcome. Be sure you come to the meeting prepared to discuss the following:

- The issues in your case
- Your desired outcome on each of the issues
- The questions you might be asked at trial by both lawyers
- The exhibits that will be offered into evidence during the trial
- The witnesses for your trial and their projected testimony
- The status of negotiations

Your meeting with your lawyer will help you better understand what to expect at trial and make the trial experience easier and less intimidating.

15.21 My lawyer says that the law firm is busy with trial preparations for my divorce. What exactly is my lawyer doing to prepare for my trial?

Countless tasks are necessary to prepare your case for trial. The following are just some of them:

- Developing arguments to be made on each of the contested issues
- Researching and reviewing the relevant law in your case
- Reviewing the facts of your case to determine which witnesses should be subpoenaed to testify
- Reviewing, selecting, and preparing exhibits
- Preparing questions for all witnesses

- Preparing an opening statement
- Reviewing rules of evidence to prepare for any objections to be made or opposed at trial
- Determining the order of witnesses and all exhibits
- Preparing your file for trial, including completion of a trial notebook with essential information

Your lawyer is committed to a good outcome in your divorce. He or she will be engaged in many important actions to fully prepare your case for trial.

15.22 How do I determine which witnesses should appear on my behalf at trial?

In preparation for trial, your lawyer will discuss with you whether other witnesses, in addition to you and your spouse, will be necessary to testify on your behalf. Witnesses may include family members, friends, child-care providers, clergy members, accountants, financial planners, psychologists, and others. When determining potential witnesses, consider your relationship with the witness, whether that witness has had an opportunity to observe relevant facts, and whether the witness has knowledge different from that of other witnesses.

You may retain expert witnesses to testify on your behalf. An expert witness will provide opinion testimony based on specialized knowledge, training, or experience. For example, a psychologist, real estate appraiser, or accountant may provide expert testimony on your behalf.

15.23 My divorce is scheduled for trial. Does this mean there is no hope for a settlement?

Many cases are settled after a trial date is set. The setting of a trial date may cause you and your spouse to think about the risks and costs of going to trial. This may help you and your spouse focus on what is most important to you and lead you toward a negotiated settlement. Because the costs of preparing for and proceeding to trial are substantial, it is best to engage in settlement negotiations well in advance of your trial date. However, it is not uncommon for cases to settle a few days before trial, or even at the courthouse before your trial begins.

15.24   Can I prevent my spouse from being in the courtroom?

No. Because your spouse is a party to the action, he or she has a right to be present. Wisconsin courtrooms are generally open to the public.

15.25   May I take a friend or family member with me to court?

Yes. Let your attorney know in advance if you intend to take anyone to court with you.

15.26   May my friends and family be present in the courtroom during my trial?

It depends on whether they will be witnesses in your case. In most cases where witnesses other than the husband and wife are testifying, the attorneys request that the court sequester the witnesses. The judge would then order all witnesses, except you and your spouse, to leave the courtroom until after they have testified.

Once a witness has completed his or her testimony, he or she will ordinarily be allowed to remain in the courtroom for the remainder of the trial.

15.27   I want to do a great job testifying as a witness in my divorce trial. What are some tips?

Keep the following points in mind when you are testifying:

- Tell the truth. Although this may not be always be comfortable, it is critical if you want your testimony to be believed by the judge.

- Listen carefully to the complete question before responding to the question. Wait to consider your answer until the full question is asked.

- Slow down. Think before you answer. Make sure you understand the question. Just answer the question. Do not volunteer additional information.

- If you don't understand a question or don't know the answer, be sure to answer that you do not know or understand the question. Do not guess.

- If the question calls for a "yes" or "no" answer, simply say so. Then wait for the attorney to ask you the next question. If there is more you want to explain, remember that you have already told your attorney all the important facts, and he or she will make sure you are allowed to give any testimony significant in your case. Your attorney will ask you follow-up questions if necessary.

- Don't argue with the judge or the lawyers.
- Take your time. You may be asked some questions that call for a thoughtful response. If you need a moment to reflect on an answer before you give it, allow yourself that time.
- Stop speaking if an objection is made by one of the lawyers. Wait until the judge has responded to the objection before you answer.

15.28 Should I be worried about cross-examination by my spouse's lawyer?

If your case goes to trial, prepare to be asked some questions by your spouse's lawyer. Many of these questions will call for a simple "yes" or "no."

If you are worried about particular questions, discuss your concerns with your attorney in advance. He or she can support you in giving a truthful response. Focus on advance preparation. Try not to take the questions personally. Remember that the lawyer is fulfilling a duty to advocate for your spouse's interests.

15.29 What happens on the day of trial?

Although no two trials are alike, the following steps will occur in most divorce trials:

- Attorneys meet with the judge in chambers to discuss procedural issues, such as how many witnesses will be called and in what order, how long the case is expected to take, and what exhibits will be filed.
- Generally, attorneys give opening statements.
- Petitioner's attorney calls petitioner's witnesses to testify.
- Respondent's attorney may cross-examine each of them.

- Respondent's attorney calls respondent's witness to testify.
- Petitioner's attorney may cross-examine each of them.
- Petitioner's lawyer calls any rebuttal witnesses, that is, witnesses whose testimony potentially contradicts the testimony of the respondent's witnesses. Respondent's attorney has the same opportunity.
- Closing arguments will be made first by the petitioner's attorney and then by the respondent's attorney.

15.30 Will the judge decide my case the day I go to court?

Often there is so much information elicited during trial that it is not possible for the judge to give an immediate ruling. The judge may want to review documents, review the law, perform calculations, review his or her notes, and give thoughtful consideration to the issues to be decided. The court may order posttrial briefs on the outstanding issues. For this reason, it may be days, weeks, or in some cases, even longer before a ruling is made.

When a judge does not make a ruling immediately at the conclusion of a trial, it is said that the case has been taken "under advisement."

16

The Appeal Process

You may find that despite your best efforts to settle your case, your divorce proceeded to trial and you now believe the judge made mistakes during the trial. You may be gravely disappointed and angered by the judge's ruling. The judge may have decided your case differently than you and your attorney predicted.

Whatever the reasons for the court's rulings, you may feel that the judge's decision was not warranted either factually or legally. If this is the case, talk to your lawyer immediately about your appeal rights. Together you may decide whether an appeal is in your best interest, or whether it is better to accept the court's ruling and to invest your money and energy in moving forward without an appeal.

It is imperative to understand that an appeal does not start the process over. It is not a second try in the hope of a different outcome. You must prove that the court abused its discretion or made a ruling that was erroneous as a matter of law. Remember that the law generally favors the finality of the judgment of divorce and an appeal is often an uphill battle.

16.1 How much time after my divorce do I have to file an appeal?

An appeal to the Wisconsin Court of Appeals generally must be initiated within forty-five days of entry of a final judgment order. This is an issue that must be addressed immediately posttrial with your attorney to make sure that all time requirements are met.

Because your attorney may also recommend filing certain motions following your trial, discuss your appeal rights with your lawyer as soon as you receive the judge's ruling. A timely discussion with your attorney about your right to appeal is essential so important deadlines are not missed.

16.2   May I appeal a temporary order?

No. Under Wisconsin law, only final orders may be appealed to a higher court. You may, however, request a *de novo review* from the circuit court if the original temporary hearing order was rendered by a family court commissioner. Your attorney may also file a motion for reconsideration under some circumstances.

16.3   What parts of the judgment of divorce may be appealed?

Decisions that may be appealed include custody, placement, child support, maintenance, property division, Section 71 payments (guaranteed payments in lieu of maintenance), role of the guardian *ad litem,* debt allocation, child removal, earning capacity, jurisdiction, family support, attorney's fees, and more.

16.4   Will my attorney recommend the appeal of specific aspects of the judgment of divorce, or will I have to request an overall appeal?

Whether to file an appeal is generally a joint decision between you and your attorney, but the ultimate determination is yours as the client. Your attorney will assist you in determining whether to file an appeal of a specific finding or conclusion of the trial court's decision or whether to file an appeal of the entire judgment. In almost all cases, only specific issues are appealed, such as allocation of maintenance for example. Your lawyer may advise you which issues have the greatest likelihood of success on appeal, based on the individual facts of your case and Wisconsin law.

You also may want to obtain a second appeal opinion from a different lawyer who was not involved in the original trial of your case.

16.5 What facts should I consider before I make the decision to file an appeal of my judgment of divorce?

An appeal should be filed only after careful consideration. You should be aware that generally appeals are not successful. That fact alone should not determine whether to file an appeal, but you want to make a decision based on a legitimate belief that you will have some likelihood of success. So discuss the potential appeal merits carefully with your attorney. Some of the factors you and your attorney should weigh in determining whether or not to file an appeal include the following:

- Whether the judge had the authority to render the decisions set forth in your judgment of divorce
- The likelihood of the success of your appeal
- The risk that your appeal may result in a counter-appeal by your former spouse
- The cost of the appeal
- The length of time an appeal will take
- The impact of any delay of the judgment pending appeal, although this is an unlikely scenario. (In almost all circumstances, the judgment of divorce remains in full force and effect until modified by a higher court.)

16.6 Are there any disadvantages to filing an appeal?

There may be disadvantages in filing an appeal, including but not limited to the following:

- Uncertainty of the outcome
- Substantial additional attorney's fees and costs
- The risk of a negative outcome, potentially worse than the current terms of the judgment of divorce
- Delay
- Prolonged conflict between you and your former spouse
- Risk of a second trial occurring after the appeal
- Difficulty in obtaining closure and moving forward with your life

16.7   Is an attorney necessary to appeal?

The appeal process is very detailed and specific, with set deadlines and specific court rules. Given the complex nature of the appellate process, you should retain an attorney to file and argue an appeal.

16.8   How long does the appeal process usually take?

An appeal may take anywhere from several months to well over a year. An appeal to the Wisconsin Court of Appeals may also lead to an appeal to the Wisconsin Supreme Court or a return to further proceedings by the trial court.

16.9   What are the steps in the appeal process?

There are many steps that your lawyer will take on your behalf in the appeal process, including:

- Identifying the issues to be appealed
- Filing a notice with the court of your intent to appeal
- Obtaining the necessary court documents and trial exhibits to send to the appellate court
- Obtaining a transcript of trial, a written copy of testimony by witnesses and statements by the judge and the lawyers made in the presence of the court reporter
- Conducting legal research to support your arguments on appeal
- Preparing and filing a document known as a "brief," which sets forth the facts of the case and relevant law, complete with citations to court transcript, court documents, and prior cases. (In some cases two briefs will be required.)
- Making an oral argument before the judges of the appellate court

16.10   Is filing and pursuing an appeal expensive?

Yes. In addition to filing fees and lawyer fees, there is likely to be a substantial cost for the preparation of the transcript of the trial testimony. The legal time generated by an appeal is always significant.

16.11   If I do not file an appeal, can I ever go back to court to change my judgment of divorce?

Certain aspects of a judgment of divorce are not modifiable, such as property division and waiver of maintenance. Other parts of your judgment of divorce, such as child support, maintenance, placement, custody, and more, may be modified if there has been a "substantial change in circumstances."

A modification of custody or placement for minor children will also generally require a determination of the best interest of the minor children, as well as a "substantial change in circumstances."

If you believe that you have a basis for modification of your judgment of divorce, contact your attorney so that he or she can review the facts and circumstances of your case.

17

After the Divorce Is Final— Steps to Take

Your divorce is completed. However, there remain a number of tasks that must be completed in order to successfully implement your divorce and move forward to a new and better future.

17.1   What steps should I take to complete my divorce?

The following is a checklist of items that should be completed after the divorce is final. This checklist is by no means a complete list, but provides you with a guideline of information. Review these items and implement those that are relevant to your divorce:

- Record any quitclaim deeds. Make sure that the deeds are signed by both parties and notarized or properly authenticated. Check the legal description to make sure it is accurate.

- If there is a division of a pension, 401(k), or other retirement plan, have drafted a qualified domestic relations order signed by the judge in your case, certified and properly approved by the plan administrator. A QDRO is generally drafted by an attorney or a specialist in that area.

- If you are receiving a transfer of funds from an account that does not require a QDRO, open a suitable account to which the funds can be transferred and take all necessary steps to allow the transfer. Talk to your financial advisor.

- Change title to cars, boats, RVs, or other vehicles by properly executing title documents. Be sure to address not only title, but all registration and license plates.
- Open new checking and savings accounts in your individual name, if you haven't already done so. Cancel any joint accounts, and make sure there are not any outstanding checks or debit cards remaining.
- Cancel any joint credit cards, cell phone accounts, and debit cards, and open new accounts in your individual name. Use these new credit cards at least occasionally, in order to establish credit in your individual name.
- If you have any automatic withdrawals or charges to joint accounts, make sure you contact the appropriate account holder prior to closing the account. Start automatic withdrawals in your new account, if applicable.
- Transfer utilities into your name, as applicable. If you are vacating the residence, make sure your name is removed from bills attached to the residence such as utilities and cable.
- Consider changing the beneficiaries on your life insurance, retirement, and other financial accounts.
- If you are undergoing a name change, get certified copies of the judgment of divorce to change your name on your driver's license, title, passport, Social Security card, and other documents.
- Put your divorce paperwork in a safe place. Generally, if any future modifications are made to your judgment of divorce, those changes must be based on a substantial change of circumstances. You will need your divorce documents to identify issues and to evaluate whether a change of circumstances has occurred.
- If you are receiving child support, check with the child-support agency to verify that it has the necessary documents, such as an interim disbursement order, to start the child-support process. If you are making or receiving payments through the Wisconsin Support Collections Trust Fund (WI SCTF), you must notify them of any address or employment changes in the

future. WI SCTF's address is P.O. Box 74200, Milwaukee, WI 53274-0200.

- Make sure all your personal property has been distributed according to the judgment of divorce. Make necessary arrangements to transfer the property as soon as possible.

- Review all health, home, auto, life, and umbrella insurance policies and make sure the terms and identification is correct on each policy. If life and health insurance is required as a part of your judgment of divorce, periodically request verification of the existence of any insurance policies required to be carried under the terms of any judgment of divorce. In the event of the death of your ex-spouse, immediately notify the life insurance carrier of the existence of any insurance policy in which you or your children have an interest.

- If you are paying or receiving maintenance, identify if your tax withholding should be changed. Go to www. irs.gov/Individuals/IRS-Withholding-Calculator and run the calculator to determine your appropriate withholding. Remember that maintenance payments are taxable to the recipient and deductible to the payor. The recipient will need to budget money for the payment of federal and state income taxes. Quarterly estimated tax payments may be required.

- You will want to prepare a new will, power of attorney for health care, general durable power of attorney, living will, trust, and/or guardianship documents. What was legal and binding during your marriage may not be legal and binding after divorce.

- Update your mailing address, if applicable, with the post office, credit card companies, banks, DMV, and insurance companies.

- Close joint safe deposit or post office boxes and open new ones, if applicable.

- Obtain a certified copy of your judgment of divorce for future reference.

- Obtain a copy of your credit report. Check it for accuracy and updating.
- Verify your health insurance coverage if you are obtaining COBRA benefits from your spouse's employer.
- Keep records of payments of maintenance, child support, and variable expenses. If you are the payor, do not pay in cash. Use a check or money order.
- You may need your spouse to sign IRS Form 8332 relative to income tax exemptions. Make sure you have the form available for signature.
- Update your children's schools and medical and dental professionals with contact information of both you and your former spouse, emergency contacts, and school pick-up/drop-off instructions.
- Keep a copy of your original marriage license if you were married for over ten years. If you were married over ten years and remain unmarried, you will be entitled to a portion of your former spouse's Social Security. You will be required to submit a copy of your marriage license, as well as a copy of the judgment of divorce, to the Social Security Administration.
- Notify your employer of your change in marital status. It may be necessary to change beneficiaries on employment documents. Review your tax claim information with your employer. Provide updated emergency contact information.
- Notify the Internal Revenue Service and Wisconsin Department of Revenue of any address change during the year of the divorce or the year following the date of divorce.
- If your judgment of divorce assigns any outstanding tax liability to your former spouse, include a copy of the relevant section of your judgment when filing your income tax returns.

This checklist is in no way comprehensive and is not applicable to all divorces. Contact your attorney to verify what steps you should take now that your divorce is final.

17.2 Now that my divorce is final, why do I need to maintain contact with my former spouse?

If you and your spouse do not share children, it is probably not necessary to maintain contact with your former spouse once you have completed the necessary steps to finalize your divorce, as identified in the checklist from the previous question. If you share children, it is usually important to parent cooperatively, which requires open lines of communication. Remember you are no longer spouses, but you remain the mother or father of your children.

17.3 What if my spouse fails to comply with the terms of the judgment of divorce?

If your ex-spouse fails to follow the terms of the judgment of divorce you may have post-judgment recourse in the form of a contempt motion or motion for modification of judgment. Contact your attorney to determine whether you have a legal basis for your position.

17.4 How soon may I get remarried after my divorce is final?

You may remarry six months after the effective date of your divorce. Wisconsin law provides that no marriage is legal until six months after that date.

17.5 What if my ex-spouse gets remarried? Do I still have to pay maintenance?

In order to terminate maintenance payments, you must apply to the court for a termination of maintenance with notice to your ex-spouse and with proof of your ex-spouse's remarriage. Subject to that verification, the court will vacate the maintenance order. Many times you and your ex-spouse will be able to stipulate to termination of maintenance on remarriage so check that option first.

In the event you are the party remarrying, you may want to consider entering into a prenuptial agreement before you remarry.

17.6 What if I have additional questions about the divorce process?

Feel free to contact Vanden Heuvel & Dineen at www.vhdlaw.com for additional information, or call toll-free (800) 805-1976.

In Closing

Divorce is difficult. Just making the decision to file for a divorce shows courage and the determination to move forward in your life. Sometimes the decision to file for divorce is not yours, it is your spouse's, but by taking an active role in responding to the divorce you are protecting your rights and accepting responsibility for the future.

Under both circumstances, you are looking more closely at your living situation, the needs of your children, your financial security, and your personal growth and healing. You are hopefully assessing your individual situation and acknowledging the truth about the changes necessary in your life. You are taking action to propel yourself into new possibilities, but also learning from your past actions.

From here, it is time to take inventory of the lessons learned, goals met, and actions yet to take. Celebrate each of those steps and understand that occasionally you will take a backward step or two. You will go through a transition period. Gone are the familiar habits of your marriage, but you will build on a new foundation. With every passing day you will move through and away from the divorce process, and you will have a better understanding of yourself. Best wishes for a happy and healthy future.

Attorney Linda S. Vanden Heuvel

Appendix

Sample Petition for Divorce

PRINT in INK

Enter the name of the county in which you are filing this case.	**STATE OF WISCONSIN, CIRCUIT COURT,** _____ **COUNTY**

For Official Use

Enter your name (you are the **petitioner**).	In RE: The marriage of **Petitioner:**
Enter your address.	First name Middle name Last name Address
On the far right, check divorce or legal separation.	Address City State Zip
Enter your spouse's name (your spouse is the **respondent**).	and **Respondent:** First name Middle name Last name
Enter your spouse's address.	Address
Note: Leave case number blank; the clerk will add this.	Address City State Zip

Petition
With Minor Children

☐ **Divorce-40101**
☐ **Legal Separation-40201**

Case No. _____

I am the petitioner in this action.

In A.1, enter your date of birth [month, day, year].	A. **I am providing the following information about myself:** 1. Date of birth _____.
	2. Immediately before filing this petition, I will have lived in this county for 30 days or more. ☐ Yes ☐ No
For 2, 3 and 4, check yes or no.	3. Immediately before filing this petition, I will have lived in the state of Wisconsin for 6 months or more. ☐ Yes ☐ No
	4. I am currently on active duty as a member of the Armed Forces of the United States of America or its allies. ☐ Yes ☐ No
In B.1, enter your spouse's date of birth [month, day, year].	B. **I am providing the following information about the respondent, my spouse:** 1. Date of birth _____.
	2. Immediately before filing this petition, the respondent will have lived in this county for 30 days or more. ☐ Yes ☐ No
For 2, 3 and 4, check yes or no.	3. Immediately before filing this petition, the respondent will have lived in the state of Wisconsin for 6 months or more. ☐ Yes ☐ No
	4. The respondent is currently on active duty as a member of the Armed Forces of the United States of America or its allies. ☐ Yes ☐ No

231

Divorce in Wisconsin

Sample Petition for Divorce   (Continued)

In C.1 and 2, enter the date [month, day, year], city, and state in which you were married.	**C. I am providing the following marriage information:** 1. My spouse and I were married on (Date) _____. 2. We were married in (City) _____ (State) _____.

3. I am filing for
   a. ☐ **Divorce.** This marriage is irretrievably broken.
   b. ☐ **Legal Separation.** This marriage is broken and the reason I am requesting a legal separation and not a divorce is _____

In 4, check a or b. If b, enter the county and state in which it was filed, the case number assigned to it, and check yes or no to indicate if the case has been dismissed.	**4. Previous Actions** This is the first time that either my spouse or I have filed for divorce or legal separation **from each other** in Wisconsin or in any other state: a. ☐ **Yes** b. ☐ **No:** County _____ State _____ Case No. _____ Has this case been dismissed? ☐ **Yes** ☐ **No**

5. This is my first marriage. ☐ **Yes** ☐ **No**

In 5, check yes or no. If no, respond to 5a-5d with information about your most recent previous marriage.	a. I was previously married to _____ b. The marriage was terminated by ☐ **divorce.** ☐ **death.** c. Date of the divorce or death _____ d. The divorce was granted in: Name of court _____ City _____ State _____

If you had an additional previous marriage, respond to 5e-5h.	e. I was also previously married to _____ f. The marriage was terminated by ☐ **divorce.** ☐ **death.** g. Date of the divorce or death _____ h. The divorce was granted in: Name of court _____ City _____ State _____ *If you had more than 2 previous marriages, repeat 5e-5h on an additional sheet.*

6. This is my spouse's first marriage. ☐ **Yes** ☐ **No**

In 6, check yes or no. If no, respond to 6a-6d with information about your spouse's most recent previous marriage, if known.	a. My spouse was previously married to _____ b. The marriage was terminated by ☐ **divorce.** ☐ **death.** c. Date of the divorce or death _____ d. The divorce was granted in: Name of court _____ City _____ State _____

If your spouse had an additional previous marriage, respond to 6e-6h.	e. My spouse was also previously married to _____ f. The marriage was terminated by: ☐ **divorce.** ☐ **death.** g. Date of the divorce or death _____ h. The divorce was granted in Name of court _____ City _____ State _____

If your spouse had more than 2 previous marriages, repeat 6e-6h on an additional sheet.

232

Appendix

Sample Petition for Divorce (Continued)

In D.1, enter the name and date of birth [month, day, year] for each **minor** child. If there are no other kids, check None.	**D. I am providing the following information regarding children:** 1. The **minor** children (age 17 or younger) born to or adopted together by me and my spouse before or during our marriage are ☐ **None.**

Name of Minor Child	Date of Birth

In 2, enter the name and date of birth [month, day, year] for each **adult** child. If you and your spouse do not have adult children together, check None.	2. The **adult** children (age 18 or older) born to or adopted together by me and my spouse before or during our marriage are ☐ **None.**

Name of Adult Child	Date of Birth

In 3, enter the name and date of birth [month, day, year] for each **other** child. If you and your spouse do not have other children, check None.	3. **Other** children born to the wife during this marriage, but not fathered by the husband are ☐ **None.**

Name of Child	Date of Birth

In 4, check a or b.	4. To the best of my knowledge, the wife in this marriage a. ☐ **is** currently pregnant. (An attorney [guardian ad litem] for the unborn child will be required if the husband is not the father.) b. ☐ **is not** currently pregnant.

In 5, check a, b, c or d. If d, enter the current address of the minor children. If the children currently reside at separate addresses, provide those addresses on an additional sheet.	5. The current address of the minor children is a. ☐ with mother at above address. b. ☐ with father at the above address. c. ☐ with both mother and father at the above addresses. d. ☐ at the address below: Address _____ Address _____ City _____ State _____ Zip _____

In 6, enter any previous addresses for the minor children living **with the parents** during the past 5 years. If none check "none." If the children have lived in more than 2 places over the past 5 years, provide those addresses on an additional sheet.	6. Previous addresses for the minor children are ☐ None (the children have lived at the current address for the last five years). Address _____ Address _____ City _____ State _____ Zip _____ Address _____ Address _____ City _____ State _____ Zip _____
In 7, check yes or no.	7. Currently, or during the last 5 years, one or more of the minor children lived with a person

233

Divorce in Wisconsin

Sample Petition for Divorce (Continued)

other than a parent.
☐ Yes ☐ No

| If yes, enter the name of that minor child and the name and address of the person with whom that child lived. | Child _____
Person _____
Address _____
Address _____
City, State, Zip _____ |

| Attach an additional sheet, if necessary. | Child _____
Person _____
Address _____
Address _____
City, State, Zip _____ |

Child _____
Person _____
Address _____
Address _____
City, State, Zip _____

In 8, check a or b.

8. I personally have been (or I am aware of others who have been) a party, witness or participated in another way in other past court proceedings concerning the custody of or physical placement or visitation with the minor children listed in **D1** or **D3**, in Wisconsin or in any other state.

If a, enter the name of the court in which it was ordered, the case number assigned to it, and date it was ordered

    a. ☐ **Yes** and the custody, physical placement, or visitation order was granted in:
        Name of court _____
        Case Number _____ Date _____
    b. ☐ **No.**

In 9, check a or b.

9. I am aware of a proceeding that could affect the current proceeding, including proceedings for enforcement and proceedings related to domestic violence, protective orders, termination of parental rights, or adoption concerning the children listed in **D1** or **D3**, in Wisconsin or any other state.

If a, enter the name of the court, the case number assigned to it, and the nature of the proceeding.

    a. ☐ **Yes**, and the proceeding that could affect the current proceeding is in:
        Name of court _____
        Case Number _____
        Nature of Proceeding _____
    b. ☐ **No.**

In 10, check a or b. If a, attach a copy of written agreement.

10. My spouse and I have made written agreements or received orders from the court about some or all of the matters in this action such as maintenance (spousal support), child support, legal custody or physical placement of the minor children, or property division.
    a. ☐ **Yes, and *I have attached a copy of the written agreement to this Petition.***
    b. ☐ **No**

If you are requesting maintenance, child support and/or family support at this time, check yes. If not, check no.

I ASK THAT THE COURT:

1. Grant a judgment as requested.

2. Enter an order granting maintenance, child support and/or family support. ☐ **Yes** ☐ **No**

3. Enter other orders as it deems just and equitable.

Appendix

Sample Petition for Divorce   (Continued)

ACTS PROHIBITED BY STATUTE

In accordance with §767.117, Wis. Stats., neither the petitioner nor the respondent to this divorce or legal separation action can participate in any of the following activities while this action is pending:

1. Harassing, intimidating, physically abusing or imposing any restraint on the personal liberty of the other party or a minor child of either of the parties.

2. Encumbering, concealing, damaging, destroying, transferring, or in any other way disposing of property owned by either or both of the parties, without the consent of the other party or an order of the court or the Circuit Court Commissioner, except in the usual course of business, in order to secure necessities or in order to pay reasonable costs and expenses of the action, including attorney fees.

3. Establishing a residence with a minor child of the parties outside the state of Wisconsin or more than 150 miles from the residence of the other party within the state without the consent of the other party or an order of the court or Circuit Court Commissioner.

4. Removing a minor child of the parties from the state of Wisconsin for more than 90 consecutive days without the consent of the other party or an order of the court or Circuit Court Commissioner.

5. Concealing a minor child of the parties from the other party without the consent of the other party or an order of the court or Circuit Court Commissioner.

A VIOLATION OF THE ABOVE PROHIBITIONS MAY RESULT IN PUNISHMENT FOR CONTEMPT, WHICH MAY INCLUDE MONETARY PENALTIES, IMPRISONMENT, AND OTHER SANCTIONS AS PROVIDED FOR IN SEC. 785.04 WIS. STATS.

A violation of paragraphs 3, 4, or 5 above is not a contempt of court if the court finds that the action was taken to protect a party or a minor child of the parties from physical abuse by the other party and that there was no reasonable opportunity under the circumstances for the party to obtain an order authorizing the action.

These PROHIBITIONS apply until the action is dismissed, a final judgment in the action is entered, or the court orders otherwise.

STOP!
Take this document to a Notary Public BEFORE you sign it.

After you have been sworn by a Notary Public, sign and print your name and date the document in front of the Notary Public.	▶ _____ Signature _____ Print or Type Name _____ Date
Have the Notary Public sign, date, and seal the document.	State of _____ County of _____ Subscribed and sworn to before me on _____ *(Seal)* _____ Notary Public/Court Official _____ Name Printed or Typed My commission/term expires: _____

Divorce in Wisconsin

Sample Petition for Divorce   (Continued)

> **Wisconsin Department of Children and Families**
> **Child Support Percentage of Income Standards**

Authority and Purpose
§49.22(9), Wis. Stats. requires the Department to adopt and publish a standard, based upon a percentage of the gross income and assets of either or both parents, to be used by courts in determining child support obligations. Chapter DCF 150 of the Wisconsin Administrative Code establishes Wisconsin's percentage of income standard for child support. It is based upon the principle that the child's standard of living should, to the degree possible, be the same as if the child's parents were living together.

Chapter DCF 150 defines the income upon which the support obligation is based, and sets the percentages of income for computing the support obligation based upon a number of children. It also explains optional procedures for adjusting the obligation when the parents share placement, when the parent has an obligation to support another family, or when the payer has particularly high or low income.

Applicability
The percentage standard applies to any temporary and final order for child support, including child support stipulations agreed to by both parents and modifications of existing child support orders. When used to calculate family support, the amount determined under the standard should be increased by the amount necessary to provide a net family support payment, after state and federal income taxes are paid, of at least the amount of a child support payment under the standard.

Definition of Income and Assets
Chapter DCF 150 defines gross income as income from any source, whether or not it is reported or taxed under federal law. The income can be in the form of money, property, or services. Public assistance or child support received from previous marriages or business expenses, which the court determines are reasonably necessary for the production of income or operation of a business are subtracted, and wages paid to dependent household member are added to determine "gross income available for child support."

The court may also determine that income may be "imputed" (assumed at a given level) based on earning capacity and/or assets, and that imputed income is added to the gross income for the calculation of the support obligation.

THE PERCENTAGE STANDARD
The percentages are:

17%	for one child
25%	for two children
29%	for three children
31%	for four children
34%	for five or more children

Wisconsin Statutes require temporary and final support orders to be expressed as fixed sum in most situations.

For further details, refer to Chapter DCF 150 of the Wisconsin Administrative Code and Wisconsin Statute 767 Actions Affecting the Family. (Choose "Wisconsin Law" on http://www.legis.state.wi.us)

Appendix

Sample Petition for Divorce   (Continued)

> **Statutory Factors Courts May Consider In Determining Child Support Awards for Paternity, Divorce, or Legal Separation**

§767.511, Child Support.

(1 m) Upon request by a party, the court may modify the amount of child support payments determined under §767.511 (1j) if, after considering the following factors, the court finds by the greater weight of the credible evidence that use of the percentage standard is unfair to the child or to any of the parties:

(a) The financial resources of the child.

(b) The financial resources of both parents.

(bj) Maintenance received by either party.

(bp) The needs of each party in order to support himself or herself at a level equal to or greater than that established under 42 USC 9902 (2).

(bz) The needs of any person, other than the child, whom either party is legally obligated to support.

(c) If the parties were married, the standard of living the child would have enjoyed had the marriage not ended in annulment, divorce or legal separation.

(d) The desirability that the custodian remain in the home as a full-time parent.

(e) The cost of day care if the custodian works outside the home, or the value of custodial services performed by the custodian if the custodian remains in the home.

(ej) The award of substantial periods of physical placement to both parents.

(em) Extraordinary travel expenses incurred in exercising the right to periods of physical placement under §767.41.

(f) The physical, mental and emotional health needs of the child, including any costs for health Insurance as provided for under sub. (4m).

(g) The child's educational needs.

(h) The tax consequences to each party.

(hm) The best interests of the child.

(hs) The earning capacity of each parent, based on each parent's education, training and work experience and the availability of work in or near the parent's community.

(i) Any other factors which the court in each case determines are relevant.

Sample Letter to Spouse

VANDEN HEUVEL & DINEEN s.c.
— ATTORNEYS AT LAW —

W175 N11086 Stonewood Drive
P. O. Box 550
Germantown, WI 53022-0550
vhdlaw.com

January 1, 2015

Ms. Jane Doe
123 Main Street
Any Town, WI 45679

RE: Doe and Doe
Case No. 00-00-00

Dear Jane:

Your husband, John, has filed for divorce. It is your husband's wish to make this difficult situation as amicable as possible.

We are required to serve you with an authenticated copy of the Summons with attached Petition with Minor Children, Order to Show Cause for Temporary Order and Affidavit in Support. As a result, your spouse has asked that I give you the opportunity to admit service on the enclosed documents by signing the enclosed Admission of Service form and returning this form directly to me in the enclosed self-addressed envelope.

If I do not receive the signed Admission of Service form from you within seven (7) days, I will make arrangements with the Sheriff's department or a private process server to serve you personally with the above-named documents.

Please be advised that this matter has been scheduled for a temporary hearing as follows:

(Location:) _____
(Date:)_____
(Time:)_____

The purpose of this hearing is to establish temporary orders which will be in effect until your divorce is finalized or otherwise amended. I will contact you in the near future to determine if we can reach a stipulated temporary agreement prior to the scheduled hearing. In the event we are able to reach a stipulated agreement, approved by the Family Court Commissioner, the temporary hearing will be removed from the court's calendar.

Appendix

Sample Letter to Spouse (Continued)

January 1, 2015
Ms. Jane Doe
Page 2

I have also enclosed a Financial Statement and Parenting Plan for your completion. Please complete and forward these documents to my office at least seven days before the scheduled hearing date. At the same time, would you also please provide me with a copy of the last twelve weeks of your payroll stubs.

John hopes we can work through the divorce in a reasonable manner, and I trust that is your desire as well. If you plan to retain an attorney, I encourage you to do so. If you do retain an attorney, please let me know the attorney's name, address, phone number, and e-mail address as soon as possible. If you do not retain an attorney, please feel free to contact me directly.

Thank you in advance for your cooperation.

Yours very truly,

VANDEN HEUVEL & DINEEN. S.C.

Linda S. Vanden Heuvel

LSVH:ejq

Enclosures

pc: Mr. John Doe

Sample Admission of Service

STATE OF WISCONSIN   **CIRCUIT COURT**   **COUNTY**

FAMILY COURT BRANCH

In re the Marriage of:

_____   Case No._____

Petitioner,

and

_____

Respondent.

ADMISSION OF SERVICE

Service is hereby admitted on the Summons with attached Petition with Minor Children and Order to Show Cause for Temporary Order with attached Affidavit in Support of Order to Show Cause for Temporary Order relative to the above-captioned matter.

Dated this_____day of_____, 20_____.

_____

Respondent

Post Office Address:
Vanden Heuvel & Dineen, S.C.
W175 N 11086 Stonewood Drive
P.O. Box 550
Germantown, WI 53022
Phone: (262) 250-1976
Fax: (262) 250-7686
E-mail: linda@vhdlaw.com

Appendix

Sample Financial Disclosure Statement

STATE OF WISCONSIN **CIRCUIT COURT** **COUNTY**
FAMILY COURT BRANCH

In re the Marriage of:

Case No._____

_____
Petitioner,

and

_____
Respondent.

PETITIONER/RESPONDENT'S FINANCIAL STATEMENT

STATEMENT OF MONTHLY EXPENSES AS OF:_____

EXPENSE	AMOUNT	EXPENSE	AMOUNT
Groceries		School tuition	
Mortgage/Rent		School transportation	
Property taxes		School special activities	
Property insurance		School tutoring	
Residence/ Apartment maintenance		School books & supplies	
Electricity		Life insurance — not employer deducted	
Gas/heat		Health insurance —not employer deducted	
Fuel/oil		Accident insurance —not employer deducted	
Sewer/garbage		Disability insurance —not employer deducted	
Water/water softener		Personal property insurance	
Telephone		Personal umbrella insurance	
Cell phone		Child-care transportation	
Internet		Babysitter	
Furniture /equipment rental		Day care center	

241

Sample Financial Disclosure Statement (Continued)

EXPENSE	AMOUNT	EXPENSE	AMOUNT
Misc. supplies (paper products, etc.)		Child's allowance	
Services/cleaning supplies		Summer/day camp	
Clothing and shoes		Lessons	
Laundry/dry cleaning		Diaper service	
Vehicle installment payment		Child support—not employer deducted	
Vehicle insurance		Maintenance—not employer deducted	
Vehicle maintenance/ repairs		Income taxes (not withheld)	
Gasoline		Entertainment	
License		Hobbies	
Parking		Vacation	
Public transportation		Gifts	
Medical (uninsured)		Membership/club	
Dental (uninsured)		Papers/books/magazines	
Orthodontist (uninsured)		Barber/beautician	
Eyeglasses (uninsured)		Cosmetics/toiletry	
Medicine/drugs (uninsured)		Donations/worship	
Therapy (uninsured)		Pets—care and maintenance	
Monthly installment payments from Debt section		Cable television	
Costs of employment		Savings	
Child-support fees		**Total Expenses**	$0.00

INCOME

Employer	Pay Period	Monthly Gross	Monthly Deductible	Monthly Net

ASSETS

Furniture/fixtures		Checking account — H/W/Joint	
Home/real estate		Savings account — H/W/Joint	
Vehicle —H		Retirement accounts — W	

Sample Financial Disclosure Statement (Continued)

Vehicle —W		Retirement accounts — H	

DEBTS

Creditor	Security/Collateral	Monthly Payments	Balance Due

LIFE INSURANCE

Company Name	Policy #	Insured	Beneficiary	Coverage Amount	Cash Value/Term

This statement is correct to the best of my knowledge.

Dated this____day of_____, 20____.

_____

John Doe
Petitioner

Subscribed and sworn before me
this_____day of_____, 20____.

_____
Notary Public, State of Wisconsin
My Commission is permanent.

Post Office Address:
W175 N 11086 Stonewood Drive
P.O. Box 550
Germantown, WI 53022
Phone: (262) 250-1976
Fax: (262) 250-7686

Divorce in Wisconsin

Sample Fee Agreement

REPRESENTATION AND FEE AGREEMENT

1. Anonymous Lawyer, S.C., Attorney at Law (hereinafter "Attorney"), is engaged to represent Anonymous Client (hereinafter "Client"), in connection with [INSERT DESCRIPTION OF SCOPE OF REPRESENTATION]. Attorney may retain associate counsel, experts, accountants, or investigators to protect Client's interests. Fees charged by associate counsel, experts, or investigators retained by Attorney shall be treated as expenses to be paid by Client on demand by Attorney. Attorney will consult with client before retaining outside counsel, experts, or investigators.

2. Client agrees to pay Attorney hourly fees at the rate of $____.00 per hour (Attorney's current hourly rate). Attorney customarily increases hourly rates on an annual basis. Attorney will provide Client with written notice of any increase in Attorney's hourly rate 30 days prior to the increase.

3. It is understood that Attorney will bill Client for work that includes, but is not limited to, the following: office conferences, telephone conversations, court appearances, reading and writing correspondence, preparing and review pleadings and documents, analyzing financial records and reports, and travel to and from court or other destinations associated with this representation.

4. Client agrees to pay on demand any actual costs or disbursements incurred or advanced on Client's behalf, such as travel, mileage, parking, photocopies, telephone calls, process service fees, court reporter fees, postage, witness and subpoena fees, filing and court fees, etc. Mileage will be charged at the rate authorized by the Internal Revenue Service (currently $_____ per mile).

5. Client agrees to pay $_____.00 on execution of this Agreement as an advanced fee for legal services of Attorney, and $_____.00 as an initial advance against costs to be incurred in this matter. Advanced costs will be placed in Attorney's trust account and disbursed as costs are actually incurred. Advanced fees will not be placed in Attorney's trust account. Advanced fees will be placed in Attorney's business account and the advanced fee of $_____.00 will serve as advanced payments for ____hours of legal services in this matter. After Attorney has provided _____ hours of legal services for Client, Attorney will provide client with a written accounting of such hours. Attorney is obligated to refund any unearned fees at the conclusion of the representation. Client hereby consents to Attorney placing advanced fees in Attorney's business account.

At the conclusion of the representation, Attorney will provide Client with a written accounting of all fees and costs incurred in the matter, or an accounting of fees and costs incurred from the date of the last billing statement sent to the Client, or a refund of any advanced fees that have not been earned or advanced costs that have not been used. If Client disputes Attorney's determination as to what amount, if any, must be refunded to the Client, Client must provide Attorney with written notice of the dispute within 30 days from the date of the final accounting. If the dispute cannot be resolved within 30 days, Attorney will submit the dispute to binding fee arbitration through the State Bar of Wisconsin Fee Arbitration Program. The State Bar's Fee Arbitration Program may be contacted c/o State Bar of Wisconsin, P.O. Box 7158, Madison, WI 53707-7158, or by phone at (800) 728-7788. [Lawyers in Milwaukee County should provide contact information for the Milwaukee Bar Association fee arbitration program.] Client is not required by this agreement to participate in fee arbitration and may pursue a dispute of Attorney's fees in other appropriate forums. Further, if Attorney fails to refund unearned fees, abide by a fee arbitration award, or abide by a final decision of a court with respect to unearned fees, Client may file a claim with the Wisconsin Lawyers Fund for Client Protection to recover

Sample Fee Agreement (Continued)

such amount. The Wisconsin Lawyers Fund for Client Protection may be contacted c/o State Bar of Wisconsin, P.O. Box 7158, Madison, WI 53707-7158, or by phone at (800) 728-7788. Client is hereby notified that Attorney reserves the right to require additional fee and cost advances during the representation.

6. STATEMENTS FOR SERVICES, COSTS, AND DISBURSEMENTS ARE DUE AND PAYABLE WITHIN 20 DAYS OF RECEIPT OF STATEMENT FROM ATTORNEY. Client agrees to pay Attorney compensation as the case progresses. Failure to make payments as agreed may provide grounds for Attorney to withdraw from further representation of Client. Fees and costs that are not paid within 20 days will be subject to a 1% monthly (12% yearly) interest charge on any unpaid balances.

7. On conclusion of this legal matter and final billing of Client's account, payments must be made in full within 30 days of receipt of Attorney's Billing Statement.

8. This agreement does not cover or apply to the filing of, prosecution of, or defense of an appeal, in which situation a new representation and fee agreement must be executed.

Dated this_____day of _____, 20____, at Hometown, Wisconsin.

Anonymous Lawyer, S.C.

_____   _____
Anonymous Client   Anonymous Lawyer

Sample Parenting Plan

STATE OF WISCONSIN   **CIRCUIT COURT**   **COUNTY**
                            FAMILY COURT DIVISION

In re the Marriage of:

_____   Case No:_____

Petitioner,

and

_____

Respondent.

PROPOSED PARENTING PLAN FOR ☐ MOTHER ☐ FATHER

INTRODUCTION — PLEASE READ CAREFULLY

> Wisconsin Law requires that a Parenting Plan be completed whenever there is a dispute regarding custody and/or placement of children. Wis. Stats 767.41(1m) & Wis. Stats. 767.451(6m)
> The purpose of this document is to provide custody/placement information to the Court, the other parent, attorneys, and other professionals involved in your case including the mediator, Family Court Social Worker, and Guardian *Ad Litem*, etc.

THIS DOCUMENT WILL BE FILED WITH THE COURT AND WILL BE OPEN TO PUBLIC REVIEW UNLESS OTHERWISE ORDERED BY THE COURT.

IF THIS DOCUMENT IS NOT TIMELY FILED, YOU MAY LOSE YOUR RIGHT TO OBJECT TO THE OTHER PARENT'S PARENTING PLAN. Wis. Stats. 767.41(im).

This parenting plan is submitted for the following purpose:

As a ☐ TEMPORARY PARENTING PLAN as to custody and/or placement

As a ☐ PERMANENT PARENTING PLAN as to custody and/or placement

As a ☐ PARTIAL PARENTING PLAN as to custody and/or placement

1.   CHILDREN:

NAME	SEX	DATE OF BIRTH

Sample Parenting Plan   (Continued)

NAME	SEX	DATE OF BIRTH

2.   CHILDREN'S CURRENT SCHOOL/PRESCHOOL:

NAME	SCHOOL	GRADE

3.   CHILDREN'S CURRENT HEALTH CARE PROVIDERS:

Doctor/Pediatrician/Clinic_____

_____

Eye/Optometrist_____

_____

Dentist/Orthodontist_____

_____

Insurance/Health plan_____

_____

Other_____

4.   INFORMATION ABOUT THE MOTHER:

NAME	DATE OF BIRTH

IMPORTANT NOTE: The next few questions require your address and your workplace. If you believe that you have been the victim of domestic abuse by the other parent or you have been the victim of battery by the other parent, you may substitute for your address, a general description of your residence, and your workplace. If you already have a domestic violence injunction, please attach a copy of the injunction to this Parenting Plan. You must advise the Court that you have a concern about possible violence if you do not provide your current address and job. Wis. Stats. 767.41(1m).

A.   Mother currently lives at_____

_____

If mother intends to move in the next two (2) years, where and when the move will take place _____

_____

B.   Optional. Mother's telephone number at home is_____
Optional. Mother's telephone number at work is_____

C.   Mother is currently employed at_____

Sample Parenting Plan   (Continued)

Mother's current days and hours of employment are_____

[If any employment changes may take place in the near future (shift, hours, or employer), please list the changes and the dates of change.]_____

5. INFORMATION ABOUT THE FATHER:

NAME	DATE OF BIRTH

IMPORTANT NOTE: The next few questions require your address and your workplace. If you believe that you have been the victim of domestic abuse by the other parent or you have been the victim of battery by the other parent, you may substitute for your address, a general description of your residence, and your workplace. If you already have a domestic violence injunction, please attach a copy of the injunction to this Parenting Plan. You must advise the Court that you have a concern about possible violence if you do not provide your current address and job. Wis. Stats. 767.41(1m).

A. Father currently lives at_____

If father intends to move in the next two (2) years, where and when the move will take place _____

B. Optional. Father's telephone number at home is_____
    Optional. Father's telephone number at work is_____

C. Father is currently employed at_____

Father's current days and hours of employment are_____

[If any employment changes may take place in the near future (shift, hours, or employer), please list the changes and the dates of change.]_____

6. LEGAL CUSTODY:

Legal custody is the ability to make major decisions for the child(ren). These decisions include the right to marry before the age 18, the right to enter the military service, as well as medical, educational, and religious decisions, etc.

Joint Legal Custody means major decision making is shared between the parents.

Sole Legal Custody gives the custodial parent the right to make the major decisions for the child(ren) even if the other parent does not agree. If sole legal custody is requested, explain to the Court why you believe joint legal custody is not the best for the child(ren).

_____

_____

Legal custody of the child(ren) should be granted as follows:
☐ Joint custody to both parents ☐ The other parent ☐ Solely to me

Sample Parenting Plan (Continued)

☐ If you believe the children should be separated from each other, which parent should have custody of which child(ren)?

_____

_____

_____

In many separated families, parents agree on most decisions but have disagreements on some issues. The Court has the power to order joint custody in general but may also make orders about which parent has control on a particular issue. You may decide that one parent should make all the major decisions. You may decide that you and the other parent will jointly make all major decisions. The third option is to list the major areas of decision making and to decide which parent will have decision-making control for an issue.

Major decisions regarding each child(ren) shall be made as follows:

Education (Parochial vs. Private)	☐ Mother	☐ Father	☐ Joint
School	☐ Mother	☐ Father	☐ Joint
Child-care provider	☐ Mother	☐ Father	☐ Joint
Non-emerg. health care	☐ Mother	☐ Father	☐ Joint
Religious upbringing	☐ Mother	☐ Father	☐ Joint
Driving	☐ Mother	☐ Father	☐ Joint
Marriage	☐ Mother	☐ Father	☐ Joint
_____	☐ Mother	☐ Father	☐ Joint
_____	☐ Mother	☐ Father	☐ Joint
_____	☐ Mother	☐ Father	☐ Joint

7. PLACEMENT:

PHYSICAL PLACEMENT is where the child(ren) is at any given time. The party with physical placement is responsible for everyday decisions. Day-to-day decisions include minor discipline, curfew, allowance, day-to-day decisions about clothing or hygiene during the time the child(ren) is with you, etc. Regardless of who makes day-to-day decisions, either parent may make emergency decisions affecting the health or safety of the child(ren).

    a.   PROPOSED PRESCHOOL PLACEMENT SCHEDULE

        ☐ There are no child(ren) of preschool age.

Sample Parenting Plan   (Continued)

☐   The child(ren) shall have placement with both parents on a 50/50 basis as follows:

_____
_____
_____

☐   The child(ren) shall have placement with the ☐ mother ☐ father, except for the following days and times when the child(ren) shall have placement with the other parent as follows:

[Day and Time] _____ to [Day and Time]

_____

☐ every week   ☐ every other week   ☐ other:_____

_____

[Day and Time] _____ to [Day and Time]

_____

☐ every week   ☐ every other week   ☐ other:_____

_____

☐ reasonable times upon reasonable notice.

b.   SCHOOL SCHEDULE
   ☐   The school schedule will start when each child(ren) begins
       ☐ 4 yr. old kindergarten ☐ 5 yr. old kindergarten ☐ first grade
   ☐   Other:_____
   ☐   There are no child(ren) of school age.
   ☐   The child(ren) shall have placement with both parents on a 50/50 basis as follows:

_____
_____
_____

The child(ren) shall have placement with the ☐ mother ☐ father, except for the following days and times when the child(ren) shall have placement with the other parent:

[Day and Time] _____ to [Day and Time]

_____

☐ every week   ☐ every other week   ☐ other:_____

[Day and Time] _____ to [Day and Time]

_____

☐ every week   ☐ every other week   ☐ other:_____

_____

☐ reasonable times upon reasonable notice.

c.   SUMMER SCHEDULE
   ☐   The child(ren) shall have placement with both parents on a 50/50 basis as follows:

_____
_____

Sample Parenting Plan   (Continued)

Upon completion of the school year, the child(ren) shall have placement with the ☐ mother ☐ father, except for the following days and times when the child(ren) will have placement with the other parent:

    ☐   Same as school year schedule.

    ☐   Other: _____

    ☐   Reasonable times upon reasonable notice.

  d.   SCHEDULE FOR HOLIDAY VACATIONS

The placement schedule of the child(ren) for the holidays listed below is as follows: (Please put "M" for Mother or "F" for Father in the even or odd year.)

HOLIDAY	TIME	EVEN YEARS	ODD YEARS
New Year's Eve			
New Year's Day			
Martin Luther King			
Easter Sunday			
Mother's Day			
Memorial Day			
Father's Day			
July 4th			
Labor Day			
Halloween			
Thanksgiving Day			
Christmas Eve			
Christmas Day			
Spring break			
Winter break			
Child's birthday			
Father's vacation			
Mother's vacation			
Father's birthday			
Mother's birthday			

    ☐   Whenever a Friday or a Monday is a school holiday or legal holiday, the adjoining weekend shall be extended to include the holiday.

Sample Parenting Plan   (Continued)

☐   Other: _____

_____

e.   PRIORITIES UNDER THE PLACEMENT SCHEDULE
☐   Does not apply.
☐   For purposes of this parenting plan the following days shall have priority:
   ☐   Parent's vacations shall have priority over holidays.
   ☐   Holidays shall have priority over the regular placement schedule.
   ☐   Other: _____

_____

f.   EXTRACURRICULAR AND RECREATIONAL ACTIVITIES
☐   The parties will jointly make the final decision regarding extracurricular and recreational activities.

☐   The ☐ mother ☐ father (check one) will have the right to make all decisions concerning extracurricular and recreational activities for the child(ren).
☐   Each parent has final decision making for activities that occur <u>only</u> during that parent's parenting time.

g.   CONTACT
☐ Mother ☐ Father shall assist the child(ren) in maintaining contact with the other parent by (check all that apply):
   ☐ Direct contact through periods of placement
   ☐ Telephone contact
   ☐ Cards/letters
   ☐ E-mail
   ☐ Other _____

_____

h.   SAFETY
☐   Neither parent shall operate a vehicle when under the influence of alcohol nor use non-prescription or mood-altering prescription drugs when the child(ren) are in the vehicle.
☐   Neither parent shall leave the child(ren) under age _____ unattended at any time.
☐   Neither parent shall use, nor allow anyone else to use, physical discipline with the child(ren).
☐   All contact between the child(ren) and _____(name) shall be supervised by_____(name)
☐   Neither parent shall allow the child(ren) to be in the presence of _____

_____

i.   MISCELLANEOUS
☐   Each parent shall inform the other parent of any change of business or residential address and/or phone number in advance OR within _____days/weeks of the change.

☐   Both parents agree that each will promptly inform the other of any emergency or other important event that involves the child(ren).

☐   Both parents will consult each other and work out an agreement regarding any extra activity of the child(ren) that affects the child(ren)'s access to the other parent.

Sample Parenting Plan   (Continued)

☐   Both parents agree that all communications regarding the child(ren) will be between the parents and that they will not use the child(ren) to convey information or to set up placement changes.

☐   Both parents agree that they will not belittle or criticize the other parent in front of the child(ren).

☐   Both parents agree that should either of them travel overnight with the child(ren), that parent will keep the other parent informed of travel plans, address(es), and telephone number(s) where that parent and the child(ren) can be reached.

☐   Both parents may participate in school conferences, events, and activities, and may consult with teachers and other school personnel.

☐   Both parents agree to advise the other parent immediately of any emergency medical/dental care sought for the child(ren), to cooperate on health matters pertaining to the child(ren), to keep each other informed as to names, addresses, and telephone numbers of all medical/dental care practitioners, and to keep each other reasonably informed.

☐   OTHER TERMS: (Add any other items regarding the child(ren) you want included in your parenting plan)._____

_____
_____

8.   **TRANSPORTATION ISSUES:**
The physical transfer of the child(ren) for placements shall be as follows:

☐   All transportation to and from placements will be provided by the ☐ mother ☐ father

☐   Transportation will be shared:

☐ Parent with the child(ren) shall deliver. ☐ Parent without child(ren) shall pick up.

☐   Transfers of child(ren) shall take place:

☐ Parent's home ☐ Halfway point: _____

☐ Other location: _____

Battery/domestic violence ☐ is ☐ is not an issue in this relationship.

If domestic violence is an issue in this relationship, complete the following:
In order to ensure the safety of the child(ren) and/or parent, transfers of the child(ren) between the parents shall be:

☐   Monitored by an agency (name of agency): _____

☐   At a neutral public site (name and location): _____

☐   At the home of the following person (name and location):_____

_____

☐   Other: _____

_____

9.   **RELIGIOUS UPBRINGING:**
The purpose of this question is to determine whether there are any serious disagreements about religious issues.

Sample Parenting Plan   (Continued)

☐ The child(ren) shall be raised in the following religion: _____

☐ No religious affiliation is planned.

10. SCHOOL SELECTION:
If a change is proposed relative to the child(ren)'s school, where do you propose that the child(ren) will go to school: _____
How will the child(ren)'s educational expenses be paid:_____

11. MEDICAL/DENTAL/OPTOMETRIC CARE AND EXPENSES:
If a change from the current arrangement is proposed, what doctor, dentist, or health care facility will provide care for the child(ren)? _____

Medical, dental, and optometric insurance for the child(ren) will be provided by:
☐ mother ☐ father

Uninsured medical/dental, optometric expenses shall be:
☐ paid by me
☐ paid by the other parent
☐ shared equally by both of us
☐ Other: _____

12. CHILD CARE:
Child care will be provided by: _____

☐ When a parent intends to leave the child(ren) in the care of someone else for a period of overnight or longer, the other parent shall be given the first choice to provide such care.

☐ The child(ren) do not require child care.

☐ The cost of child care (if needed) will be paid by:

☐ mother ☐ father ☐ shared equally by both
☐ Other: _____

13. CHILD SUPPORT:
How much do you suggest the other parent will pay for child support to start this parenting plan?
The ☐ mother ☐ father shall be responsible for child support as follows:
☐ as required by the state support guidelines
☐ Other: _____

14. RESOLVING DISAGREEMENTS:
If there are disagreements between the parents on issues where the Court has ordered joint decisions, the disagreements will be resolved as follows: (check all that apply)
☐ The parent who has primary physical placement will decide.
☐ The parent who has actual physical placement at the time of the disagreement will decide.

Sample Parenting Plan   (Continued)

☐ The parents will request assistance from friends, relatives, clergy, counselors, or others who can be neutral and fair. The following person(s) are suggested to serve as a third-party neutral(s): _____

☐ Contact the _____ County Family Court Mediation program.

☐ Other: _____

The cost of this process shall be allocated between the parties as follows:

_____ Mother _____ Father

☐ The counseling, mediation, or arbitration process shall be commenced by notifying the other party by:

    ☐ written request ☐ certified mail ☐ Other: _____

☐ A written record shall be prepared of any agreement reached in counseling or mediation and shall be provided to each party.

OTHER PROVISIONS

☐ There are no other provisions.

☐ There are the following other provisions:_____

_____

YOUR SIGNATURE BELOW INDICATES THAT YOU HAVE READ AND AGREE WITH EVERYTHING IN THIS DOCUMENT.

_____

Signature

_____

Date

Resources

The following is a list of websites that may be of assistance to you.

FAMILY LAW:

Vanden Heuvel & Dineen, S.C.
www.vhdlaw.com

American Academy of Matrimonial Lawyers
www.aaml.org

American Bar Association Section of Family Law
www.abanet.org/family/home.html

Child Support Guidelines Calculator
http://dcf.wisconsin.gov/bcs/order/guidelines_tools.htm

Collaborative Family Law Council of Wisconsin
www.collabdivorce.com

Kelley Blue Book
www.kbb.com

Restraining Orders Wisconsin (how to obtain)
www.doj.state.wi.us/ocvs/victim-rights/restraining-orders

U.S. Department of Justice, Office on Violence Against Women
www.ovw.usdoj.gov

Wisconsin Child Support Online Services
http://dcf.wisconsin.gov/bcs/payments/logon.htm

The Wisconsin Child Support Program
http://dcf.wisconsin.gov/bcs/

Wisconsin Family and Custody Law Statutes and Code
http://docs.legis.wisconsin.gov/statutes/prefaces/toc
and
www.legis.state.wi.us/rsb/stats.html

Wisconsin Circuit Court Forms
www.wicourts.gov/forms1/circuit/ccform.
jsp?FormName=&FormNumber=&beg_date=&end_
date=&StatuteCite=&Category=6

Wisconsin Circuit Court
www.wicourts.gov/courts/circuit/ccsites.htm

Wisconsin Department of Children and Families
http://dcf.wisconsin.gov/

Wisconsin Fathers for Children and Families
www.wisconsinfathers.org

Wisconsin State Law Library
http://wilawlibrary.gov/

MISCELLANEOUS:

Annual credit reports service (free)
www.annualcreditreport.com/index.action

Avvo
www.avvo.com

Better Business Bureau
www.bbb.org

Community Justice, Inc.
www.communityjusticeinc.org

Community Mental Health Counseling Centers, Inc.
www.communitymhccenters.com

Internal Revenue Service
www.irs.gov

Lawyers USA
http://lawyersusaonline.com

Legal Action of Wisconsin
www.legalaction.org

Legal Aid Society of Milwaukee
www.lasmilwaukee.com

Martindale-Hubbell
www.martindale.com

Merriam-Webster Dictionary
www.merriam-webster.com

Northern Wisconsin Legal Advice Project
www.nwlap.org

Social Security Administration
www.ssa.gov/

State of Wisconsin
www.wisconsin.gov

United States Bankruptcy Court
www.wieb.uscourts.gov

United States Postal Service Zip Code Lookup
https://tools.usps.com/go/ZipLookupAction!input.action

University of Wisconsin Family Court Clinic
www.law.wisc.edu/eji/familycourt/index.html

Wisconsin Bar Association
www.wisbar.org

Wisconsin Bar Association Modest Means Program
http://www.wisbar.org/forPublic/INeedaLawyer/Pages/Modest-Means.aspx

Wisconsin Circuit Court Access (WCCA)
www.wcca.wicourts.gov/index.xsl

Wisconsin Commissioner of Insurance
www.oci.wi.gov

Wisconsin Court System
www.wicourts.gov/courts/index.htm

Wisconsin Department of Financial Institutions
www.wdfi.org

Wisconsin Department of Health Services
www.dhfs.state.wi.us

Wisconsin Department of Safety and Professional Services
http://dsps.wi.gov/Home

Wisconsin Department of Transportation
www.dot.state.wi.us

Wisconsin Department of Workforce Development
www.dwd.state.wi.us

Wisconsin Judicare, Inc.
www.judicare.org

Glossary

Affidavit: A written statement of facts made under oath, signed before a notary public, and submitted to the court in support of a pleading. Your attorney will prepare an affidavit to present relevant facts. The person signing the affidavit may be referred to as the *affiant*.

Allegation: A statement that one party claims is true.

Appeal: The process by which a higher court reviews the decision of a lower court.

Child support: Financial support for a child usually paid by the noncustodial parent to the custodial parent.

Contempt of court: The willful and intentional failure of a party to comply with a court order or judgment. Contempt may be punishable by a fine or jail.

Contested divorce: Any divorce in which the parties cannot reach a full agreement. A contested divorce will result in a trial to the court, which will decide all disputed issues.

Court order: A court-issued document setting forth the judge's orders. An order may be issued based on the parties' agreement or the judge's decision. An order may require the parties to perform certain acts or set forth their rights and responsibilities. An order is put in writing, signed by the judge, and filed with the court.

Cross-examination: The questioning of a witness by opposing counsel during trial or at a deposition in response to questions asked by the other lawyer.

Custody: Joint legal custody means the conditions under which both parties share legal custody and neither parent's legal custody rights are superior, except with respect to specified decisions as set forth by the court or the parties in the final judgment or order. The award of legal custody grants any person having legal custody of children the right and responsibility to make major decisions concerning the children, except with respect to specified decisions as set forth by the court or the parties in the final judgment or order.

Deposition: Testimony under oath. A party or witness will be asked questions by an attorney, and all questions, answers, and comments will be recorded by an official court reporter or videotape.

Direct examination: The initial questioning of a witness in court by the lawyer who called him or her to the stand.

Discovery: A process used by attorneys to discover information from the opposing party and third parties for the purpose of fully preparing a case for settlement or trial. Types of discovery include interrogatories, requests for production of documents, requests for admissions, depositions, releases, and more.

Dissolution: The act of terminating or dissolving a marriage.

Ex parte: The term used to describe an appearance of only one party before the judge, without the other party being present.

Findings of fact, conclusions of law, and judgment of divorce: A formal written document usually prepared by the petitioner's attorney, approved by the respondent's attorney, and signed by the judge that sets forth the formal findings of fact, conclusions of law, and judgment of divorce. This is the actual legal document that grants a divorce and specifically sets forth the terms and conditions of the divorce whether by a negotiated settlement or trial to the court.

Guardian *ad litem* (GAL): An attorney appointed by the court to represent and advocate for the children's best interest.

Hearing: Any proceeding before the court for the purpose of resolving disputed issues between the parties through presentation of testimony, affidavits, exhibits, or argument.

Hold-harmless provision: A term in a court order that requires one party to assume responsibility for a debt and to protect the other spouse from any loss or expense in connection with it, as in to hold harmless from liability.

Interrogatories: Formal written requests directed to the other party for the production of truthful answers to relevant questions. Interrogatories are used in preparation for trial to obtain information not otherwise available. Interrogatories must be answered under oath by the party to whom they are directed.

Maintenance: Court-ordered spousal support payments paid from one party to another.

Mediation: A process by which a neutral third party facilitates negotiations between the parties on a wide range of issues.

Motion: A request to the court to make some type of order. A hearing will generally be held to determine whether or not the motion should be granted.

Motion for relocation: A parent's written request to the court seeking permission to relocate with the children to another state or more than 150 miles in Wisconsin from the other parent.

Motion to modify: A party's written request to the court to change a prior order regarding custody, child support, maintenance, or other issues set forth in the judgment of divorce.

No-fault divorce: No-fault divorces do not require evidence of marital misconduct. This means that abandonment, cruelty, or adultery are neither relevant nor required to be proven for the purposes of granting the divorce.

Party: The person in a legal action whose rights or interests will be affected by the action. For example, in a divorce the parties include the wife and husband.

Pending: During the case. For example, the judge may award you temporary support while your case is pending.

Petition for divorce: The petition sets forth many statistical facts about the marriage and the parties and also states that the marriage is irretrievably broken. The petition is served with the summons.

Petitioner: The person who filed the petition for divorce initiating the divorce action.

Pleadings: Formal, written documents filed with the court.

Pro se: To proceed in a legal matter without representation.

Property division: The method by which real and personal property and debts are divided in a divorce.

Qualified domestic relations order (QDRO): A type of court order that provides for direct payment from a retirement account to a former spouse.

Qualified medical support order (QMSO): A type of court order that provides a former spouse certain rights regarding medical insurance and information.

Request for production of documents: A formal written request for documents sent from one party to the other during the discovery process.

Respondent: The responding party to a divorce; the party who did not file the petition initiating the divorce.

Response and counterclaim: A written response to the petition for divorce. It serves to admit or deny allegations in the petition and may also make claims against the petitioner.

Sequester: To order prospective witnesses out of the courtroom until they have concluded their testimony.

Setoff: A debt or financial obligation of one spouse that is deducted from the debt or financial obligation of the other spouse.

Settlement: The agreed resolution of disputed issues.

Stipulation: A formal written agreement between the parties and/or their attorneys. It can cover any subject. If there is a complete, written stipulation regarding all terms of the final judgment, the parties will be able to schedule a "default" divorce.

Subpoena: A document authorized by the court or an attorney, as an officer of the court, which requires a person to appear and give testimony at a hearing, trial, or deposition or to produce documents. Failure to comply may result in punishment by the court. A subpoena requesting documents is called a *subpoena duces tecum*.

Summons: The pleading that provides initial notice of the divorce.

Temporary order: An order of the court or of the family court commissioner setting forth orders that are in effect prior to the final hearing on the divorce. It usually covers such items as custody, placement, support, temporary use of the home and other property of the parties, and payments of bills and mortgages.

Temporary restraining order (TRO): An order of the court prohibiting a party from a certain behavior. For example, a temporary restraining order may order a person not to transfer any funds during the pendency of a pending divorce action.

Trial: A formal court hearing and examination of evidence before a judge, including testimony, exhibits, and arguments from the parties and witnesses, setting forth each party's trial evidence.

Glossary

Under advisement: A term used to describe the status of a case, usually after a court hearing on a motion or a trial when the judge has not yet made a decision.

Index

Index

communication
  with attorney, 46–47, 53–55
  during mediation, 89
  with spouse, 127
Community Justice, Inc., 69
compensation, 79, 138
competition, 29
conclusions of law, 6, 44
confidentiality, 27, 39, 46
conflict, 90
confusion about getting divorce, 36
contested divorce, 44
contributions to retirement, 179
coping
  with divorce, 28–29
  with stress, 25–36
cost-of-living allowance (COLA), 180
costs, *see* fees
counseling, 31–32
counterclaim, 3, 44
country requirements, 103
county requirements, 11
court, 203–207, *see also* hearings; trial
  appearing in, 52, 203–204, 207
  child/children's presence during, 119
  going to, 202–216
  Indian tribal court, 12
  judge's role in, 6, 216
  jury's role in, 205
  marital settlement agreement and, 21
  personal support during, 214
  property and, division of, 157, 168
  spouse's attendance in, 204, 214
  talking to attorney during, 210

court order
  domestic abuse temporary restraining, 100
  ex parte, 16, 100
  for house/home, 158
  for life insurance, 182
  for mediation, 6
  motion for, 16
  pretrial, 211
  restraining, 100
  temporary, 3–4, 43–44, 52
  temporary restraining, 99–100
court order acceptable for processing (COAP), 178
court reporter, 207
credit cards, 186–188
cross-examination, 215

D

dating, 120, 125
death, 79, 181–182
  child custody and, 132
  property and, division of, 175
  spousal maintenance and, 154
debt
  allocation of, 189
  disclosure of, 76–77
  division of (*see* debts, division of)
  premarital, 188
  property and, division of, 175
debts, division of, 185–191
  bankruptcy and, 190–191
  credit cards, 186–188
  during divorce process, 188
  hold-harmless provision and, 189
  of house/home, 189
  of premarital debt, 188
  refusal to, 191

Index

About the Author

 **Linda S. Vanden Heuvel** is an attorney practicing in southeastern Wisconsin. She devotes a majority of her practice to representing individuals involved in family law matters. She has practiced family law for more than thirty years representing parties in cases involving divorce, collaborative divorce, legal separation, annulments, mediation, custody and placement, maintenance, child support, property division, grandparents' rights, paternity, prenuptial and postnuptial agreements, post-judgment modifications, domestic abuse, and restraining orders. Linda is able to save her clients time, money, and emotional distress through settlement negotiations, but is a recognized litigator with the ability to effectively litigate cases if settlement efforts fail. Linda is skilled at handling complex divorces including large estates, contentious custody/placement disputes, and property division litigation.

Attorney Vanden Heuvel has been recognized as one of the top Wisconsin family law litigators and is recognized statewide as a leading divorce and family law attorney. She has received the highest possible rating from Martindale-Hubbell for over twenty consecutive years.

Linda S. Vanden Heuvel

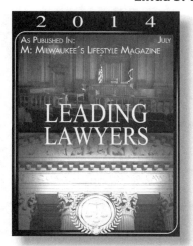

2014—Rated a Leading Divorce and Family Law Attorney

2014—Top-Rated Divorce and Family Law Attorney *M Magazine*

AV Rated Martindale-Hubbell

2014—Client Distinction Award

2014—Women's Preeminent Attorney

Divorce Titles from Addicus Books

Visit our online catalog at www.AddicusBooks.com

Divorce in Alabama: The Legal Process, Your Rights, and What to Expect $21.95

Divorce in Arizona: The Legal Process, Your Rights, and What to Expect. $21.95

Divorce in California: The Legal Process, Your Rights, and What to Expect $21.95

Divorce in Connecticut: The Legal Process, Your Rights, and What to Expect $21.95

Divorce in Georgia: The Legal Process, Your Rights, and What to Expect $21.95

Divorce in Hawaii: The Legal Process, Your Rights, and What to Expect $21.95

Divorce in Illinois: The Legal Process, Your Rights, and What to Expect $21.95

Divorce in Louisiana: The Legal Process, Your Rights, and What to Expect $21.95

Divorce in Maine: The Legal Process, Your Rights, and What to Expect $21.95

Divorce in Michigan: The Legal Process, Your Rights, and What to Expect. $21.95

Divorce in Mississippi: The Legal Process, Your Rights, and What to Expect. $21.95

Divorce in Missouri: The Legal Process, Your Rights, and What to Expect $21.95

Divorce in Nebraska: The Legal Process, Your Rights, and What to Expect—2nd Edition $21.95

Divorce in Nevada: The Legal Process, Your Rights, and What to Expect. $21.95

Divorce in New Jersey: The Legal Process, Your Rights, and What to Expect $21.95

Divorce in New York: The Legal Process, Your Rights, and What to Expect $21.95

Divorce in Tennessee: The Legal Process, Your Rights, and What to Expect $21.95

Divorce in Virginia: The Legal Process, Your Rights, and What to Expect $21.95

Divorce in Washington: The Legal Process, Your Rights, and What to Expect $21.95

Divorce in West Virginia: The Legal Process, Your Rights, and What to Expect $21.95

Divorce in Wisconsin: The Legal Process, Your Rights, and What to Expect $21.95

To Order Books:
Visit us online at: www.AddicusBooks.com
Call toll free: (800) 888-4741

Addicus Books
P. O. Box 45327
Omaha, NE 68145

*Addicus Books is dedicated to publishing books
that comfort and educate.*